GRAINS IN CHINA

T0372540

The Chinese Economy Series

This series examines the immense importance of China within the global economy. Books in the series view the Chinese economy in many ways, such as: a transition economy, a bridge between the developing and developed nations, a vital member of the WTO, and even as a potential rival to the US.

Providing readers with high quality monographs and edited volumes by authors from the East and West, this series is a truly global forum on one of the world's key economies.

Series Editors

Aimin Chen, Indiana State University, USA
Shunfeng Song, University of Nevada-Reno, USA

Recent Titles in the Series

Critical Issues in China's Growth and Development
Edited by Yum K. Kwan and Eden S. H. Yu
ISBN 0 7546 4270 4

Urban Transformation in China
Edited by Aimin Chen, Gordon G. Liu and Kevin H. Zhang
ISBN 0 7546 3312 8

Urbanization and Social Welfare in China
Edited by Aimin Chen, Gordon G. Liu and Kevin H. Zhang
ISBN 0 7546 3313 6

Technology and Knowledge Transfer in China
Richard Li-Hua
ISBN 0 7546 3928 2

China's Economic Development and Democratization
Yanlai Wang
ISBN 0 7546 3620 8

Grains in China

Foodgrain, Feedgrain and World Trade

Edited by
ZHANG-YUE ZHOU
James Cook University

WEI-MING TIAN
China Agricultural University

Routledge
Taylor & Francis Group

LONDON AND NEW YORK

First published 2005 by Ashgate Publishing

Reissued 2018 by Routledge
2 Park Square, Milton Park, Abingdon, Oxon OX14 4RN
605 Third Avenue, New York, NY 10017

First issued in paperback 2021

Routledge is an imprint of the Taylor & Francis Group, an informa business

A Library of Congress record exists under LC control number: 2004030115

Notice:
Product or corporate names may be trademarks or registered trademarks, and are used only for identification and explanation without intent to infringe.

Publisher's Note
The publisher has gone to great lengths to ensure the quality of this reprint but points out that some imperfections in the original copies may be apparent.

Disclaimer
The publisher has made every effort to trace copyright holders and welcomes correspondence from those they have been unable to contact.

ISBN 13: 978-0-815-38933-0 (hbk)
ISBN 13: 978-1-351-15708-7 (ebk)
ISBN 13: 978-1-138-35702-0 (pbk)

DOI: 10.4324/9781351157087

Contents

INTRODUCTION

PART I: FOODGRAIN AND FEEDGRAIN

PART II: GRAIN TRADE

CONCLUSION

List of Figures

List of Tables

List of Maps

Contributors

Xi-An Liu is Senior Research Associate at the Griffith Asian Institute of Griffith University in Australia. Dr Liu's main research interests include China's political and economic institutional issues, grain issues, and rural development. He has participated in a number of research projects related to China's agricultural and rural development. Currently, Dr Liu is engaged in a research project concerning China's globalisation strategies.

Xiao-Yun Liu is Associate Professor at the Centre for Integrated Agricultural Development of China Agricultural University in Beijing. Dr Liu's major research interests lie in applied econometric analysis, agricultural policies, rural development and gender issues. She obtained her doctoral degree from China Agricultural University in 1999.

Wei-Ming Tian is Professor and Director of the Institute of Agricultural Economics at the College of Economics and Management of China Agricultural University in Beijing. He has published extensively on China's agricultural economic issues, both in Chinese and English. His major research areas include production economics, agricultural marketing and price policies, agricultural trade, and agribusiness development. In recent years, he has worked extensively on markets of agricultural commodities and on issues of China's WTO accession and agricultural development. He has led a number of national and international research projects.

Guang-Hua Wan is Senior Research Fellow and Project Director at the World Institute for Development Economics Research (WIDER), United Nations University (UNU-WIDER), which is located in Finland. Dr Wan has been conducting research on the Chinese economy for the past 20 years. His area of expertise covers rural development, efficiency and productivity measurement, household consumption and demand, food production and marketing, poverty alleviation, and income distribution. He has published extensively in these areas and has been frequently invited to referee papers for some of the world's leading journals.

Ji-Min Wang is Director of the Division of Animal Husbandry Economy in the Institute of Agricultural Economics of the Chinese Academy of Agricultural Sciences in Beijing. Professor Wang's major research areas include agricultural marketing and price policies, agricultural trade, and livestock economics. He has led a number of projects related to China's animal husbandry industries and consumption of animal products in China. He has also participated in research projects on China's grain issues and poverty alleviation. He is also a consultant to several ministries of the Chinese government in Beijing.

Yan-Rui Wu is Associate Professor in Economics of the Business School at the University of Western Australia. Dr Wu's research interests include the Chinese and Asian economies, and he specialises in development economics, consumption economics, and applied econometrics. He has developed strong expertise in demand analysis, household survey design and survey analyses. Dr Wu has worked on several food-related projects funded by the Australian Centre for International Agricultural Research, AusAID, and the Grains Research and Development Corporation. His work has led to the publication of several books and a number of journal articles.

Xian Xin is Deputy Dean of the College of Economics and Management of China Agricultural University in Beijing. Professor Xin's major research interests lie in agricultural markets, agricultural research and development policies, and econometrical modelling. He has worked on a number of projects funded by the Ministry of Agriculture and the Ministry of Science and Technology on China's agricultural policy issues. He obtained his doctoral degree from a special Ph.D. training program jointly conducted by China Agricultural University and Winrock International (1996 to 1998). Dr Xin is chief journal editor of *China Agricultural Economic Review*.

Zhen-Hai Yang is Director of the Feed Division, National Feed Industry Office of China's Ministry of Agriculture. During the past two decades, Mr Yang has been heavily involved in administrative work in such areas as feed resource development, quality control, legislation and law making and its execution. He has also actively participated in feed-related macro policy research and has frequently made presentations to grains and feed markets conferences in China and other Asian countries in the past few years. During 1999-2000, Mr Yang was in charge of formulating China's feed industry development program for 2001-2005.

Zhang-Yue Zhou is Associate Professor in Business Studies at the School of Business at James Cook University in Australia. Previously, he taught at the University of Sydney and was the Director of the Asian Agribusiness Research Centre of the University of Sydney. His research interests include grain economics, food consumption, comparative economics, agricultural prices and marketing, and rural development. He has published extensively in these areas. Most of his recent publications are in the areas of grain economics of India and China. Currently Dr Zhou is working on projects concerning China's feedgrain market, China's animal product consumption, foodgrain production and marketing in China and India, and international agricultural trade issues.

Preface

This book contributes to the literature by addressing the dynamics of China's grain production, consumption and trade with a particular focus on examining China's demand for feedgrain vis-à-vis its demand for foodgrain and likely implications on grain trade, given that China is now a member of the WTO.

We have written this book primarily for researchers, officials in government trade departments, and food traders who are interested in China's food issues in general and foodgrain and feedgrain issues in particular. The book will also be of great interest to university students who study broad agricultural trade and agricultural policy issues such as grain demand and supply, foodgrain consumption trends, feedgrain market developments, and grain trade.

The book is a result of extensive collaborative work. In the past two decades we have devoted much effort to studying China's grain issues. Our passion for this topic is rooted in our personal experience in China during the 1960s and 1970s of not having enough food. We have developed our understanding of important grain issues through our discussions, evident in various parts of this book. Apart from our own collaborative work, our colleagues, experts in their respective fields, have also made invaluable contributions to the completion of the book. We are most grateful for their contribution and collaboration.

Much of the discussion on China's feedgrain issues benefited from a research project on "China's Regional Feedgrain Markets: Development and Prospects", funded by Australia's Grains Research and Development Corporation (GRDC). GRDC's funding support enabled us to examine China's feedgrain market in great detail and is greatly acknowledged. In particular, we wish to thank Dr Mike Taverner, GRDC Program Consultant, for being instrumental in the design and implementation of that project.

Over the past years, many of our colleagues and research students at the University of Sydney and China Agricultural University have provided us with much needed support and assistance for our research work. Worth particular mention are Professors John Chudleigh, Ross Wilson, Kevin Parton, Xiu-Rong He, Fu Qin and Xiu-Qing Wang who have given us constant support and encouragement for our research endeavour.

Dr Brendan George, Senior Editor in Business and Economics at Ashgate Publishing, and Professors Aimin Chen and Shunfeng Song, the Chinese Economy Series Editors, provided us with invaluable and constructive comments that helped greatly in shaping the book. We are also most grateful to a number of other staff at Ashgate Publishing for their help in bringing this book to publication.

Last but not least, we thank Ms Marjorie Wilson and Ms Penny Marr of the University of Sydney for editing our drafts and for desktop publishing. We owe them a great deal for their skills and patience.

Zhang-Yue Zhou
Wei-Ming Tian

INTRODUCTION

Chapter 1

China's Grain: An Issue that Concerns Many

Zhang-Yue Zhou and Wei-Ming Tian

China's grain will always be an issue – unless grains can be produced in hydroponic systems without much reliance on arable land. Too much grain in China can be a problem, causing a depressed price and income for grain farmers both in China and overseas. Too little grain can also be a problem, causing the Chinese government great concern about food security and driving up the world grain price due to increased imports – an undesirable consequence for many developing importers. Hence, China's grain problem is indeed an issue not only for China but also for the rest of the world. Not surprisingly, it has attracted attention worldwide.

In the past several years, however, interest in China's grain issue has somewhat relaxed, because of China's relative grain surplus. During the past five years (1999-2003), China exported about 50 million tonnes of grains net. Even after its accession to the WTO in December 2001, China still net exported some 30 million tonnes of grains during 2002-2003, contrary to the expectation by many that it would import a large amount of grains. China exported grains during these years even when its grain output had consecutively dropped each year by about 60 million tonnes from its peak in 1998. This unforeseen surplus seems to have led to a degree of complacency about China's grain problems.

The complacency, however, was short-lived. In late 2003, prompted by increased domestic grain prices, concerns about China's grain problems were renewed. Price fluctuations are a normal phenomenon in the market; nonetheless, the fact that an increase in grain prices can cause so much concern to the government, traders and consumers confirms that China still has a grain problem. There may be short-term comfort in China's grain demand and supply situations; but long-term comfort is not warranted.

Indeed, China's grain problem is far from over, and it will continue for a long time. However, it is no longer a simple issue of total quantum, matching total supply with total demand. Increased consumer income in the past two decades has resulted in significant structural changes in grain consumption in China, e.g., increased demand for higher quality foodgrains and for animal products – thus, the derived demand for feedgrains. To respond to changes in consumer demand, China's grain industries have made adjustments to the varieties of grains. In addition, major grain production has tended to shift from the southern to the northern regions in the past two decades.

These changes, together with the accession by China to the WTO at the end of 2001, pose various important questions related to the future development of the Chinese grain economy. What are the structural changes in foodgrain consumption in both rural and urban areas of China? How is foodgrain consumption affected by animal product consumption? Is China producing enough grains to meet both the demand for foodgrain and the increasing demand for feedgrain? How will the further opening up of the grain market affect China's grain production and domestic trade? How will the WTO accession and the Doha Round negotiations affect China's international grain trade and, in turn, the overall international grain market?

1.1 Why This Book

While there is no shortage of literature on China's grain issues, studies that incorporate recent important developments and examine the above-mentioned issues from a systematic perspective are scarce. Studies with an up-to-date assessment of the Chinese grain economy will be useful. This book attempts to fill the void in the literature. It examines how China's foodgrain and feedgrain demand and supply have evolved in the past two decades and how such changes will impact on China's grain trade in the era of its WTO membership. In view of the increasing importance of China's feedgrains, this book pays particular attention to addressing China's feedgrain issues in the broad context of grain demand and supply in China and the world.

Why is it important to address feedgrain demand in the broader context of overall grain demand? Globally, the next three decades will see a strong increase in demand for feed, especially cereal feed. The increasing demand for feed is driven by the increasing demand for animal products, especially in developing countries. According to a recently released report by FAO, *World Agriculture: Towards 2015/2030*, per capita meat consumption in developing countries rose by 150% and that of milk and dairy products by 60% between 1964-66 and 1997-99 (FAO 2002, p. 5). Increase in animal product consumption is projected to continue, in both developing and developed countries (Bruinsma 2003, p. 159).

The increased consumption of animal products will require more animal feed. However, pasture has only limited potential as a source of additional feed in the future. Mixed crop–livestock production systems will also have limited potential for increasing animal products.

An increasing share of livestock production will come from intensive industrial livestock production systems. In recent years, production from these systems has grown twice as fast as that from traditional mixed farming systems, and more than six times faster than from grazing systems. Increased intensification will require more feedgrain, and the demand for feedgrain will be strong.

The FAO report suggests that, by 2030, global aggregate consumption of all cereals should increase by about one billion tonnes from the 1.86 billion tonnes of

1997/99. Of this increment, about 50% will be used for feed, 42% for food, and the remainder for other uses (e.g., seed, industrial non-food and waste) (Bruinsma 2003, pp. 65, 74). Thus, feed use of cereal grains will be the most dynamic element driving the world cereal economy and will account for an ever-growing share in aggregate demand for cereal grains.

In short, increasing demand for animal products will drive a strong demand for feedstuff, especially feedgrains, to produce additional livestock. However, globally it seems there is a lack of awareness of this emerging trend. It is important to address feedgrain demand in the broader context of overall grain demand.

It is even more important to examine China's feedgrain demand and its increasing importance in China's overall grain economy. According to FAO, the rapid expansion of worldwide livestock production is, to a large extent, attributable to the remarkable growth of livestock industries in China. During 1989-99, world annual growth rate of total livestock production was 2%. Excluding China, this rate, however, was merely 0.8%. Hence, the demand for feedgrain by China's fast expanding livestock industries deserves particular attention and needs to be addressed in the context of China's broader grain economy.

1.2 Objectives and Features

Our book is written with a view to making a contribution to the literature by addressing the dynamics of China's grain production, consumption and trade with a particular focus on China's demand for feedgrain *vis-à-vis* its demand for foodgrain and the likely implications on international grain trade. Through this book, we attempt to achieve the following major objectives:

1. To highlight the trends in China's grain production, consumption and trade and to examine forces that drive these changes
2. To simulate China's regional feedgrain demand, supply and trade flows after the WTO accession
3. To predict China's future grain demand in the context of international trade reforms
4. To draw implications on international grain trade.

This book has the following major features:

- China's grain issues are examined from a systematic perspective with a particular attention to factors peculiar to China that affect grain demand and supply.
- It highlights the most recent developments in China's grain economy and provides the latest assessments on consumption trends of foodgrain, feedgrain, and animal products in China.
- A special emphasis has been placed, in view of the increasing importance of feedgrains, on examining China's feedgrain issues in the broad context of grain demand and supply in China and the world.

- It provides comprehensive accounts of China's feedgrain demand, supply, marketing and regional trade flows.
- It constructs a regional feedgrain demand and supply balance sheet for China: this is the first of its kind, and is invaluable for future studies.
- It offers projections on China's grain imports by 2010.

1.3 Outline

Apart from this introductory chapter (Chapter 1) and the final conclusions chapter (Chapter 13), the book comprises another eleven chapters grouped into two parts. Part One (Chapters 2-8), 'Foodgrain and Feedgrain', deals with issues related to China's foodgrain and feedgrain demand and supply, while Part Two (Chapters 9-12), 'Grain Trade', deals with issues concerning China's grain trade domestically and internationally.

In the second chapter, we highlight the policy environment in which China's grain economy operates, thus placing the subject matter into perspective. Issues examined in this chapter include recent developments in the Chinese grain policies that affect grain production, consumption, reserves and trade. The chapter also sheds light on how China's grain policies may evolve given the changing grain demand and supply situations both domestically and internationally, and especially given that China is now a member of the WTO.

Having established a broad picture of the policy environment, we turn in Chapters 3, 4 and 5 to examine China's grain production and consumption. Chapter 3 highlights the recent trends in China's grain production. Important issues covered in this chapter include changes in the level and composition of grain production, dynamics in grain production patterns at the regional and crop levels, the use of technologies in grain production, and changes in production costs. This chapter will also identify important factors that may affect China's long-term grain supply capacity. Chapters 4 and 5 look into the dynamics of foodgrain consumption in rural and urban areas, respectively. Direct consumption of grains by the Chinese has started to decline, not only in urban areas but also in rural areas. We examine the changing patterns of direct human consumption of grains and discuss causes that have led to such changes.

Increase in income is mainly responsible for the decline in direct human use of grains, as consumers can afford to buy more relatively expensive foods, such as fruits and animal products. Increased demand for animal products leads to increased demand for grains to feed the animals. Indeed, many have argued that any future increase in total grain demand in China will be mainly caused by an increasing demand for feedgrains. In this context, it is important to understand which animal products and how much of them the Chinese are consuming as this provides a foundation to examine future demand for animal products and thus feedgrains. This is the subject of Chapter 6.

In Chapter 7, we pay particular attention to the current status of China's feedgrain production and consumption. Firstly, the patterns of China's feedgrain production are highlighted. This is followed by a discussion about where, how, and how much feedgrains are used in China. In this chapter, we also offer our views on the prospects of China's future feedgrain production and consumption.

Believing that feedgrain demand in China will become the major component of China's total grain demand in the future, a number of studies have been devoted to projecting China's feedgrain demand and supply. However, there exist substantial discrepancies in demand and supply projections and the subsequent quantity of imports required. In Chapter 8, we review these studies and explore the reasons for the vast discrepancies in their findings. We then highlight the areas for which research priority should be given in order to derive more plausible projections for policy formation and marketing activities. These considerations also serve our own modelling work in later chapters.

In the second part of the book (Chapters 9-12), we deal with China's foodgrain and feedgrain trade. In Chapter 9, we present an overview of China's recent foodgrain and feedgrain trade both domestically and internationally. We first focus on the changing patterns of domestic grain trade. We then examine the sources and destinations of China's grain imports and exports, and changes in the composition of grains imported and exported. In addition, major provinces that provide exports and those that absorb imports will also be identified.

Given that China is now a member of the WTO, its grain market operations are subject to WTO rules. Further reforms are expected to the domestic market and it will increasingly operate under a free trade regime. It is thus useful to see how China's domestic feedgrain markets will evolve, particularly at the regional level. In Chapter 10, we construct a regional feedgrain demand and supply balance sheet, which is a pioneer effort and fills a gap in this important area. Based on this balance sheet (where free trade is assumed), we simulate the effects on regional feedgrain demand, supply, price, and trade flows under various scenarios (e.g., technological improvements in feedgrain production and animal raising; increase in income; increase in animal product export; and imposition of regional trade restrictions, i.e., if free trade was not completely allowed). Based on the simulation framework, we also present the 2010 scenarios of China's feedgrain demand, supply, trade flows and imports.

Since joining the WTO, China has been in the process of carrying out trade reforms including grain trade. Consequently, China's future grain demand and supply will be increasingly linked to and affected by the international market. In Chapter 11, we examine China's grain demand and supply in the context of the world market, taking into consideration the possible impacts of China's WTO membership and the new round of WTO negotiations. In this chapter, how the world grain market will evolve and how this will affect China's grain production, import and export is simulated under a number of scenarios (e.g., China's fulfilment of its WTO commitment; all regions cut their import tariff rates; all developed economies remove their export subsidies on agricultural products completely; and all developed economies remove their domestic support to agricultural products completely). Simulation results on China's grain production, import and export are given for 2010.

In relation to findings in the earlier chapters, Chapter 12 looks at China's grain issues from various angles. In particular, it sheds light on relationships between feedgrain requirement and foodgrain consumption in China. It also examines the impact of economic growth and demographic changes on demand for foodgrain and feedgrain with reference to a number of other countries in Asia and other regions. The findings are used to draw implications for China's future foodgrain and feedgrain consumption and for international grain trade.

References

Bruinsma, J. (ed.) (2003), *World Agriculture: Towards 2015/2030, An FAO Perspective*, Earthscan, London.
FAO (Food and Agriculture Organization of the United Nations) (2002), *World Agriculture: Towards 2015/2030*, Summary Report, FAO, Rome.

PART I
FOODGRAIN AND FEEDGRAIN

Chapter 2

Developments in China's Grain Policies

Wei-Ming Tian and Zhang-Yue Zhou

In this part of the book, we address issues related to the production and consumption of foodgrain and feedgrain in China. To better understand how grain production and consumption have evolved in China in the past decade or so, it is useful to have an overview of the developments in China's grain policies. Such an overview will also facilitate our understanding of China's grain trade that will be the focus of the next part of the book. This chapter is devoted to highlighting the developments of China's grain policies since the early 1990s.[1]

2.1 Evolution of Grain Production, Procurement and Trade Policies

The most important function of agriculture in China has been to supply food for its huge population, a function repeatedly emphasised by the government and researchers. At the time of its founding in 1949, the People's Republic of China encountered severe shortages of grain. Since then, the government has made great efforts to ensure an adequate grain supply for its people, and over the past five decades has significantly improved the supply situation, particularly since the mid-1980s. In the meantime, the grain policies have also evolved from a more strict control over production, consumption and trade by means of administrative measures to a less controlled regime using increasing market forces. In this section, we first trace the major government policy developments related to grain production since 1990. Given that the government's policy on grain procurement and trade has been closely related to fluctuations in grain production, it is useful to discuss grain procurement and trade policy changes in conjunction with grain production policy developments.

In the early 1980s, China experienced consecutive bumper grain harvests. This significantly eased China's grain supply situation and in some areas there were even complaints of difficulty in selling and storing grains. In 1985, the coercive unified grain procurement system, which had been in use for more than thirty years, was replaced by a "contractual grain procurement system". The implementation of this new system discouraged farmers from growing and selling more grains, resulting in a sharp drop in both yield and sown area of grain in 1985. While sown area to grain crops dropped, sown area to most of the major cash crops (except cotton) increased (SSB 1986, p. 174).

The policy-makers became alarmed by the fall in production and in 1986 efforts were made to increase grain production. One measure was to deploy extensive administrative manpower to "persuade" millions of farmer households to sign contracts to sell grains to the government. A moderate increase in grain production was registered in 1986 but was mainly brought about by an increase in sown area to grain and came at the cost of reduced cash crop cultivation (SSB 1989, p. 192).

In the following years, various other policy measures were also initiated to encourage farmers to produce more grains, including reduced contractual procurement quota, a "three-link" scheme, an increase in contractual procurement prices, extension of new technologies, and improvement in infrastructure. In 1989, grain production increased and for the first time exceeded its 1984 level, though very marginally. In late 1990, some changes were brought to the grain procurement policy: farmers were again obligated to deliver the required amounts of grains to the state. However, they were allowed to sell remaining grains through other channels (Delfs 1990; Hu 1990; State Council 1991a).

In the early 1990s, a fast increase in input price levels, led by fertilisers, became a burning issue.[2] While there were procurement price increases (two major ones were in April 1992 and June 1994), input prices also increased and rapidly. Often the level of input price increases was higher than that of output price increases (Deng 1993; Liu 1995). This greatly affected farmers' earnings.

To restrict input price level rises, the government reinstated disciplines on ceiling prices in 1993 for several major agricultural inputs. Due to a lack of reinforcement measures, there were cases where these ceiling prices were broken. Since the input price level was so high, farmers complained bitterly and the issue was repeatedly reported in the media at that time.[3]

As a result of good harvests in 1989 and 1990, there was plenty of grain available in the market. The market was sluggish from late 1989 to mid 1993. Farmers again suffered from "difficulties in selling grain". In some areas, market prices dropped below the government quota prices. The low output prices but high input prices further dampened farmers' returns from grain production. To protect farmers' interests, a new minimum support price policy was started in 1990 (State Council 1990a). The government promised to purchase all grains (after the fulfilment of quota delivery) offered by farmers at no lower than announced support prices. To facilitate this operation, the government decided to establish a special national grain reserve scheme to absorb the extra grains bought under the support price. In the meantime, the State Grain Reserve Bureau was established, an administration directly under the State Council, to manage reserve stocks (State Council 1990b).

In view of the fact that market availability was good and that the unified grain sale system had almost disappeared in China by September 1993, the government in October 1993 decided that, from 1994, the government would procure a certain amount of grain but the price would be determined by the market. However, the sluggish grain market revived in late 1993. Market prices rose quickly and sharply, starting from the southern part of the country but soon spread all over the country. Panic buying and hoarding co-existed.

Given this situation, the 1993 new measures could not be put into practice in 1994. The government emphasised the importance of government-held grain and asked local governments to increase grain procurement. In addition to the 50 million tonnes quota purchase, another 40 million tonnes were to be purchased at negotiated prices. The government insisted that 70% to 80% of the marketed grains should be traded by its agents.

Pressured by the high market price level, procurement prices of four major grain crops (wheat, paddy, corn and soybean) were raised in June 1994 by about 44% (from 72¥/100 kg to 104¥/100 kg). However, the market price level increased even further, making it difficult for government agents to procure grain at the target level. To fulfil the assigned tasks, some local governments had to increase prices even for quota purchases, with the gap between the central government price and the actual price being borne by themselves (Zhou and Chen 1995).

Early in 1995, the central government introduced a "provincial governor responsibility system" to handle the grain economy within their jurisdiction in an attempt to achieve regional balances of grain supply and demand. Among other expectations, provincial governors were required to take responsibility to procure 70-80% of the marketed grains, to organise grain supply, and to keep prices under control within their provinces. However, the quota procurement price for 1995 remained the same as in 1994. This was the case, perhaps, due to the following three considerations. (1) The price increases in 1994 were quite substantial and there would be a lag in farmers' response to price signals and thus there was no need to increase further in 1995. (2) Many still held that an increase in grain prices could trigger an increase in the overall price level. By not increasing the procurement price further, it would help to curtail the high level of inflation at that time. (3) Further increasing procurement price would also increase the government's fiscal burden.

Throughout 1994 and into early 1995 market prices remained high. The government increased the release of grains from the reserves through the wholesale market in order to curb the price rise. The impact was limited and grain prices continued to rise. Consequently, in 1995 the government increased grain imports substantially. The net import was 19.9 million tonnes, a record high. This helped to keep prices for the rest of 1995 fairly stable. At the macro economic level, the government imposed a series of restraining programs on government spending and took various other measures to reduce money supply.

During 1994 and 1995, the central government also made efforts to increase grain production capacity, such as designation of some counties as grain production bases, land reclamation and improvement under agricultural development projects, increased investment in rural infrastructure, increased assistance to agricultural extension, stricter protection of cultivated land, and increased support to farm input industries. As a result of various government measures along with high prices, grain output leapt, reaching a new record high of over 500 millions tonnes in 1996 and remained high in the following three years.

In 1997, the grain market again became sluggish. Grain prices started to decline due to both domestic and external factors. Domestically, the supply was plentiful. Internationally, the world grain prices also declined. The government believed the decline in the world grain prices would be a short-term phenomenon. In order to protect farmer income and also maintain grain production capacity, it began to implement guaranteed procurement of grains at state-set floor prices in late 1997. State grain marketing enterprises (SGMEs) were ordered to buy whatever amounts farmers wanted to sell. These measures were later developed to become a new grain policy package issued in June 1998. The new package consisted of three policy measures: (1) purchase at floor prices all grains that producers want to sell, (2) sell purchased grains at prices covering all operating costs, and (3) ensure an enclosed circulation of working funds within China Agricultural Development Bank (CADB), i.e., all transactions of the SGMEs must go through their accounts at CADB.

However, this policy package never worked as intended. The distorted price signal induced farmers to hand over lower quality grains not in high demand, leading to overstocking by the SGMEs. Apart from limited storage capacity, the SGMEs lacked incentive to purchase at the floor prices due to sluggish market prospects. Granted a monopolistic position in local markets, the SGMEs often abused their power to reject or downgrade grains using various excuses and make purchases based on their own interests. Low domestic and world market prices made "sale without loss" difficult. The operations of SGMEs resulted in huge financial losses. In order to cope with the situation, the government controlled grain imports and exports through its state trading system. This measure restricted imports while providing support to exports, helping to dispose of overstocked grains (mainly corn). The slowdown in China's WTO accession negotiation in the late 1990s and hence its delayed acceptance to the WTO enabled China to subsidise its corn export.

Starting from 1999, the government adjusted floor prices downward and removed low quality varieties out of guaranteed procurement. Price margins were allowed to better reflect quality differences and seasonal handling costs. Some food-processing firms were allowed to sign grain purchase contracts directly with producers to ensure supply of products with the required quality attributes. Facing the consequences of the unsuccessful 1998 policy package, coupled with abundant grain supply, the government initiated further market-oriented reforms starting in 1999. Some of the major initiatives and measures are as follows.

In 1999, the government started a program to turn grain fields back to tree plantation or pasture in areas where the land was not suited for grain production. Popularly known as "Grain for Green", the program aims to rehabilitate degraded environments or natural resources that have been badly damaged by inappropriate usage or overexploitation, especially in western China. The trial was initially started in Sichuan, Shaanxi and Gansu. Since 1999, the program has been rapidly extended to cover most provinces. By 2003, about 8 million hectares of cultivated land was planted to trees (State Forestry Bureau 2004). Under this program, the government provides participating farmers with grains and money as compensation for income foregone. The program became possible partially due to the need to ease the downward pressure on grain prices as a result of the relative grain surplus in the domestic market but also partially due to the increased public awareness for a better environment. The short-term effect from such a program includes the reduction of the grain supply and stockpile. If the program can be sustained, it will also deliver a long-term effect: an improved natural environment. How long this program will be implemented is yet to be seen. Two major factors that will affect its life are: whether the government will allocate sufficient funds to sustain the program; and what the government may decide to do if China's grain supply turns from the recent relative surplus to a shortage in the future.

Other measures were also undertaken to signal farmers to produce less low quality grain. One was to reduce the varieties of grain crops covered under the guaranteed procurement scheme (for example, spring wheat in 1999; low quality early-season indica rice in 2000). In February 2002, corn produced in southern China was also phased out. In the same year, many provinces also reduced their coverage of grain crops under the guaranteed procurement scheme and reduced prices for those still under the scheme.

China became a WTO member in late 2001. Further deregulation of grain marketing was on the agenda. In 2002 eight grain-deficit provinces started to liberalise their regional grain markets, initiated by local governments and approved by the central government in 2001. Since then, other provincial governments have also decided to liberalise their markets either as a whole or in some major grain-deficit areas within their provinces. For example, Shandong liberalised grain marketing in Qingdao, Yantai and Weihai in April 2002.

Further reforms involving more provinces were planned for 2003. However, in late 2003, there were sharp and sudden grain price increases. Compared with prices in the same period of 2002, the price increases in wholesale markets in late October 2003 were 14% for white wheat, 24% for yellow corn, 10% for japonica rice and 40% for soybean. These price increases caused some uncertainty in the direction and speed of further grain market reforms. In early 2004, grain prices continued to increase. Compared with prices in the same period of 2003, in March 2004 price increases were 40% for white wheat, 17% for yellow corn, 45% for japonica rice, and 30% for soybean. There were a number of reasons for the grain price increases, including reduced level of grain stocks in China due to lower grain output, but net grain exports in four consecutive years (2000-03) increased world grain prices, and speculations in the market. The government was again alarmed and immediately began to take actions to investigate the causes of the grain price increase and to boost domestic grain production.

Several major measures undertaken by the government to increase grain production included the strictest control over the conversion of cultivated land into non-agricultural uses; prevention of undue increases of agricultural input prices; the use of protective floor prices for major grain crops; increased investment for agricultural extension; subsidies for the purchase of some inputs such as agricultural machinery and improved seeds; and direct payments to grain farmers. Direct payments are linked to areas planted to grains, and thus may not be fully decoupled. The source of the funds for such direct payments is from the "grain risk funds". The grain risk funds used to be used to cover the losses of those SGMEs in their marketing operations, but are now used to provide direct support to the farmers. A number of provinces such as Jiangsu, Heilongjiang, Henan, and Beijing have already started to provide direct payments to their farmers. This is a national policy but provincial governments are required to determine the amount of payments and criteria used to distribute the payments.

In early 2004, the government announced that agricultural taxes would be reduced and eventually abolished in five years' time. This measure is likely to have limited impact on the level of grain output, but will increase rural incomes in the short term. The government has recently adopted one other major policy measure. On 3 June 2004, the State Council issued a new regulation relating to grain marketing. This regulation declared that China would further liberalise its grain market in 2004. All types of entities are now allowed to purchase grains in the market provided they meet the requirements for registering as grain traders with local governments.

Since the early 1990s, there have also been important changes to grain imports and exports and related policies. At the beginning of the 1990s, trade of grains was subject to central government's planning and management. Both imports and exports were determined in line with annual economic plans and implemented by the designated state trading enterprises (STEs), for example, the Cereal, Oil & Foodstuffs Importing and Exporting Corporation, and some regional STEs. Distribution and pricing of imports and exports were also centrally determined. In 1993, the government reduced the coverage of agricultural products subject to quotas and licenses, but major grain products were still managed by STEs. On the export side, licenses were issued at different levels based on the importance of exported grain items, such as rice, corn, and soybean.

Despite the fact that the state trading system for grains largely remained intact as a result of the reforms in 1993, regulations became more transparent. The STEs were essentially transformed into entities responsible for their own operating results, which induced them to also become profit-seeking enterprises. As a result of stopping import subsidies and transforming the STEs into agents, linkages between domestic prices and the world market prices were established. This has become an important factor affecting reforms to grain policies in later years.

With consecutive good harvests for four years starting from 1996, there was much downward pressure on prices in the grain market, which affected farmer income. There was also pressure on storage space, and the need for turnover to avoid deterioration of stored grains. In addition to the increased use of grains as feed, exporting grains was a major solution. A subsidy was provided to encourage the export of grains. China has since 1997 net exported grains to the world market, chiefly corn. Meanwhile, China increased imports of soybean. Following China's joining the WTO at the end of 2001, China ended direct subsidies to grain export in 2002 in line with the WTO accession commitment. However, in the interim, some indirect support was provided. For example, the government collects a railway construction fee on all goods shipped through railways, but for all grains shipped for exporting, this fee was waived till May 2004. The government also gave a full refund of value-added taxes for exported grains. These measures, along with rising corn and wheat prices in the world market since mid-2002, facilitated China's continued large-scale grain exports after its accession to the WTO.

China's net grain exports since 1997, coupled with reduced grain outputs since 2000, must have led to reduced grain stocks. However, the exact level of grain stocks is not available, and the government has still not started to publicise the level of its reserve stocks. Nonetheless, the reduced level of stocks seems to be one of the triggers that have prompted the increase in grain prices in late 2003 – as a result of speculations of likely increases in China's grain imports. In late 2003, China placed some orders of wheat imports partially in response to domestic demand and partially in response to pressure from the US government on China to open up its market. As a result, wheat imports in 2004 will increase. In the longer term, China will increase its grain import. However, it is likely that the amount and composition of imports may vary to a great extent between years and the amount in general is unlikely to be large in the near future. Although China will increasingly follow market rules to decide where and how much to import, some non-market factors may have some impacts on China's import behaviour.

2.2 Grain Consumption Policies

As mentioned earlier, in the late 1940s and early 1950s, China experienced a severe shortage of foodgrain. When there is an overall grain shortage, control over grain distribution is often essential. To ensure that people receive a fair amount of grain, the Chinese government introduced a rationing system at the end of 1953 when the unified grain procurement scheme was implemented. The system primarily covered non-agricultural population or agricultural population who were engaged in non-grain businesses or who produced grain but not enough for home use. The ration was set by the government according to age and occupation (labouring strength). The use of grain coupons was an important element of the rationing system.

From its inception until the early 1990s, the system underwent few significant changes. Only minor alternations were made occasionally in the supply standard and prices or in coverage of the system. Since the mid-1980s, grain procurement prices were raised several times to encourage greater production. However, the unified grain sale price under the rationing system was not raised or only raised very marginally, leaving the sale price below the procurement price. This led to increased government subsidy on grain consumption. The steadily increasing subsidy on grain consumption became increasingly unaffordable. Starting from the mid-1980s, much attention was paid to seeking ways to reduce the subsidy. In spite of the increasing pressure to curtail the size of the subsidy, the government, nevertheless, left the unified sale price of grain largely untouched in order to maintain social stability. However, urban consumers were able to buy grains from free markets or from government stores at negotiated prices if they wished to buy beyond the ration amount. Also, urban residents could sell rationed low quality grains or sell the coupons and buy high quality grain at a higher price.

A major change in grain consumption policy took place in May 1991, when the government moved to reduce urban subsidies for rationed grain by increasing the unified grain sale price (State Council 1991b). After this increase, the sale price was, however, still lower than the procurement price.

In April 1992, the sale price was further increased to equal the grain procurement price (State Council 1992). The total subsidy on grain consumption was reduced significantly, from 47 billion yuan in 1991 to 35 billion yuan in 1992, a reduction of 12 billion yuan. By about mid-1993, the unified grain sale system disappeared in most areas of the country, leaving the urban dwellers responsible for the purchase of their own grain at market prices.[4] In 1993, the subsidy was consequently further reduced to less than 19 billion yuan.[5]

From October 1993, the grain price in the free market increased sharply with the situation aggravated by panic buying. Having been so sensitive about grain price, the Chinese government immediately mobilised various resources to cope with this price surge, including placing a ceiling price on grain traded in the free market. Grain price was brought under control by about early December of that year with heavy administrative intervention.

In the first half of 1994, price fluctuations continued in some areas. From July 1994, grain prices again rose quickly throughout China. In view of the sharp fluctuations in grain prices in late 1993 and mid-1994, the Chinese government tried very hard to bring prices under control. From late 1994, some local governments restored rationing methods to supply grain to urban consumers at a subsidised rate.

During 1995, there were no worrying price surges, thanks to increased grain imports by the government and increased grain supply through government shops at subsidised prices. Some areas started to reintroduce coupons and by September 1995 about half of the provinces restored the use of coupons ('What does the reintroduction of coupons mean?', *Beijing Economic News*, 17 September 1995; Ka 1995). The reintroduction of coupons lasted, however, only for a short period.

During 1995 and 1996, local governments were increasingly required by the central government to assume primary responsibilities to handle grain matters under their jurisdiction. Consequently, although they still procured grains under a quota regime at a government-set price, the methods of grain distribution were not identical across regions. Some cities sold subsidised grains through government shops without a ration; others did so with a ration. But, as with the earlier centrally administered rationing system, few used any targeting except in a few cities such as Shanghai and Beijing ('Shanghai adopts new grain and cooking oil distribution methods', *Grain and Cooking Oil Market News*, 8 March 1996; 'Beijing raised grain sale prices', *Beijing Economic News*, 2 July 1996).

As a result of increased grain production in 1996 and in subsequent years, there was plenty of grain in the market and the price was relatively stable and low. For the first time in China's recent history, having enough grain to eat ceased to be a problem. Most consumers had no difficulty affording grains. Indeed, many consumers' direct consumption of grains had declined, especially in urban areas. Coupled with their increased income, the expenditure share of grains had become relatively small (see Chapters 4 and 5 for details). On the other hand, their consumption of foods of animal origin had increased (see Chapter 6), which led to a rapid increase in the consumption of feedgrains in China in recent years (see Chapter 7). Hence, the government no longer needed to take direct responsibility to ensure the provision of grains to individual consumers.[6] Subsequently, the need for an active government grain consumption policy also disappeared. However, the government continues to closely monitor the price situations in the market. It still strongly believes that it is important to maintain grain price stability in order to ensure social stability, especially in the urban areas.

2.3 Policies Concerning Grain Reserve Stocks

Prior to the 1980s, the government continuously emphasised the need to have grain reserves in order to be prepared for any wars (with the western countries earlier and later with the former USSR). However, government reserve policies and the amount of reserves were top secret and not available to the public. There exists very limited literature on the composition of operational turnover stocks and buffer reserves and on how grain reserves were managed. In the mid-1980s, following changed grain demand and supply situations, more grains could be spared for reserve purposes. Indeed, there was increased demand for storage capacity. Increased reserve levels led to the demand for a more clearly defined grain reserve policy and to separate operations of normal turnover stocks from buffer reserves.

A more tangible reserve policy started to emerge in the early 1990s due to the good harvests in 1989 and 1990. The good harvests led farmers to experiencing another "difficulty in selling grain". To protect farmers' interests, the government promised to purchase all grains offered by farmers at support prices, and the extra grains bought under support prices were to be absorbed by a special national grain reserve scheme newly established by the government (State Council 1990b). The operations were carried out by the State Grain Reserve Bureau. However, due to problems such as limited purchasing funds and limited storage capacity, implementation was ineffective. Farmers were often given IOUs for the grains they sold. Some purchased grains were stored in the open due to insufficient storage (Wang 1991; Zhu 1991).

The government in early 1993 attempted to establish "grain risk funds" that would be used for the operation of grain procurement at the support price and the accumulation of grains for the special national grain reserve scheme. Both the central government and provincial governments were to establish their "grain risk funds". In practice, obtaining the funds was often a problem.

During the 1990s, the State Grain Reserve Bureau had two major responsibilities related to China's grain operations: (1) policy functions of grain reserves (for the nation's grain security) and (2) commercial operations of grain reserves (normal market operations). Grain bureaus under various local government levels carried out the actual marketing operations. Very often the two different functions were carried out at the local level by the same group of personnel but with two different organisation names. Two separate accounts were required, one for each of the two organisations. Any losses associated with the implementation of policy functions were attributed to the account of the organisation for policy functions. On the other hand, any losses associated with market operations should be attributed to the account of the organisation for normal market operations, as the latter was supposed to be an autonomous commercial entity. In reality, however, because both of the operations were carried out by the same group of people, there was a tendency for the losses from normal market operations to be attributed to the policy function account or for the costs for their normal market operations to be charged to the policy function account to boost their profit level. In the late 1990s, there were voices recommending increasingly that the two grain-reserve related operations be strictly separated. Those in charge of these two operations have no incentive to see them separated.

In April 2000 the government reorganised the State Grain Reserve Bureau, which led to the creation of two new organisations for two different operations. One was named the State Grain Bureau, responsible for policy functions of grain reserves. The other was named the State Grain Reserve Management Corporation, responsible for commercial operations of grain reserves. The former is a policy-oriented decision-making agency that manages China's grain reserve strategies and implements various other policy initiatives to ensure China's grain security. The latter conducts grain trade operations like a commercial entity. One of the major objectives for this reform is to separate the market operations function from the State Grain Reserve Bureau. It was expected that this would help avoid conflicts of interest between policy operations and commercial operations. As noted above there were strong incentives for some to attribute the costs of their market operations to the policy operations account for personal gains. This then becomes the government's budget burden.

Closely related to China's grain reserve policy is the capacity of China's grain storage. In the 1980s, there was a severe shortage in grain storage capacity, and the quality of the grain storage facilities available was low. From the early 1990s, the government began to pay much attention to increasing China's grain storage capacity and improving grain marketing facilities. Apart from funds from government budget, foreign funds were also borrowed for these purposes. For example, the World Bank provided a loan of $490 million for the China Grain Market Project. The Chinese government also allocated 33.7 billion yuan between 1998 and 2001 for construction of 51.5 million tonnes of storage facilities (State Grain Bureau 2002, p. 1).

Grain reserve data used to be, and perhaps are still, regarded by some as being of crucial importance for national strategic security. They are kept secret and are generally not available to the public. However, the secrecy surrounding Chinese grain reserves is perhaps no longer as crucial to China's national strategic security as it might have been in the past. In fact, a relaxation of secrecy would be beneficial to market stabilisation not only in China but also globally as this would discourage speculation. There is a need for China to regularly publicise its grain reserve stocks, but when it may choose to do so is uncertain. On the other hand, whether the government even knows accurately the amount of reserve stock in hand is also a question. It has happened that local agents of the State Grain Reserve Bureau have sometimes provided inaccurate reserve reports to the government in an attempt to request more government funding for their operations.

2.4 Concluding Comments

A review of China's grain policy developments since the early 1990s clearly shows that production and procurement policies are the centrepiece in China's overall grain policies. All other components revolve around them. Given the fact that some 60% of China's grain output is still consumed on-farm, the amount of grains available for sale in the market to the non-agricultural population and the amount of grains in the government's hand draw much attention from the policy makers. Changes in these amounts often trigger changes to procurement policies. When the government feels uncomfortable about the amount of grains available to the market (too much or too little), modifications are often made to procurement policies, and this then results in changes in production policies and other components of the grain policies.

Since the mid-1980s when the government began to reform the unified grain procurement system, China's grain policies have generally evolved from a more strict control approach to a less controlled regime using increasing market forces. In the near future, China's grain economy and market is likely to become more liberalised. Consequently, there will be further changes to the approach that the government uses to procure grains. The government is likely to increasingly procure grains in the market. In particular, when the agricultural tax is finally phased out, the government has to rely on market operations to procure grains for its own disposal, chiefly, for market stabilisation, for protecting farmers' income, and for use by military personnel. Given the fact that, in normal situations, urban residents purchase grains from the market and do not need the government to supply them with grains any more, the amount of grains that the government needs to procure will gradually decrease.

When the government becomes more proficient in using the market to secure grains for its own disposal and to influence the market, it may become the case that grain policy changes will be less abrupt than has often happened in the past.

However, achieving grain security – primarily through domestic resources – will continue to be the paramount objective of the government's future grain policy. It is possible that the government will do whatever is allowable to achieve China's grain security chiefly by relying on domestic resources. The recent declining trend in the direct consumption of grains is likely to make it easier for China to manage its grain security. That is, China can choose to chiefly use domestic resources to ensure the supply of foodgrains but import grains from the international market to meet any feedgrain shortages. With such a strategy, should there be any unforeseen events that prevent China's imports of grains from the international market, the supply of foodgrains in the domestic market will not be jeopardised.

When China's grain security is reasonably assured, the government's grain policy will also increasingly accommodate the needs for (1) raising farmer income and reducing poverty incidence, (2) fulfilling WTO commitments to further opening up its grain market, and (3) protecting and rehabilitating environment and natural resources.

Having provided a broad overview of the developments in China's grain policy in the recent decade, we now turn to more detailed aspects of production and consumption of China's foodgrain and feedgrain and their trade. In the next chapter, we examine the grain production trend in China.

References

Delfs, R. (1990), 'China returns to coercive grain quotas: state incentives', *Far Eastern Economic Review*, 22 November, pp. 62-63.

Deng, Y.M. (1993), 'Predicament and wayout of commercial grain bases: a survey of the grain problems in Changtu County, Liaoning Province', in Deng, Y.M., Chen, J.S. and Yuan, Y.K. (eds), *Grain Marketing: Commercialisation and Government Macro Adjustment*, Economic Management Press, Beijing.

Hu, P. (1990), 'Speech at the National Grain Meeting [extract]' (November 1990), in *Chinese Grain Economy*, 1991, No. 1, p. 9.

Ka, L. (1995), 'How to comprehend the reintroduction of coupons', *Economic Daily*, 22 February, p. 2.

Liu, X.G. (1995), 'Happiness and concerns of grain specialist households', *Economic Daily*, 16 December, p. 1.

SSB, *China Statistics Yearbook*, various issues, China Statistical Press, Beijing.

State Council (1990a), 'Decisions on strengthening grain procurement and distribution', *Chinese Grain Economy*, No. 5, pp. 1-3.

State Council (1990b), 'Decisions on establishing national special grain reserve system', *Chinese Grain Economy*, No. 6, pp. 1-2.

State Council (1991a), 'Circulation on issues regarding the adjustment of grain procurement and supply', *Chinese Grain Economy*, No. 2, pp. 1-3.

State Council (1991b), 'Decision on the adjustment of the unified sale prices of grain and cooking oil', in the Editorial Board of Grain Economy and Management Series (ed.) (1992), *Review and Outlook of the Reforms of the Grain Marketing System*, Chinese Commerce Press, Beijing, pp. 109-13.

State Council (1992), 'Decision on the increase of the unified grain sale price', in the Editorial Board of Grain Economy and Management Series (ed.) (1992), *Review and Outlook of the Reforms of the Grain Marketing System*, Chinese Commerce Press, Beijing, pp. 255-59.

State Grain Bureau (2002), *Study on Construction of Grain Storage Facilities in the Northeast*, China Planning Publishing House, Beijing.

State Forestry Bureau (2004), '60 million *mu* of land will be returned from grain production to forestry this year', available at http://news.xinhuanet.com, 6 April 2004.

Wang, J.L. (1991), 'Grain losses and the urgency to build up grain storage facilities', *Chinese Grain Economy*, No. 3, pp. 39-40.

Zhao, F.S. and Qi, X.Q. (eds) (1988), *Grain in Contemporary China*, Chinese Social Sciences Press, Beijing

Zhou, Z.Y. (1997), *Effects of Grain Marketing Systems on Grain Production: A Comparative Study of China and India*, The Haworth Press, New York.

Zhou, Z.Y. and Chen, L.B. (1995), 'Reforms in China's grain procurement system in 1994: an appraisal', *Reform*, No. 5, pp. 55-58.

Zhu, T.B. (1991), 'National special grain reserve system is yet to be improved', *Chinese Grain Economy*, No. 4, pp. 35-36.

Notes

[1]   For details of China's grain policy developments before 1990, see Zhao and Qi (1988); Zhou (1997). Discussion on China's grain policy before the mid-1990s is largely based on Zhou (1997).

[2]   In the early 1980s, production, distribution and trade of farm inputs were managed under the central planning system. Starting from 1985, as an incentive, a scheme of twin-track prices was formally introduced into the chemical fertiliser industry, which allowed the state-owned large factories to sell their extra output at market prices. Meanwhile, the government continued to impose ceilings on ex-factory prices in order to control the price level.

[3]   Controlling input prices has been an issue for the government in recent years, causing it to take a number of measures to curtail input prices such as providing subsidies to manufacturers of agricultural chemicals. Nonetheless, until 1997, the input price had been increasing and its level had been always higher than that of grains except in 1994 when grain prices increased sharply. From 1998 to 2003, the input price level started to decline but the grain price level also declined resulting in the former being still higher than the latter. In early 2004, input prices have been increasing following price increases in grains.

[4]   It is noted that, for each major grain sale price increase, some cash payment was made to city workers to compensate the price increase.

[5]   Although the ration system was abolished, the government still procures grain through both quota and market purchases. This grain is used for central reserves and other government purposes and sold through government-owned shops at market prices.

[6]   Admittedly, there was a small pocket of the population who had difficulty buying their staple food. However, since the mid-1990s, various levels of government in China paid increased attention to the institution of a social security system, which had played a role in providing a safety net to those who experience difficulty buying staple food. In the meantime, family members and relatives also provided assistance to those in need.

Chapter 3

Trends in Grain Production

Zhang-Yue Zhou and Wei-Ming Tian

Grain is China's most significant agricultural product, its output being the most watched indicator by government officials, traders and researchers both inside and outside China. In this chapter, we examine China's grain production trends in the recent decade. To understand China's grain production and how its trend evolves, it is useful to appreciate the characteristics of China's grain production, the subject of the next section. In Section 3.2, we examine changes in total grain output and in grain crop composition. Section 3.3 highlights the dynamics in regional distribution of grain production. Changes in production technologies and costs are presented in Section 3.4. In Section 3.5, we address a number of emerging issues that are likely to affect future grain production.

3.1 Characteristics of China's Grain Production

China's grain production has some unique features. Such features affect not only short-run land and labour productivities, but also long-term prospects of the grain sector's development and grain supply potential. Some major features of China's grain production are highlighted below.

The most striking feature of China's grain production is the very small scale of production. The huge amount of grains is produced by millions of small household farms. Following the rural economic reforms in the early 1980s, rural households again became the basic units of agricultural production. Land was distributed among farmers largely according to the number of people in a household. This resulted in a very small land area per household. Also the area may be composed of several small blocks due to the need to distribute land of varying quality to all farmers in an equitable manner. Farmers use these small blocks to produce a wide range of farm produce. In 2002, there were about 248 million household farms. Land area cultivated by each farm is extremely small (Figure 3.1). Over 90% of household farms work on an area that is under 1 hectare while those that have a land area over 3.4 hectares account for less than 1%. Yet most of China's grain output in the vicinity of 500 million tonnes is produced by these small farms.

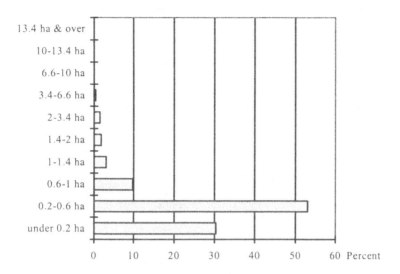

Figure 3.1 Scale distribution of cultivated land of farm households

Source: Office for National Agricultural Census (1998, p. 43).

Most of China's grain is produced for on-farm consumption. According to SSB (2003, p. 441), each agricultural labourer produced on average about 1400 kg of grains, of which less than half was sold either to the state or on the market with the rest being retained for on-farm consumption. China's grain production is still largely semi-subsistence.

Producing grains of the desired quality is difficult. The small scale of production coupled with inadequate grain marketing facilities make it very difficult to produce grains of the desired quality at the desired quantity for specific usages. First, the quality of grains varies from farm to farm. Second, grains of similar quality are often not handled separately, due to either lack of facilities or the small quantity.

There tends to be an over-utilisation of land resources. Due to limited land resources and high demand for grains, China has to make full use, and sometimes overuse, of its land resources in order to produce enough grains. Multiple cropping has been widely practised throughout China as a way to raise land productivity. Intensive land use often leads to soil degradation.

Regional patterns are distinct. Being such a vast country, China has diverse agronomic conditions. In line with local conditions, Chinese farmers produce different crops in various ways, resulting in distinct regional patterns of grain production. For example, rice is produced chiefly in southern China and wheat in northern China (see Section 3 later in this chapter for details of regional distribution of various grains). Farmers also adopt various cropping systems according to local conditions. For instance, rice-based double or even triple cropping is a common practice in the tropical and subtropical areas and multiple cropping of upland crops is widely used in the temperate zone.

Grain production is still strongly affected by government policies. Although the Chinese government has in the past two decades tried to liberalise its grain economy, it still maintains a strong degree of control over grain production. As discussed in Chapter 2, the degree of control depends on China's grain output and the amount of grains that is in the government's hand. The government intervenes in grain production whenever it is deemed necessary.

Given the above features of China's grain production, it may be appreciated that how China's grain production will evolve in the future is likely to be complicated and will be affected by various factors. Particularly in relation to government policy, any dramatic changes may overshadow predicted general trends of grain production as happened in the past two decades. Keeping this in mind, in the rest of this chapter, we examine major trends in China's grain production since the early 1990s and identify important factors that will affect its longer term development.

3.2 Grain Production and Crop Composition

Closely related to structural changes that have taken place in China's broader agricultural sector since 1990, China's total grain production has also fluctuated. Changes in the production of grains have typically exhibited a reversed "U" shape (see Figure 3.2).

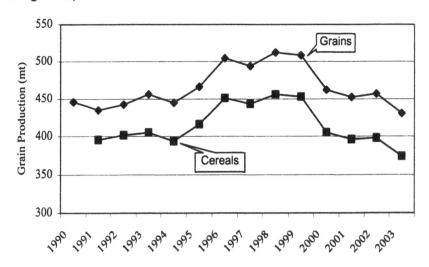

Figure 3.2 Trends in China's total grain production

Source: SSB (2003, p. 430)

The promotional policies and the high prices since 1994 stimulated grain production strongly. As a result, grain output rose notably in subsequent years until 1998 when China registered a record high of 512 million tonnes of grains. The strong growth in domestic supply, coupled with declining world grain prices, resulted in stockpiling of grains in government reserves, usually grains of low quality. In response, the government encouraged farmers to adjust their production according to market demand. Grain prices, including state procurement prices, have declined to varying extents since 1998 (MOA 2003). Consequently, China's grain output dropped in 1999 by 4 million tonnes and during 2000-02 total grain output remained 50-60 million tonnes lower than the 1998 level. The consecutive lower grain output since 1999, further prompted by a rising price since September 2003, caused Chinese policymakers to deploy various measures in early 2004 in order to promote grain production (see Chapter 2 for details).

Grain in China includes cereals (rice, wheat, corn, sorghum, millet and other miscellaneous grains), tuber crops (sweet potatoes and potatoes only, not including taro and cassava), as well as pulses (soybeans only). The output of tuber crops (sweet potatoes and potatoes) was converted on a 4:1 ratio, i.e., four kilograms of fresh tubers were equivalent to one kilogram of grain, up to 1963. Since 1964, the ratio has been 5:1. The output of beans refers to dry beans without pods. Grain production level as presented in Figure 3.2 includes all these "grains". Cereals, however, occupy an overwhelming importance in grain production, accounting for about 89% of the total grain output. Since 1991, the government has issued separate statistics for cereals. In the future, cereals will receive ever-increasing attention in the discussion of grains.

In this section, we focus on the production changes in cereals. Table 3.1 indicates three major changes in cereal production since 1991: (1) decline in area sown to cereal crops, (2) fluctuation in cereal output, and (3) changes in the composition of cereal crops.

In the late 1990s, the government was bothered by an overstock of cereals, which represented a heavy fiscal burden at both the national and regional levels. To reduce both the stock level and the downward pressure on the price in the grain market which had suppressed farmer income, the government took various measures to encourage farmers to adjust their crop production. One major measure was the "Grain for Green" program (see Chapter 2 for more details). Under this program, farmers in areas where resources are not conducive for grain production are provided with incentives to restore their cultivated land to forests, pastures or lakes, in an effort to rehabilitate the degraded or damaged environment. By 2003, about 8 million hectares of cultivated land had been planted to trees (State Forestry Bureau 2004).

During 1999-2002, total area planted to cereals deceased from 91.6 million hectares to 81.5 million hectares, a reduction by 11%. Apart from land set aside for conservation purposes under the "Grain for Green" program, relatively low return from cereal crops, rapid urbanisation and increased use of arable land for non-agricultural purposes (e.g., highway construction) are major causes of the reduced areas sown to cereals.

Grains in China

Table 3.1 Trends in cereal production

Year	Sown area (million hectares)				Output (million tonnes)			
	Total	*Rice*	*Wheat*	*Corn*	*Total*	*Rice*	*Wheat*	*Corn*
1991	94.07	32.59	30.95	21.57	395.7	183.8	96.0	98.8
1992	92.52	32.09	30.50	21.04	401.7	186.2	101.6	95.4
1993	88.91	30.36	30.24	20.69	405.2	177.5	106.4	102.7
1994	87.54	30.17	28.98	21.15	393.9	175.9	99.3	99.3
1995	89.31	30.74	28.86	22.78	416.1	185.2	102.2	112.0
1996	92.21	31.41	29.61	24.50	451.3	195.1	110.6	127.5
1997	91.96	31.77	30.06	23.78	443.5	200.7	123.3	104.3
1998	92.12	31.21	29.77	25.24	456.2	198.7	109.7	133.0
1999	91.62	31.28	28.86	25.90	453.0	198.5	113.9	128.1
2000	85.26	29.96	26.65	23.06	405.2	187.9	99.6	106.0
2001	82.60	28.81	24.66	24.28	396.5	177.6	93.9	114.1
2002	81.47	28.20	23.91	24.63	398.0	174.5	90.3	121.3

Source: SSB (2003, pp. 425, 430).

There is a clear trend of devoting more land area to corn production at the expense mainly of wheat. In 2002, the share of corn area in total area planted to cereals rose to 30%, compared with 23% in 1991. Meanwhile, the share of rice remained at about 35%, but the share of wheat declined from 33% to 29%. Apart from strong domestic demand for corn as feed, the increase in sown area to corn is induced by the relatively high price of corn in the domestic market, which is partially attributed to government policies in the late 1990s to subsidise corn export (see Chapter 9). The decline in wheat output is mainly due to reduction of spring wheat, which is of inferior quality. In 1990, the output of spring wheat was 13.3 million tonnes, but it declined to 7.4 million tonnes in 2000 (MOA 2004).

The fluctuation in cereal output largely matches that of total grain output. China's cereal output increased sharply in 1996, then remained at a level around 450 million tonnes before the decline in 1999 (Table 3.1). The decline in cereal production in recent years is attributed to the reduction in planting areas as discussed above and also to a reduction in yields.

Figure 3.3 shows that although the yields of major cereal crops in recent years were higher than that in the early 1990s, they are lower than the respective peak levels. Lower yields are partially due to low prices in recent years that did not entice farmers to use more inputs. Apart from this, a shift towards producing cereal varieties of higher quality is another, perhaps more important, reason. The area planted to high quality varieties rose from 22.7 million hectares in 1998 to 38.7 million hectares in 2002 for early indica rice, from 16.0 million hectares to 72.7 million hectares for wheat, and from 19.3 million hectares to 59.3 million hectares for corn (MOA 2003, pp. 1-2).

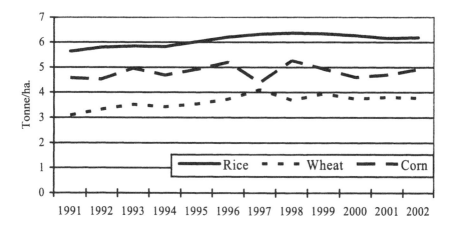

Figure 3.3 Changes in yields of major cereals

Source: Calculations based on SSB, various issues.

Although total cereal output has fluctuated over time, the proportion of each of the major cereals (wheat and corn and unmilled rice) in the total output has remained fairly stable (see Figure 3.4). However, the change in proportion does exhibit certain trends. That is, the share of rice in total cereal output tends to decline slightly over the years. The share of wheat remained at about 25% till 2000 but seems to have experienced a notable decline since 2001. The share of corn generally shows an increasing trend, increasing at the expense of rice and wheat shares. At the aggregate level, the proportion of these three major cereals continues to dominate the total cereal output, accounting for 97% in recent years compared to 95% in the early 1990s.

The other 3-5% of the cereal output is for minor cereal crops. Factors responsible for the decline in the share of minor cereal crops from 5% to 3% are: (1) only high quality minor cereals can sell at remunerative prices. However, such products are usually site-specific and cannot be planted widely. (2) Change in the alcohol industry also has an impact. The reduction of alcohol content of spirits and a shift from spirits to beer and wine has reduced the demand for minor cereals (such as sorghum and millet). (3) Large imports of higher quality barley for brewery purposes reduce the demand for domestically produced barley. Limited efforts have been devoted to improving domestic barley varieties and production techniques.

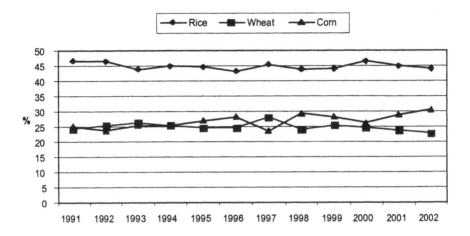

Figure 3.4 Proportion of major cereals out of total cereal output

Source: Calculations based on data in SSB (2003, p. 430).

The changes in the composition of the three major cereals are chiefly induced by market forces. The key driving force is the reduced direct human consumption of grains and increased use of grains as animal feed. In urban areas, per capita grain consumption has declined sharply from 131 kg in 1990 to 78 kg in 2002 (SSB 2003, p. 352). Per capita consumption of grains in rural areas has also declined (for details, see Chapters 4 and 5). Accompanying this reduced direct consumption of grains, consumer demand shifted to higher quality of grains. Farmers have responded by producing more grains of higher quality. However, higher quality grains generally have lower yields, thus contributing to lower rice and wheat output and to lower shares of the total cereal output. On the other hand, increased demand for food of animal origin has boosted China's demand for feedgrains in the past decade or so (see Chapters 6 and 7). This has encouraged farmers to produce more corn.

3.3 Regional Distribution of Grain Production

Map 3.1 shows regional distribution of grain production in China in 2002. In the past two decades, however, there have been changes in regional distribution of grain production. At the more aggregate level, grain production has shifted from the south to the north. In 1978, about 59% of China's grains were produced by 14 provinces south of the Yangtze River (including Jiangsu, Anhui and Hubei, part of which are in north of the Yangtze River; in 1978, Chongqing and Hainan had not yet been separated from Sichuan and Guangdong). The 15 provinces north of the

Yangtze River produced the other 41%. However, by 2002, the proportion of grains produced by those provinces south of the Yangtze River had dropped by about seven percentage points, to being less than 52% while the proportion of grains produced by northern provinces had increased to 48.5%. This has resulted in a change from "transporting grains from the south to the north" (*nan liang bei diao*) to "transporting grains from the north to the south" (*bei liang nan yun*).

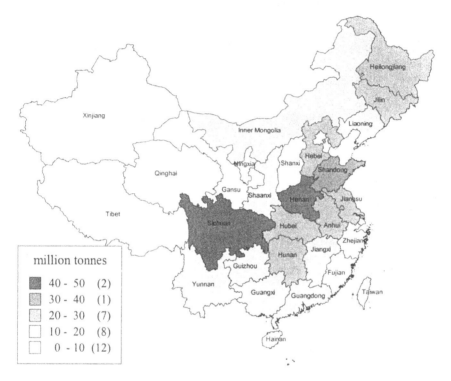

Map 3.1 Regional distribution of grain production, China, 2002

Source: Based on SSB (2003, p. 430).

At the less aggregate level, the decline in grain production in southern China took place mainly in the wealthier south-east coastal region. From 1978 to 2002, this region registered a decline in the proportion of grain production out of the national total by 6.7 percentage points, while the four north-east provinces gained about five percentage points (see Table 3.2, Panel A). The other major gaining region is the four provinces in north Central China, by 2.7 percentage points. Changes in the share in all other regions seem to be marginal. Hence, it can be concluded that grain production has been declining in China's south-east coastal region but increasing in the north-east region.

Grains in China

Table 3.2 Changes in regional distribution of grain production, 1978-2002 *

A. All Grain					
Region	*1978*	*1980*	*1990*	*2000*	*2002*
Beijing-Tianjin	1.0	1.0	1.0	0.6	0.5
North-east	12.8	12.3	15.3	14.2	17.7
South-east	20.7	20.7	17.9	15.8	14.0
Central China	41.3	40.9	42.9	44.2	43.2
Central China – North	21.1	21.0	22.2	24.5	23.8
Central China – South	20.2	19.8	20.7	19.6	19.4
South-west	18.0	19.3	16.7	18.9	18.1
North-west	6.2	5.8	6.1	6.3	6.6
North of Yangtze River	41.1	40.1	44.6	45.7	48.5
South of Yangtze River	58.9	59.9	55.4	54.3	51.5
Output (mt)	304.8	320.6	446.2	462.2	457.1
B. Rice					
Region	*1978*	*1980*	*1990*	*2000*	*2002*
Beijing-Tianjin	0.3	0.4	0.3	0.1	0.1
North-east	3.0	3.0	5.3	9.9	10.0
South-east	34.2	34.4	30.4	27.3	25.8
Central China	39.0	37.8	40.4	37.8	39.4
Central China – North	2.3	2.4	2.4	2.7	2.9
Central China – South	36.7	35.3	38.0	35.1	36.5
South-west	22.6	23.4	22.6	23.6	23.5
North-west	1.0	1.0	1.1	1.2	1.2
North of Yangtze River	6.5	6.9	9.0	13.9	14.2
South of Yangtze River	93.5	93.1	91.0	86.1	85.8
Output (mt)	136.9	139.9	189.3	187.9	174.5
C. Wheat					
Region	*1978*	*1980*	*1990*	*2000*	*2002*
Beijing-Tianjin	2.1	1.2	1.7	1.3	0.8
North-east	6.9	9.0	8.1	3.3	2.6
South-east	10.0	12.9	11.1	8.9	7.6
Central China	55.7	50.7	56.2	65.1	66.4
Central China – North	45.4	39.1	45.8	55.4	56.9
Central China – South	10.3	11.6	10.4	9.8	9.5
South-west	11.1	11.9	8.9	9.3	8.9
North-west	14.3	14.3	14.0	12.1	13.7
North of Yangtze River	68.6	63.7	69.5	72.0	74.0
South of Yangtze River	31.4	36.3	30.5	28.0	26.0
Output (mt)	53.8	55.2	98.2	99.6	90.3

D. Corn					
Region	*1978*	*1980*	*1990*	*2000*	*2002*
Beijing-Tianjin	1.6	2.3	2.1	0.9	1.0
North-east	32.6	29.1	38.5	28.0	35.4
South-east	2.9	2.6	2.7	3.3	2.9
Central China	36.3	38.8	36.2	42.1	38.3
Central China – North	33.4	36.5	33.1	36.7	32.8
Central China – South	2.9	2.3	3.1	5.4	5.5
South-west	17.0	19.1	13.3	16.5	13.9
North-west	9.5	8.0	7.1	9.2	8.5
North of Yangtze River	77.2	75.9	80.9	74.8	77.6
South of Yangtze River	22.8	24.1	19.1	25.2	22.4
Output (mt)	55.9	62.6	96.8	106.0	121.3

* The grouping of provinces into regions for this table is somewhat arbitrary. We carried out the grouping largely on the basis of local geographical conditions and the level of economic development. Beijing and Tianjin, two minor grain-producing areas, are placed into one group. The provinces included in each of the other groups are given below:

- North-east: Inner Mongolia, Liaoning, Jilin and Heilongjiang. Inner Mongolia is included in the north-east region because its grain production is concentrated in the east.
- South-east: Shanghai, Jiangsu, Zhejiang, Fujian, Guangdong and Hainan.
- Central China: Shandong, Shanxi, Henan, Hebei, Anhui, Jiangxi, Hunan and Hubei. These provinces are further divided into two sub-regions. The former four provinces are placed into the north Central China group and the latter the south Central China group.
- South-west: Guangxi, Chongqing, Sichuan, Guizhou, Yunnan and Tibet.
- North-west: Shaanxi, Gansu, Qinghai, Ningxia and Xinjiang.

Sources: SSB, various issues.

Table 3.2 also shows that Central China remains the major grain-producing region in China. Among other reasons, changes in the level of economic development between regions are primarily responsible for changes in regional distribution of grain production. Rapid economic development in the south-east coastal region made grain production a less attractive industry. Governments in such regions are keen to promote agricultural structural adjustments.

If we divide China into east, middle and west, then the proportion of grain production in each region out of the national total has little changed (Table 3.2, Panel A). In the west provinces, the proportion had marginally increased by a mere 0.52 percentage points. In Central China, it gained 1.83 percentage points. In the east provinces, altogether their proportion declined by only 2.35 percentage points. The decline in the proportion of grain production in the south-east coastal provinces has been chiefly offset by an increase in the proportion in the north-east provinces as shown earlier.

Changes have also occurred in regional distribution of grain production at the crop level. An overwhelming proportion of China's rice (86%) is still produced by those provinces south of the Yangtze River. Nonetheless, there has been an increasing trend in rice production in those provinces north of the Yangtze River, an increase by almost 8 percentage points in 2002 compared to 1978 (see Table 3.2, Panel B). However, this increase has taken place mainly in the four north-east provinces (mainly in Heilongjiang) (by 7 percentage points). On the other hand, the proportion of rice production in those south-east coastal provinces has fallen by 8.4 percentage points. The proportional change in all other regions is relatively small. As mentioned earlier, the declining comparative advantage in grain production in the south-east region is largely responsible for the drop in the region's rice production share. The north-east provinces are most suitable for the production of premium quality japonica rice, which has been in high demand by domestic consumers and also in demand for exports.

Wheat production has become increasingly concentrated in Central China, especially in the four provinces north of the Yangtze River (namely, Shandong, Shanxi, Henan and Hebei) (Table 3.2, Panel C). In 1978, about 56% of China's wheat was produced in the eight provinces in Central China. By 2002, this proportion has increased to 66%, with 57% being produced by the four northern provinces. Measurable changes have also occurred in the distribution of wheat production in most other regions. Compared to other regions, those north-east provinces experienced a larger reduction in wheat production (by 4.3 percentage points). Winter wheat cannot be produced in most parts of these provinces. While spring wheat production is possible, the quality is not good. In these provinces, wheat production has been to some extent substituted by rice and corn production.

No drastic changes have occurred in the distribution of corn production in southern and northern China (see Table 3.2, Panel D). The proportion of corn produced in 2002 in provinces south of the Yangtze River has remained at a level similar to that in 1978, though there were some fluctuations in years in between. In south-east provinces, the proportion of corn production in the national total has been at around 3%. This proportion has increased by 2.6 percentage points in the four Central China provinces that are south of the Yangtze River. This is largely due to substitution of corn production for rice production driven by the growing demand for feedgrain. Feedgrain has been in short supply in many southern provinces. Transporting corn from north-east China to south China is not only expensive but also places strain on the transportation capacity. The proportion of corn production in north-east China fluctuated quite significantly. Changing market prices and unfavourable weather conditions are largely responsible for the unstable corn production in these provinces. South-west China is a major corn-consuming area, due to pork production. Its corn production has, however, fluctuated and tended to decline. In the meantime, this region's pork production out of the national total has also tended to decline.

An examination of changes in grain production at the provincial level further confirms that grain production patterns have been evolving largely in accordance with changed market demand and supply situations and local comparative advantages. Table 3.3 presents the share of grain output of each province out of the national total in 2000-2002 (three-year average) and changes in this share as compared with those in 1989-1991 (three-year average).

Table 3.3 Changes in distribution of cereal production

Region	2000-02 share in national total (%)				Difference from early 1990s (%)			
	Rice	*Wheat*	*Corn*	*Total*	*Rice*	*Wheat*	*Corn*	*Total*
Beijing	0.0	0.5	0.5	0.3	-0.1	-0.6	-0.9	-0.4
Tianjin	0.1	0.5	0.5	0.3	-0.1	-0.1	-0.2	-0.1
Hebei	0.3	12.1	9.0	5.7	-0.2	2.6	0.2	0.9
Shanxi	0.0	2.4	3.2	1.5	0.0	-0.8	0.3	0.0
Inner Mongolia	0.3	1.5	6.5	2.4	0.2	-1.0	2.5	0.7
Liaoning	2.1	0.2	6.5	2.9	0.2	-0.2	-1.0	0.0
Jilin	2.1	0.1	11.3	4.3	0.7	0.0	-3.1	0.0
Heilongjiang	5.5	1.0	7.9	5.1	3.9	-3.4	-2.1	0.7
Shanghai	0.7	0.2	0.0	0.4	-0.3	-0.1	0.0	-0.2
Jiangsu	9.6	7.6	2.2	7.0	0.5	-1.4	-0.4	-0.5
Zhejiang	4.9	0.4	0.2	2.4	-2.4	-0.4	0.1	-1.4
Anhui	6.9	7.5	2.5	5.8	0.4	2.4	0.9	0.8
Fujian	3.3	0.1	0.1	1.6	-0.8	-0.2	0.1	-0.5
Jiangxi	8.2	0.1	0.1	3.8	-0.2	0.0	0.0	-0.4
Shandong	0.6	17.8	12.6	8.3	0.2	0.1	-0.8	0.3
Henan	1.6	23.9	10.0	9.5	0.2	7.0	0.5	2.1
Hubei	8.2	2.1	1.8	4.8	-1.0	-2.0	0.5	-1.1
Hunan	12.7	0.2	1.1	6.2	-0.7	-0.1	0.8	-0.6
Guangdong	7.3	0.0	0.6	3.5	-1.6	-0.2	0.4	-0.9
Guangxi	6.8	0.0	1.5	3.6	0.3	0.0	0.3	0.1
Hainan	0.8	0.0	0.0	0.4	0.0	0.0	0.0	0.0
Sichuan*	11.2	6.1	6.2	8.5	-0.5	-1.1	-0.9	-0.9
Guizhou	2.4	1.0	2.9	2.2	0.4	0.3	0.9	0.5
Yunnan	3.2	1.5	4.1	3.0	0.5	0.5	1.0	0.7
Tibet	0.0	0.3	0.0	0.1	0.0	0.1	0.0	0.0
Shaanxi	0.5	4.3	3.3	2.3	0.0	-0.5	-0.3	-0.1
Gansu	0.0	3.1	1.8	1.3	0.0	-0.7	0.4	0.0
Qinghai	0.0	0.5	0.0	0.1	0.0	-0.3	0.0	-0.1
Ningxia	0.4	0.9	0.8	0.6	0.1	0.1	0.4	0.2
Xinjiang	0.3	4.1	2.6	1.9	0.1	0.1	0.4	0.2

* Sichuan includes Chongqing.

Source: Calculations based on data from SSB, various issues.

Provinces having a large share in rice production are Hunan (12.7%), followed by Sichuan (11.2%), Jiangsu (9.6%), Jiangxi and Hubei (8.2% for both). For wheat, the province having the largest share is Henan (23.9%), followed by Shandong (17.8%), Hebei (12.1%), Jiangsu (7.6%) and Anhui (7.5%). Shandong had the largest share in corn production in 2000-2002 (12.6%), followed by Jilin (11.3%), Henan (10%), Hebei (9%) and Heilongjiang (7.9%). Both Liaoning and Inner Mongolia produced 6.5% of China's corn in 2000-2002. In terms of total cereal production, Henan is the largest producer (9.5%), followed by Sichuan (8.5%), Shandong (8.3%), Jiangsu (7%) and Hunan (6.2%).

According to Table 3.3, a general trend is emerging that production has become increasingly shifted to regions with greater comparative advantages. In terms of regional shares in the national output for rice, the largest increase occurred in Heilongjiang followed by Jilin, while the largest decline occurred in Zhejiang followed by Guangdong. As for wheat, during the 1990s, the output share increased fastest in Henan, followed by Hebei and Anhui, while the share declined fastest in Heilongjiang, followed by Hubei, Jiangsu, and Sichuan. Changes in distribution of corn are somewhat complicated. While Inner Mongolia registered an increase in the output share, the share of corn production in all the other three north-east provinces declined. On the other hand, the share of corn production in some southern provinces increased, led by Anhui, Hunan and Yunnan. Changes in the regional pattern of grain production suggest that market forces have begun to play a role in influencing the distribution of grain production in China, thanks to various policy and market reforms by the government, which made such regional adjustments possible.

In recent years, the government has strongly encouraged farmers to adjust their grain production (to produce higher quality grains) in order to solve the relative surplus problem. The extent to which farmers have used this opportunity varies from province to province (see Table 3.4), depending on their ability to use such an opportunity together with the comparative advantage their region possesses. Farmers in wealthier regions, such as in Beijing, Tianjin, Shanghai and Zhejiang, tend to have made greater adjustments to the level of their grain production and also to the composition of their grain crops, compared to their counterparts in less wealthy regions, such as Guangxi, Yunnan, Guizhou and Xinjiang. In economically developed regions, farmers have better access to non-agricultural activities and also to markets that allow them to alter their farm production. Farmers in poorer regions have limited such access. In some major agricultural provinces, land was deviated from cereal production to cash crops, such as vegetables and oilseeds. Table 3.4 also demonstrates to some extent that Chinese farmers are quite responsive to external changes. This suggests that if the government policies allow them to adjust their grain production and there is demand in the market for certain kinds of products, Chinese farmers will respond accordingly. How China's future grain production patterns will evolve will be largely determined by market forces unless the Chinese government reverts to stricter administrative controls, which is less likely.

3.4 Production Technologies and Costs

China's arable land area is not only very limited but has also been declining at an alarming rate in recent years. This places much pressure to develop production technologies that help to improve yields and to raise cropping intensity. Indeed, raising yields and cropping intensity has been the major approach to increase grain output. By international standards, China's cropping intensity is among the highest in the world. In southern China, two or even three crops are produced in the same piece of land within a year. To accommodate this, China has developed varieties with a shorter period of growth. Practical timesaving techniques, such as plastic mulching of seedlings and intercropping, are also available. The use of farm machinery has tended to increase in recent years and has also contributed to saving time on farm. Such technologies have played a major role in maintaining China's level of grain output, though they have some drawbacks. For example, shorter growth periods result in relative lower quality of cereals; intensive use of materials and labour inputs lead to higher production costs. Intensive cropping also depends heavily on reliable infrastructure, such as irrigation and drainage facilities. Reliable supply of inputs such as good quality fertilisers, pesticides, and cheaper labour is also critical. Also intensive cropping often produces negative externalities on the environment (e.g., land degradation, soil erosion, etc.) which tends to undermine sustainability of China's grain production in the long run.

Table 3.4 Proportional changes in cereal outputs and areas between 1999 and 2002

Region	Output %				Area %			
	Cereals	*Rice*	*Wheat*	*Corn*	*Cereals*	*Rice*	*Wheat*	*Corn*
Beijing	-62.0	-77.5	-74.6	-46.8	-63.1	-76.6	-71.8	-56.0
Tianjin	-23.4	-72.1	-38.4	26.3	-30.3	-75.6	-33.0	-13.1
Hebei	-11.6	-40.1	-14.1	-4.9	-9.7	-28.2	-10.3	-3.2
Shanxi	7.3	-39.4	-8.7	16.0	-9.7	-41.1	-13.2	-3.5
Inner Mongolia	-9.3	-18.6	-55.5	6.5	-17.9	-23.1	-50.5	-0.6
Liaoning	-10.5	-2.0	-80.6	-12.9	-11.1	10.9	-67.4	-14.7
Jilin	-9.0	-8.8	-50.9	-9.0	10.1	43.2	-65.9	8.6
Heilongjiang	-13.0	-2.5	-68.5	-12.9	-18.7	-3.1	-72.6	-13.8
Shanghai	-38.5	-29.2	-72.9	-38.8	-44.8	-33.7	-67.7	-38.7
Jiangsu	-19.7	-11.7	-39.8	-1.2	-18.2	-17.4	-23.8	-3.9
Zhejiang	-33.3	-31.2	-64.9	32.7	-42.4	-39.6	-63.5	11.5
Anhui	0.3	2.1	-19.8	67.3	0.4	-4.7	0.0	10.7
Fujian	-22.2	-21.7	-53.5	2.8	-22.1	-21.1	-53.2	-1.4
Jiangxi	-10.7	-10.4	-55.2	-26.7	-9.9	-8.6	-53.7	-38.5
Shandong	-22.0	-16.7	-26.9	-15.2	-13.1	-20.7	-15.2	-8.6
Henan	0.0	1.1	-1.9	2.9	0.7	-7.7	-0.6	5.8
Hubei	-17.5	-12.8	-50.4	-8.2	-20.3	-15.4	-34.8	-15.2
Hunan	-9.9	-10.2	-17.2	-6.0	-10.8	-11.1	-23.1	-2.6
Guangdong	-25.4	-25.5	-27.3	-26.2	-14.7	-14.2	-29.7	-20.1
Guangxi	-5.5	-5.1	-30.8	-6.2	-2.2	1.0	-35.2	-12.4
Hainan	-17.1	-17.6		3.2	-11.0	-11.9		-10.6
Chongqing	-6.2	-7.8	-11.9	3.2	-11.9	-4.2	-27.0	-8.3
Sichuan	-14.7	-10.9	-15.5	-18.0	-11.0	-4.6	-19.9	-11.1
Guizhou	-13.6	-24.0	-19.1	2.5	-6.6	-1.8	-16.4	-3.0
Yunnan	-4.0	-1.5	-15.3	0.4	-2.4	19.9	-16.7	-2.7
Tibet	6.5	7.1	-10.9	18.1	-2.9	65.0	-18.1	18.8
Shaanxi	-7.6	-6.7	0.0	-15.0	-15.3	-15.6	-14.6	-11.0
Gansu	-9.2	2.8	-2.6	-14.1	-14.4	-10.4	-11.7	-5.2
Qinghai	-28.1		-23.9	-45.0	-29.1		-22.1	-27.1
Ningxia	6.4	1.5	22.9	-3.1	12.0	7.7	38.6	-4.7
Xinjiang	3.0	38.2	-11.2	16.4	-4.6	-0.7	-15.6	15.9

Source: Calculations based on data from SSB, various issues.

There is a tendency for farmers to substitute labour-day inputs with more other inputs when higher earnings can be made elsewhere. Labour-day inputs in cereal production have tended to decline, especially in more developed regions where non-farming employment opportunities are greater. According to a production cost survey by the State Planning Commission (State Planning Commission 2003), at the national average, labour-day input per hectare in 2002 was 203 labour-days for japonica rice, 179 labour-days for early indica rice, 140 labour-days for wheat, and 176 labour-days for corn. These represent a reduction in labour-day input, compared with the 1991 level, of 35%, 40%, 28% and 20%, respectively. The reduction of labour-day input is much greater in economically developed regions, such as Jiangsu, Zhejiang, Fujian, and Guangdong, as well as in the municipal cities, i.e., Beijing, Shanghai, and Tianjin. For example, between 1991 and 2002, the labour-day input in early indica rice declined by 54% in Zhejiang, compared to 31% in Jiangxi (an economically less developed province next to Zhejiang). The labour-day input in wheat declined by 57% in Jiangsu, compared to 30% in Henan (an economically less developed province in Central China). The labour-day input in corn declined by 49% in Jiangsu, but by only 15% in Hebei (an economically less developed province surrounding Beijing).

The production cost survey reveals that cereal production costs have shown a general pattern of reversed U-shape movement (see Table 3.5). The costs peaked during the mid-1990s when the Chinese government took strong measures to promote grain production. When grain prices began to decline after 1998, producers reduced input use. However, it is worth noting that labour costs tended to rise even though labour-day inputs had declined, indicating that labour had become more and more expensive. Increased labour cost has raised the proportion of labour cost out of the total cost. For example, in the case of japonica rice, this proportion has increased by 10 percentage points. The corresponding increases for indica rice, wheat and corn are 17, 10 and 12 percentage points.

3.5 Emerging Issues Affecting Grain Production

During 1996-99, China's total cereal output was maintained at about 450 million tonnes (Table 3.1). Since 2000, total cereal output has been around 400 million tonnes, 50 million tonnes lower compared to that in the previous four years. This suggests that China has the potential to increase its cereal output. We acknowledge that China's arable land area would have declined; however, raising yields is still possible and, in addition, if prices are favourable, substitution between crops is also possible. Then, in years to come, what will be the trend in China's cereal production? The following factors are likely to affect China's future cereal production.

Quantity and quality of water. Per capita water availability in China is very low, the second lowest in the world. In recent years, many water bodies have also become polluted. China is increasingly facing a shortage of water. Lower water availability and poor quality for agricultural use will restrain China's grain production. If the comparative advantage in China's grain production continues to decline, crucial resources such as water may be further diverted to other industries. A more comprehensive water use policy, most likely leading to higher fee charges for using water in agriculture, will be developed in the near future, increasing agricultural production costs.

Table 3.5 Changes in production costs of major cereals (¥/kg)*

Year	Japonica rice		Early indica rice		Wheat		Corn	
	Material cost	*Total cost*	*Material cost*	*Total cost*	*Material cost*	*Total cost*	*Material cost*	*Total cost*
1991	0.49	0.69	0.46	0.67	0.64	0.85	0.34	0.49
1992	0.51	0.72	0.39	0.63	0.63	0.83	0.34	0.55
1993	0.48	0.70	0.39	0.63	0.57	0.79	0.30	0.49
1994	0.56	0.80	0.44	0.71	0.64	0.88	0.37	0.58
1995	0.58	0.84	0.47	0.77	0.58	0.87	0.40	0.66
1996	0.55	0.85	0.46	0.83	0.64	0.96	0.37	0.62
1997	0.52	0.80	0.47	0.90	0.58	0.89	0.41	0.72
1998	0.46	0.79	0.48	0.89	0.69	1.04	0.37	0.65
1999	0.48	0.73	0.48	0.89	0.68	1.02	0.39	0.67
2000	0.48	0.82	0.43	0.81	0.65	0.96	0.39	0.69
2001	0.45	0.74	0.43	0.82	0.61	0.94	0.36	0.65
2002	0.46	0.75	0.43	0.83	0.62	0.95	0.37	0.64

* Costs have been deflated by the farm input price index into 2002 constant prices. Total costs include both material and labour costs.

Source: State Planning Commission, various issues.

Environment and natural resource protection. As a result of growing public awareness of environmental issues, there is increasing pressure to protect the environment and natural resources, especially in those areas where there has been serious damage. Such protection will come at the expense of reduced sown areas to grain crops due to the limited land available. For example, either continuation or discontinuation of the current "Grain for Green" program will affect China's total grain output.

Increasing opportunity cost of labour in grain production. The opportunity cost of rural labour in farming is rising as a result of broader economic development, especially in economically more developed regions. As shown earlier, although labour-day input in cereal production has declined, the labour cost has actually increased. This may lead to higher production cost, thus eroding price-competitiveness of domestic products.

Demand for higher quality grain products. There has been a trend in China towards demanding higher quality grains. For example, in the case of wheat, in order to procure better quality grains, some enterprises contract farmers to produce wheat (*ding dan nong ye*). Under such arrangements, firms usually provide farmers with technical assistance to produce wheat with desired attributes. According to the Ministry of Agriculture (MOA 2003, p. 8), by 2002, about 22 million hectares of crops were produced under contract arrangements, including 3.3 million hectares of wheat. Clearly farmers have responded to the market trend by producing more higher quality grains. However, higher quality grains generally tend to have lower yields.

Feedgrain versus foodgrain. In addition to structural adjustments resulting from increased demand for higher quality of foodgrains, further crop structural adjustments are likely to take place in that increased acreage may be devoted to the production of cereals for feed purposes. Further, an emerging trend worth noting is that in some areas a growing share of land is used for production of hays or crops for silages, other than harvesting the crops for cereals. This is the case especially in those areas with fast development of dairy cattle. Hence, it is possible in the near future that outputs of cereals may not increase greatly, and that total nutrients produced with domestic resources for human and animals may actually continue to increase.

Decline in arable land. Urbanisation and use of arable land for non-agricultural purposes have contributed to the recent rapid decline in arable land, especially the most productive land adjacent to suburban areas. Although the government has issued various documents stating that restrictive measures will be applied when approving arable land for non-agricultural uses, it is yet to be seen whether the rapid decline in arable land can be stopped. If the effect of reduced sown area to grain crops cannot be offset by an increasing yield, the level of total grain output will be affected.

Land fragmentation. There were about 248 million household farms in China in 2002, working on extremely tiny blocks of land. If land consolidation is possible in the future, there are likely to be changes in farming practices to produce grain and in the demand for technologies. However, how this may affect China's total grain output level is uncertain.

Grain market integration. China's transportation and marketing infrastructures have improved and will continue to do so, thus promoting greater grain market integration. More integrated markets will further facilitate the allocation of resources to grain production based on regional comparative advantages. Hence, grain production will be increasingly concentrated in regions with comparative advantages and further shifts in grain production between regions are expected.

Technological progress. Technological progress will become increasingly important in determining China's future grain production growth. Recently, the government has tended to increase its investment in agricultural research, development and extension. Increased attention to technological progress will lead to greater growth in grain production.

World market. When China fulfils its commitments made upon WTO accession, whether the imports of cereals and animal feeds into China will increase greatly is yet to be seen. If the imports surge, domestic prices may be depressed which in turn will dampen Chinese farmers' interest in producing grains. On the other hand, if major exporting countries reduce or stop their domestic support and export subsidies, the world market prices of grains may rise. If this happens, the pressure on Chinese grain producers would be smaller and the Chinese farmers may be even encouraged to produce more grains.

Government policy. This remains the most uncertain factor that can abruptly and significantly affect China's grain production. For example, in view of the recent grain price increases in late 2003 and early 2004, the government has taken a number of measures to boost grain production. The 2004 total grain output is expected to increase. Some other policy changes may also indirectly affect grain production, for example, policies on environment and natural resource protection; policies on market reforms.

We have shown that a number of issues will affect China's future grain production. While some factors will promote China's grain production level, others will work in the opposite direction. Hence, it remains a most challenging task to anticipate China's future grain output level. However, in the near future, based on the current policy settings, China's grain output level is likely to be slightly higher than the current level and will continue to increase by a small extent for some years to come. On the other hand, China's future grain production will also be affected by its demand for grains, which in turn is dynamically affected by the demand for foodgrains and feedgrains. In the following chapters, we examine China's demand for foodgrains and feedgrains.

References

MOA (Ministry of Agriculture) (2003), *China Agricultural Development Report 2003* (and previous issues), China Agricultural Press, Beijing.

MOA (2004), website, http://www.agri.gov.cn, accessed on 28 May 2004.

Office for National Agricultural Census 1998, *Highlights of China's First Agricultural Census*, China Statistical Press, Beijing.

SSB (State Statistical Bureau) (2003), *China Statistical Yearbook 2003* (and previous issues), China Statistical Press, Beijing.

State Forestry Bureau (2004), '60 million *mu* of land will be returned from grain production to forestry this year', http://news.xinhuanet.com, 6 April 2004.

State Planning Commission (2003), *Compilation of Agricultural Production Costs and Returns* (and previous issues), State Planning Commission, Beijing.

Chapter 4

Rural Foodgrain Consumption

Zhang-Yue Zhou, Yan-Rui Wu and Wei-Ming Tian

Foodgrain consumption has dropped in both rural and urban China in recent years. In this chapter we look into the dynamics of foodgrain consumption in rural China and discuss the causes that have led to such dynamics. It is noted that changes in the direct consumption of foodgrains are closely related to the consumption of other foods; hence, it is necessary to examine foodgrain consumption patterns in the broad context of food consumption. Further, Chinese rural and urban residents are two distinct consumer groups. It is useful to analyse the consumption dynamics of the two groups separately. We will discuss foodgrain consumption in urban China in the next chapter.

4.1 Review of Literature

A number of factors can cause changes in household consumption. These can be economic (e.g., income and price changes), social (e.g., urbanisation leading to dietary changes), cultural (e.g., influences by exotic lifestyles), and market development that makes new foods available. Among these factors, however, income is seen to be the most influential. Studies show that the level of income affects not only the level but also the composition of food consumption (Regmi et al. 2001; Jones et al. 2003). The increase in consumer income in fast-growing developing countries such as China tends to induce drastic changes in the composition of food consumption (Cranfield et al. 1998; Guo et al. 2000; Gould 2002).

Because of the significant and wide implications of China's food consumption changes, researchers from both within and outside China have paid increased attention to this issue from various perspectives. A number of studies have used the popular almost ideal demand system (AIDS) to identify factors that affect consumption behaviours and to derive parameters such as price and income elasticities: for example, Halbrendt and Tuan (1994), Fan et al. (1995), Wu and Li (1995), and Huang and Rozelle (1998). Wan (1998), using a nonparametric framework developed by Sakong and Hayes (1993), examines taste changes in food demand in rural China. Focusing on structural change in the impact of income on food consumption in China, Guo et al. (2000) follow a two-step process proposed by Haines et al. (1988). To identify determinants of expenditures on food for at-home consumption, Gould (2002) uses an econometric model specification that consists of (1) the system of share equations in which the shares are based on at-home food expenditures and (2) an auxiliary at-home food expenditure function. When reliable price information is unavailable, Engel functions may be used (Wu 1999).

Obtaining data for China's consumption analyses used to be a challenge. In recent years this situation seems to have improved, although gaining quality data remains a major challenge. In earlier attempts, researchers often resorted to cross-section data (e.g., Halbrendt and Tuan 1994, rural household survey data collected by China's State Statistical Bureau (SSB), 2560 households of Guangdong province for 1990; Huang and Rozelle 1998, 433 rural household surveys of SSB in Hebei province for 1993) or highly aggregated data (e.g., Fan et al. 1995, provincial aggregates for 1982-90; Wu and Li 1995, aggregated data from 33 cities for 1990; Wan 1998, provincial aggregates for 1982-90). In more recent studies, Guo et al. (2000) used the data (for 1989, 1991, and 1993) from the China Health and Nutrition Survey data; the survey is conducted biannually and covers eight provinces with a little over 3000 households. On the other hand, Gould (2002) managed to secure three consecutive years of urban household survey data (1995-97) from SSB for Jiangsu, Shandong and Guangdong provinces.

Earlier studies have made important contributions to an understanding of consumption behaviours in China. Most of the studies generate key parameters such as income and price elasticities of demand for various food items. Useful observations include: (1) demand is price-inelastic for most commonly consumed food items; (2) there is a tendency to shift away from coarse grains to fine grains and, in some regions, from rice to wheat consumption; and (3) Chinese consumers will consume more meats as their income increases.

There have also been conflicts between the findings of earlier studies. Besides the different analytical methods used, data type (i.e., the use of cross-sectional or very aggregated data) is probably a major source of difference in the findings. To analyse consumer behaviours, cross-section and time-series data at the household level are ideal. Such micro-level panel data allow for constructing and testing more complicated behavioural models than purely cross-section data (Baltagi 1995, p. 5). Many variables can be more accurately measured at the micro level and biases resulting from aggregation over individuals are eliminated (Blundell 1988; Klevmarken 1989). Further, the time span of the panels used by some studies, e.g., Guo et al. (2000) and Gould (2002), seems short. When panels involve annual data covering only a short span of time, this means that asymptotic arguments rely crucially on the number of individuals tending to infinity (Baltagi 1995, p. 7).

It is also noted that data used in the existing studies are somewhat "dated". Consumption behaviours have experienced rapid changes in the past decade in China, driven chiefly by increased consumer income and external cultural influences. Related to income growth are the likely changes in income elasticities. For some food items such as animal products income elasticities may increase when consumers' incomes increase from a very low level. However, after income has reached a certain high level, income elasticities may decline with further increase in consumers' income. For example, Shono et al. (2000) note that income elasticities decreased as income and consumption levels of some meats increased over time. Zhou (2001) reveals that the income elasticity of demand for milk tends to decline when income rises further from a very high level. Recent empirical evidence by Chu (2003), where she modelled urban meat consumption patterns, shows all animal products tend to exhibit a trend of declining income elasticities. As such, researchers have argued that some parameters derived on the basis of data of a decade ago are less adequate for policy purposes in China and new estimates based on recent data are called for (He and Tian 2000; Zhou et al. 2003).

This chapter contributes, in several ways, to the literature concerning China's rural food consumption in general and foodgrain consumption in particular. First, it uses the most up-to-date household-level survey data with a longer span of time (1995-2002). Second, for better representation, it selects three provinces of different levels of economic development (Guangdong represents an economically developed region, Hubei a medium developed region, and Yunnan an economically less developed region). Third, while the SSB household survey data have been used fairly extensively for study on China's food consumption, the household survey data collected by the Research Centre for Rural Economy of the Ministry of Agriculture remains little exploited. This chapter makes use of this data source. Finally, in addition to examining those common determinants of food expenditure, this chapter will also explore the likely impacts of some other factors on food consumption such as family type, family major business operations, tax and fee burden, and influences of family members not working on the land; these factors have been so far left largely untouched in the literature.

4.2 Describing Rural Foodgrain Consumption

Household-level survey data are used. These data are collected by the Research Centre for Rural Economy (RCRE) of China's Ministry of Agriculture. The survey first began in 1986 and was carried out annually, except in 1992 and 1994. In each village, some 100 households were surveyed. The survey instruments have evolved over the years. Those used for 1986-91 were the same (with 312 variables), but they were expanded for the 1993 survey (with 394 variables) and further expanded for the surveys since 1995 (with 439 variables). Data between 1995 and 2002 are used in this study to ensure consistency of variables over years.

Three provinces, Guangdong, Hubei and Yunnan, are selected for this study.[1] They represent different levels of economic development, Guangdong representing the most developed, Yunnan the least developed, and Hubei at a level of development in the middle of these two. Three villages were then selected from each province according to the level of economic development as measured by per capita net income. Brief information about the region where the villages chosen are located is given in Table 4.1, together with per capita income in each village.

In the surveys, there are nine categories of major family business activities: 1) cropping, 2) forestry, 3) animal husbandry, 4) fisheries, 5) industry, 6) construction, 7) transportation, 8) tertiary services, and 9) others.[2] In this study, activities belonging to categories 1-4 are considered as farming and the rest (i.e., categories 5-9) as non-farming. To minimise errors in the data, we applied various criteria to a number of variables to crosscheck the data. Whenever doubt arose or when an observation had a non-legitimate entry, the relevant observations were eliminated. Results of preliminary analyses of the survey data are reported on the following pages, but, in summary, these are the findings:

- Food expenditure still accounts for a large portion of total living expenditure.
- The proportion of food expenditure on staple food is declining but that on food consumed away from home is increasing.
- Consumption of foodgrains is declining and that of food of animal origin is slowly increasing.
- Income level is the major determinant on the composition and the level of food consumption.
- Other factors also affect rural consumption.

Table 4.1 Sample regions and per capita income, 2002

Province and rural per capita income (¥)	City from which sample village is drawn	Village-level per capita income (¥)	Brief description of the region
Hubei (2444)	Hanyang (Village 1)	4089	A relatively developed region within the province with good transportation
	Hanchuan (Village 2)	2890	Similar to Hanyang
	Changyang (Village 3)	1799	A hilly area with a less developed economy and market
Guangdong (3912)	Dongguan (Village 1)	26225	Highly industrialised area close to Guangzhou and Hong Kong
	Dianbai (Village 2)	2756	Relatively less developed area within Guangdong province
	Wuchuan (Village 3)	2253	Similar to Dianbai but in a coastal area
Yunnan (1609)	Yuxi (Village 1)	7039	A wealthier area with much injection from a highly developed tobacco industry
	Lanchang (Village 2)	578	Very remote and mountainous area, one of the poorest regions in the province and in China
	Dali (Village 3)	2130	Very remote and mountainous area, one of the poorer regions but with tourist resources

Sources: SSB (2003); RCRE survey data.

Food expenditure still accounts for a large portion of total living expenditure
Table 4.2 shows that over 55% of total living expenditure is spent on food. This proportion is higher for the poorer province, Yunnan. In Table 4.2, the proportion of Guangdong, the more economically developed province, is not significantly lower than that of Yunnan due to the following reasons. (1) The income level of Yunnan's Village 1 is very high, thus pulling up the provincial average. (2) Although the income level of Guangdong's Village 1 is very high, that of the other two villages is low, pushing down the provincial average. At the village level, about 66% of total living expenditure was spent on food in these two villages of Guangdong in 2002. Village-level analyses show that in the poorest village, Village 2 of Yunnan, by 2002, some 75% of total living cost was still spent on food.

While the proportion of expenditure on food is slowly declining, the proportion of expenditure on other items is increasing, chiefly, houses, tertiary services, and culture. However, there are distinct regional differences. In the poorer province, Yunnan, the proportion of expenditure on culture is small and also increases at a very slow pace. This same proportion in the other two provinces is almost three times that in Yunnan (Table 4.2).

The proportion of food expenditure on staple food is declining but that on food consumed away from home is increasing At the three-province level (Hubei, Guangdong and Yunnan, combined), over the past decade, expenditure on staple food (chiefly foodgrains in China) among total food expenditure is declining (from 39% in 1995 to 35.3% in 2002) while expenditure on food consumed away from home has steadily increased (from 7% in 1995 to 11.7% in 2002) (Table 4.3). Expenditure on non-staple food declined slightly from 54% in 1995 to 53% in 2002.

Consumption of foodgrains is declining and that of food of animal origin is slowly increasing Table 4.4 indicates that, as rural income increases over the past decade, there is a clear declining trend in direct consumption of foodgrains. However, at the three-province level, the increase in the consumption of food of animal origin is not notable except in the case of poultry meat, where there is a 28% increase in 2002 compared with 1995. At the more disaggregated levels, a slow increase in the consumption of most animal products can be established (see Table 4.4, at the provincial level).

However, while there is a general trend in reduced consumption of foodgrains and increased consumption of animal products, there are clear regional differences both in the level and the composition of animal product consumption. Village-level analyses show that in Village 2 of Yunnan province, the poorest village among the nine villages chosen, consumption of animal products is very low and in some cases declining. Consumption of aquatic products and poultry eggs is almost nil in this village. The consumption of animal products in the two poorer Guangdong villages, Villages 2 and 3, also experienced stagnation or even reduction.

On the other hand, the increase in the consumption of animal products in the two richer villages, Village 1 of Guangdong and Village 1 in Yunnan, is most notable. The level of consumption of various animal products in these two villages is also much higher than that in other villages. (Higher level consumption of aquatic products in the villages of Guangdong is also related to local dietary habits.) This tends to confirm that, in addition to some regional influences on dietary habits, consumer income is a most important determinant affecting the composition and level of food consumption. The analysis between income level and food consumption, following, provides further confirmation.

Income level is the major determinant on the composition and the level of food consumption Table 4.5 clearly shows that, as income increases, the proportion of living expenditure spent on food declines. For those living in poverty, a very high portion (almost 80%) of their living expenditure is spent on food.[3] This same proportion is only a little over 30% for those very wealthy residents with a per capita income of more than 20000 yuan. On the other hand, as income increases, the Chinese rural residents spend more on improving their dwelling conditions and obtaining more tertiary services. Proportionally, the expenditure on culture tends to increase first and then start to decline (Table 4.5).

Table 4.5 further shows that, as income increases, the proportion of food expenditure on staple food, chiefly foodgrains in China, declines rapidly while that on non-staple food and on food consumed away from home increases, suggesting that the composition of their food consumption changes and diversifies. This is clearly reflected in Table 4.6. An increase in income from a very low level leads initially to increased direct consumption of foodgrains. This is not surprising as the poor have difficulty in getting enough to eat and they will consume more foodgrains before they commit their limited resources to luxury food. However, as income further increases, the consumption of foodgrains starts to decline while that of other food items continue to increase (Table 4.6).

While most other food items, chiefly animal products, further increase as income goes up, some other food items do not follow the same pattern. The consumption of animal oil increases and then declines – most likely due to health concerns. The consumption of vegetables exhibits a similar pattern to animal oil – perhaps due to increased consumption of fruits. Sugar consumption tends to stabilise as income reaches a certain level – again likely due to health concerns. On the other hand, the consumption level of other food items by higher income groups of rural residents (namely, pork, beef and mutton, milk, poultry meat and eggs, and aquatic products) is significantly higher than that of lower income rural groups.

Table 4.2 Changes in the composition of living expenditure in rural China (%)

Year	Per capita income (¥)	Food	Clothing	Housing	Fuel	Daily consumables	Services	Culture	Other
All three provinces									
1995	3121	62.6	7.3	6.2	3.7	6.4	4.9	7.2	1.7
1996	3596	63.3	6.4	6.9	3.7	5.7	4.7	8.2	1.1
1997	3692	60.8	7.2	6.6	3.5	6.0	5.8	8.4	1.8
1998	3575	62.3	6.8	5.1	3.8	5.4	5.8	8.8	1.9
1999	3634	61.8	6.3	5.7	4.1	5.3	6.3	8.8	1.7
2000	4106	57.2	6.7	7.9	4.3	5.7	6.9	9.7	1.6
2001	3905	58.1	6.3	7.1	4.2	5.3	7.8	9.5	1.6
2002	5940	55.5	5.7	8.7	4.1	6.9	8.6	8.9	1.5
Hubei									
1995	2556	57.9	7.9	5.9	4.8	7.1	5.3	8.9	2.3
1996	2238	59.2	6.6	5.5	5.2	5.1	6.8	11.4	0.1
1997	2630	58.5	7.6	5.0	4.4	5.5	6.8	10.7	1.7
1998	2408	59.9	7.6	3.0	5.5	4.5	7.5	9.9	2.1
1999	2489	55.3	7.1	5.4	5.8	6.3	6.9	10.9	2.3
2000	2685	49.6	8.2	8.3	6.6	5.6	8.7	12.4	0.6
2001	2707	50.5	7.3	5.7	6.0	5.7	12.1	11.2	1.5
2002	2911	49.1	7.3	4.1	5.5	7.6	11.6	12.7	2.0

Table 4.2 (continued)

Year	Per capita income (¥)	Food	Clothing	Housing	Fuel	Daily consumables	Services	Culture	Other
				Guangdong					
1995	4546	61.0	5.7	8.2	2.9	6.4	4.9	9.6	1.3
1996	5019	60.9	5.4	7.4	2.9	7.6	3.8	10.3	1.6
1997	5262	58.4	5.3	7.9	3.0	7.4	4.8	11.0	2.2
1998	4649	63.0	4.9	5.8	3.1	4.4	4.6	12.4	1.9
1999	4881	63.5	4.8	5.9	3.3	4.2	4.8	11.7	1.8
2000	5533	58.2	5.0	9.6	3.4	5.1	4.7	12.7	1.3
2001	5514	60.5	4.9	6.5	3.5	4.2	5.8	13.2	1.4
2002*	10552	56.7	4.4	6.5	3.5	7.3	9.1	11.3	1.2
				Yunnan					
1995	2014	67.2	8.7	4.3	3.8	6.0	4.7	3.6	1.8
1996	2934	68.2	7.2	7.3	3.6	4.0	4.2	4.3	1.2
1997	2825	64.2	8.7	6.2	3.4	5.1	6.2	4.6	1.6
1998	3189	63.1	8.3	5.8	3.5	6.8	6.1	4.6	1.8
1999	3046	63.9	7.4	5.6	3.9	5.9	7.5	4.7	1.1
2000	3515	60.6	7.6	5.9	3.9	6.3	7.9	5.1	2.5
2001	3018	60.1	7.0	8.5	3.9	6.3	7.4	4.8	2.0
2002	3199	58.0	6.0	13.3	4.0	6.2	6.5	4.4	1.6

* The per capita income of Guangdong suddenly almost doubled in 2002. This was caused by an abrupt increase in per capita income (more than double) in Village 1 of Guangdong.

Source: Calculations based on RCRE survey data.

Table 4.3 Composition of food expenditure (%)

Year	Staple food	Non-staple food	Away-from-home consumption
1995	39.0	54.0	7.0
1996	39.0	52.7	8.1
1997	36.5	55.0	8.5
1998	36.4	54.2	9.0
1999	37.2	52.7	10.1
2000	35.4	53.3	11.3
2001	36.8	52.0	11.2
2002	35.3	53.0	11.7

Source: Calculations based on RCRE survey data.

Other factors also affect rural consumption Other factors may affect food consumption, though indirectly, through their influence on income level. In Table 4.7, family heads of those with lower per capita income tend to have a lower education level. Table 4.7 also indicates that a family's ability to earn income off-farm has a very strong impact on their income level and hence their consumption patterns. Those families with a very high per capita income derive a very small portion of their income from agriculture. Their living expenditure is over 35 times that of the poorest group. It is also interesting to note that these very poor families proportionally pay much higher taxes and charges, which eats into their very limited means. Cross-tabulation was carried out to examine whether family type had any impact on the patterns of food consumption in rural China. No clear relationships between the two could be established although extended families do tend to have slightly higher milk consumption, perhaps because larger families tend to have more children and elderly and thus higher milk consumption. Family size and the age of family head were also found to have little impact on the patterns of food consumption.

The preliminary analyses of the data reveal some useful trends in relation to food consumption in rural China. These trends confirm that important changes are taking place in rural food consumption. The preliminary analyses also pinpoint some factors that may have contributed to the changes in food consumption patterns in rural China. In the next section, based on econometric modelling, we identify and confirm some of these important factors.

4.3 Modelling Rural Foodgrain Consumption

Major factors that may affect the level and composition of food consumption in rural China can be placed into the following groups:

1. Price of food
2. Per capita net income
3. Tax and fee burden [4]
4. Regional difference
5. Other non-price and non-income factors, chiefly, family characteristics, including:
   - family size
   - family type [5]
   - age of household head
   - education level of household head
   - proportion of non-rural labour out of total family labour
   - proportion of income from non-farming sources [6]

The RCRE household survey data only collect the quantity of various food items consumed by households without the corresponding consumption expenditure. This makes it impossible to infer any price information. Various other alternatives have been attempted but they are little help in deriving any meaningful price information. The absence of price data is rather unfortunate and limits our ability to analyse various effects related to price changes such as income effect and substitution effect. Nonetheless, our database still contains much useful household information that enables us to discover the effects associated with many other factors as enumerated above. Our econometric modelling will focus on these factors.

4.3.1 Analytical Framework

The choice of analytical framework for our study is dictated by the availability of data. Because our database does not contain food price information, the following simple linear demand model is employed for the empirical analysis:

$$Q_{ij} = \alpha_i + \beta_i Y_j + \varepsilon_i \qquad (1)$$

where Q_{ij} and Y_j represent the quantity of demand for the ith commodity by the jth household and the total expenditure of the jth household, respectively; and α and β are the intercept and slope coefficients to be estimated.

Given Equation (1), the expenditure elasticity of demand for the ith commodity, η_i, can be computed as follows:

$$\eta_i = \beta_i \frac{\overline{Y}}{\overline{Q}_i} \qquad (2)$$

where $\overline{Y}$ is the average expenditure per capita and $\overline{Q}_i$ is the average quantity of the ith commodity consumed.

Table 4.4 Trends in per capita consumption of major food items, rural China (kg)

Year	Per capita income (¥)	Foodgrains (unmilled)	Vegetables	Vegetable oil	Animal oil	Pork	Beef and mutton	Milk	Poultry meat	Eggs	Aquatic products	Fruits	Sugar
					All three provinces								
1995	3121	201.3	120.8	5.7	2.3	20.1	1.0	0.09	4.0	2.8	12.4	13.4	2.5
1996	3596	201.3	121.8	5.8	2.3	20.4	1.1	0.09	4.0	2.9	12.0	11.8	2.4
1997	3692	194.4	116.5	6.1	2.3	20.0	1.0	0.13	4.0	2.8	12.9	13.4	2.4
1998	3575	193.1	117.8	6.3	2.8	20.3	1.3	0.09	4.5	2.9	12.4	13.1	2.6
1999	3634	189.8	106.8	6.0	2.5	19.5	1.1	0.07	4.6	2.8	11.9	13.8	2.5
2000	4106	188.8	112.3	6.8	2.5	21.2	1.3	0.14	5.1	3.1	12.4	15.6	2.4
2001	3905	184.8	113.0	6.6	2.6	20.7	1.1	0.15	5.0	3.1	12.4	13.5	2.1
2002	5940	180.1	117.3	7.5	2.6	20.6	1.1	0.43	5.1	3.0	12.3	13.2	2.5
					Hubei								
1995	2556	210.2	158.1	11.9	2.3	23.9	0.8	0.02	1.5	4.2	11.3	14.1	1.8
1996	2238	210.5	168.5	11.5	2.3	25.1	0.7	0.02	1.5	3.9	10.6	8.1	1.7
1997	2630	208.6	169.2	12.6	2.4	24.6	1.0	0.08	2.0	3.6	11.4	18.1	1.9
1998	2408	207.4	154.8	12.4	2.8	24.6	0.7	0.07	1.8	3.4	10.8	13.6	1.9
1999	2489	210.3	149.8	11.9	2.5	22.1	0.9	0.07	1.7	3.4	9.0	14.7	1.8
2000	2685	200.3	139.4	13.8	3.0	24.4	1.1	0.05	1.9	4.1	9.3	21.7	2.0
2001	2707	188.1	128.0	13.0	3.1	24.0	1.1	0.09	2.1	3.8	8.7	12.0	1.9
2002	2911	176.0	125.4	15.5	2.4	22.2	1.1	0.07	2.3	4.0	8.4	9.3	1.6

Table 4.4 (continued)

Year	Per capita income (¥)	Foodgrains (unmilled)	Vegetables	Vegetable oil	Animal oil	Pork	Beef and mutton	Milk	Poultry meat	Eggs	Aquatic products	Fruits	Sugar
						Guangdong							
1995	4546	177.1	69.4	5.3	1.4	26.6	1.4	0.15	7.1	3.1	24.0	15.2	3.2
1996	5019	188.8	70.7	6.0	1.3	25.8	1.5	0.14	7.0	3.5	23.7	12.7	3.1
1997	5262	181.7	71.0	6.1	1.4	26.3	1.2	0.18	7.1	3.7	26.5	13.2	3.2
1998	4649	188.8	73.5	6.0	1.4	25.1	1.2	0.09	7.6	3.7	24.5	13.1	3.0
1999	4881	192.2	74.3	5.9	1.3	24.3	1.2	0.07	8.0	3.9	24.2	13.7	2.7
2000	5533	196.0	75.6	6.1	1.4	25.4	0.9	0.18	8.7	3.9	25.0	14.6	2.6
2001	5514	197.2	79.7	6.4	1.7	25.8	1.0	0.15	9.1	4.3	25.9	15.1	2.2
2002	10552	200.2	87.8	6.9	2.0	26.2	0.9	0.35	8.8	4.0	25.6	15.6	2.4
						Yunnan							
1995	2014	220.6	149.8	2.2	3.3	10.9	0.7	0.08	2.5	1.6	1.0	11.2	2.1
1996	2934	208.7	146.8	2.4	3.3	12.2	0.8	0.09	2.4	1.6	1.0	13.1	2.1
1997	2825	198.1	129.2	2.5	3.1	11.4	0.9	0.12	2.3	1.4	1.0	11.0	1.8
1998	3189	189.0	140.1	3.2	4.3	13.1	1.7	0.10	3.0	1.7	1.3	12.8	2.5
1999	3046	175.7	114.8	2.8	3.8	13.4	1.2	0.07	2.9	1.4	1.2	13.4	2.7
2000	3515	174.8	133.0	3.3	3.3	15.1	1.8	0.16	3.3	1.7	1.6	13.0	2.5
2001	3018	170.7	136.9	3.2	3.2	13.9	1.2	0.20	2.6	1.5	1.3	12.8	2.1
2002	3199	163.0	141.1	3.6	3.2	14.4	1.4	0.70	3.1	1.6	1.7	13.2	3.1

Source: Calculations based on RCRE survey data.

Table 4.5 Per capita income and proportion of living expenditure on food and other items, rural China

Income group (¥)	Expenditure on food consumption (%)				Clothing	Housing	Fuel	Expenditure on other items (%)			
	Total food expenditure	Staple food	of which (%) Non-staple food	Away-from-home consumption				Daily consumables	Expenditure on tertiary services	Culture	Other
≤500	79.1	69.4	29.0	1.6	6.5	4.3	3.9	2.5	2.0	1.6	0.1
501–1000	71.4	52.5	43.6	3.1	7.0	4.7	4.6	3.7	4.1	4.4	0.2
1001–2000	65.0	38.5	53.3	7.5	6.0	4.7	4.1	4.4	5.1	9.8	0.9
2001–3000	59.1	33.8	54.4	11.4	6.7	5.5	4.2	5.3	6.3	11.3	1.5
3001–4000	55.7	29.7	56.7	13.1	7.0	6.2	3.8	6.0	7.8	11.0	2.5
4001–6000	51.0	27.4	59.1	13.4	7.3	9.1	3.6	7.7	9.0	9.4	2.9
6001–10000	50.0	23.0	62.5	14.5	6.7	9.7	3.4	9.1	9.2	8.3	3.6
10001–20000	44.5	22.1	64.8	13.1	5.9	15.7	2.8	12.4	8.9	6.7	3.2
>20000	33.4	19.3	64.3	16.5	5.3	23.9	2.4	13.3	13.7	6.8	1.4

Source: Calculations based on RCRE survey data.

Table 4.6 Per capita income and level of consumption of different food items, rural China

Income group (¥)	Foodgrains (unmilled)	Foodgrains (bought)	Vegetables	Vegetable oil	Animal oil	Pork	Beef and mutton	Milk	Poultry meat	Eggs	Aquatic products	Fruits	Sugar
							Consumption (kg)						
≤500	199.4	29.3	107.6	0.4	0.4	3.4	0.4	0.01	1.4	0.2	0.2	2.9	0.7
501-1000	195.8	38.6	108.8	3.0	1.9	13.5	0.6	0.00	2.0	0.9	2.6	7.0	1.3
1001-2000	206.4	62.6	106.8	5.7	2.6	20.3	0.8	0.04	3.4	2.4	9.7	9.1	2.3
2001-3000	203.3	78.3	108.9	7.7	2.6	19.8	1.1	0.05	4.4	3.1	13.9	9.9	2.6
3001-4000	191.3	82.5	127.8	8.2	3.4	22.7	1.3	0.10	4.6	3.7	15.4	15.2	2.7
4001-6000	179.0	81.4	136.2	8.3	3.3	26.7	1.8	0.14	6.4	4.4	16.8	20.8	3.2
6001-10000	161.5	97.4	129.8	8.0	2.8	27.7	1.8	0.42	7.8	5.0	18.3	25.6	3.3
10001-20000	143.7	117.2	122.3	8.5	1.9	27.4	2.0	0.52	9.1	4.5	24.8	30.7	3.1
>20000	140.8	127.7	115.7	9.4	1.4	31.2	3.0	2.31	12.5	5.4	30.7	40.5	3.3

Source: Calculations based on RCRE survey data.

Table 4.7 Relationships between per capita income and other family attributes

Income group (¥)	No. of obs	% of total	Per capita income (¥)	Education level of family head*	Non-agric. income out of total income (%)	Per capita living expenditure (¥)	Tax/fee payments per capita (¥)	Tax/fee payments out of income per capita (%)
≤500	432	7	354	1.3	24.1	481	28	8.5
501-1000	606	10	747	1.7	32.3	855	43	5.8
1001-2000	1532	26	1513	2.3	56.0	1412	65	4.4
2001-3000	1134	19	2448	2.5	70.4	1889	108	4.3
3001-4000	658	11	3462	2.5	80.3	2510	145	4.3
4001-6000	624	11	4898	2.5	87.7	4121	171	3.5
6001-10000	457	8	7681	2.6	91.1	4603	202	2.6
10001-20000	298	5	13412	2.7	94.6	7647	288	2.1
>20000	110	2	41532	2.6	97.3	17295	2584	4.8

Source: Calculations based on RCRE survey data.

* Education level of family head: 1 = illiterate or semi-literate
2 = finished elementary school (6 years schooling)
3 = finished junior high school (9 years)
4 = finished senior high school or higher (>12 years)

The above models can be extended to incorporate household-specific characteristics, Z_k, such as the age and schooling of household heads, size of the household, and so on. Symbolically, the extended model can be presented as follows:

$$Q_{ij} = \alpha_i + \beta_i Y_j + \Sigma(\alpha_{ik} + \beta_{ik} Y_j)Z_k + \varepsilon_i \qquad (3)$$

where Z_k often appears as a dummy variable. Thus, the estimated expenditure elasticity of demand, η_{ik}, for the ith commodity associated with the kth household characteristic is

$$\eta_{ik} = (\beta_i + \beta_{ik})\frac{\overline{Y}_k}{\overline{Q}_{ik}} \qquad (4)$$

where $\overline{Y}_k$ and $\overline{Q}_{ik}$ are, respectively, the average expenditure per capita and the average quantity of the ith commodity consumed for the group associated with the kth household characteristic.

4.3.2 Estimating Procedures

To estimate the above models (3) and (4), the following sets of dummy variables are defined:

Region 1	Hubei province
Region 2	Guangdong province
Region 3	Yunnan province
Size 1	Up to three persons in the household
Size 2	Four or five persons in the household
Size 3	Six or more persons in the household
Education 1	Head of household with junior high school education or higher
Education 2	Other education level
Age 1	Head of household is 30 years or under
Age 2	Head of household is between 31 to 50 years
Age 3	Head of household is 51 years or above
Male 1	The number of employed males is less than 50% of the total number of farm workers in the household.
Male 2	The number of employed males is 50% of the total number of farm workers in the household.
Male 3	The number of employed males is greater than 50% of the total number of farm workers in the household.
Non-farming 1	The number of non-farming workers or part-time farm workers is less than 50% of the total number of workers in the household.
Non-farming 2	The number of non-farming workers or part-time farm workers is 100% of the total number of workers in the household (that is, there are no full-time farm workers in the household).
Non-farming 3	The number of non-farming workers or part-time farm workers is between 50% and 100% of the total number of workers in the household.

Farming 1	Farming income is less than 20% of the household's total net income.
Farming 2	Farming income is between 20% and 60% of the household's total net income.
Farming 3	Farming income is more than 60% of the household's total net income.
Tax and fees 1	Proportion of tax and other fee payments is less than 1% of the household's total net income.
Tax and fees 2	Proportion of tax and other fee payments is greater than 1% but less than 3% of the household's total net income.
Tax and fees 3	Proportion of tax and other fee payments is greater than 3% of the household's total net income.
Income 1	Less than 1500 yuan (according to household net income per capita)
Income 2	Between 1500 and 2700 yuan
Income 3	Greater than 2700 yuan

To avoid the dummy variable trap, only two of the variables in each set (one dummy variable for schooling) are included in the regressions. Therefore, a maximum of 36 independent variables (including the intercept) are included in each of the 96 regressions for the 12 food products over the period 1995-2002. The estimation results are then used to calculate the expenditure elasticities as specified in Equation (4).[7]

4.3.3 Interpretation of the Findings

Table 4.8 presents the estimated expenditure elasticities calculated at the corresponding mean values of each group. Based on Table 4.8, the following important observations can be derived.

- The expenditure elasticities of demand for foodgrain have the smallest values in most cases – even negative values in two cases. Thus, it seems that demand for this food item may be less elastic than that for other products. The magnitudes of the elasticities imply that foodgrain is becoming very much an inferior good in rural China. We may conclude that direct consumption of grain is saturated even in rural China according to the sample used here.
- The expenditure elasticities of demand for animal products (pork, beef and mutton, animal fat and poultry meat and eggs), fruits and sugar are relatively large in value, implying that demand for these products is more elastic.
- Though there are exceptional cases where elasticity of demand for animal products is too small or even negative, the findings in Table 4.8 imply substantial growth in the consumption of animal products and hence indirect demand for grain in rural China.
- As expected, there are observable variations in expenditure elasticities between regions. It is noted, however, because there are extreme rich and poor villages in the sample provinces, especially in Guangdong and

Yunnan (see Table 4.1), the grouping according to three provinces may have to some extent "weakened" regional variations.

- It seems that demand is less responsive to income changes for low-income households but more for high-income households. One explanation is that low-income families have many needs to be met and they have only obtained a subsistence level. With a rise in their income, those households probably want to spend on non-food items such as clothing and education. With a fall in their income, they still have to keep their subsistence level of consumption.

- Demand for animal products in male-dominated households appears to be less elastic. Male-dominated households distinguish themselves from other families because of the substantial costs of boys finding brides in rural China. Parents of rural boys often have to save hard for their sons' marriages.

- Table 4.8 also shows that demand for meat tends to be less elastic for young families. This may be due to the fact that young families have to budget for more non-food items such as baby needs and housing.

- The proportion of non-farming income plays a role in determining household consumption patterns, but a strong relationship between consumption behaviour and the number of non-farm workers within the household was not borne out. Intuitively, the more non-farm workers, the higher the non-farm income in a family. Perhaps much of the influence of the number of non-farm workers on consumption behaviour is captured by the level of non-farming income. Based on Table 4.8, the demand for animal products and aquatic products by households with relatively more non-farming income is less elastic. There are two possible explanations for this: first, those households often have members serving in local government or private enterprises who frequently dine away from home due to private and official functions. Secondly, those households may have members working in the cities part-time or full-time. These members' consumption is not accounted for in the family budget.

- Although earlier preliminary analysis shows that very poor families pay proportionally much higher taxes and charges, our modelling results did not confirm that the level of taxes and fees is a significant effect on consumption behaviour. Nonetheless, higher tax and fee payments from their net family income must affect the ability of poorer families to meet basic food needs.

- According to the estimates in Table 4.8, the size of households does not seem to have a major bearing on consumption pattern. This is consistent with earlier descriptive analyses presented in Section 4.2. Our modelling results also show that education does not appear to be an important influence either on rural consumption. Nonetheless, high-income families tend to have heads of households with more schooling (see Table 4.7).

Table 4.8 Estimated expenditure elasticities

Variable	Foodgrain	Vegetables	Vegetable oil	Animal oil	Pork	Beef and mutton	Poultry meat	Eggs	Aquatic products	Fruits	Sugar
Region 1	0.24	0.08	0.19	-0.01	0.16	0.52	0.29	0.26	0.51	-0.10	0.27
Region 2	0.18	0.06	0.34	0.60	0.33	-0.61	0.97	0.48	0.59	0.21	0.63
Region 3	0.05	0.24	0.40	0.47	0.86	0.43	0.89	0.71	1.81	0.65	0.93
Size 1	0.12	0.33	0.14	0.50	0.51	0.21	0.93	0.25	0.44	0.82	1.31
Size 2	0.06	0.35	0.27	0.59	0.62	0.37	1.21	0.58	0.36	0.83	1.19
Size 3	0.03	0.33	0.26	0.79	0.60	0.23	0.73	0.56	0.29	1.62	0.96
Education 1	0.06	0.44	0.18	0.63	0.76	0.66	1.13	0.82	0.36	1.30	0.96
Education 2	0.04	0.26	0.24	0.63	0.62	0.30	0.80	0.50	0.30	1.03	1.03
Age 1	0.25	-0.26	0.18	0.35	0.40	0.53	0.02	-0.21	-0.49	0.89	1.08
Age 2	0.04	0.26	0.26	0.90	0.72	0.20	0.91	0.54	0.34	1.19	1.14
Age 3	0.04	0.28	0.21	0.77	0.62	0.31	0.81	0.50	0.24	1.18	1.10
Male 1	0.01	0.37	0.31	0.74	0.78	0.63	1.01	0.61	0.39	0.92	1.19
Male 2	0.01	0.36	0.21	0.80	0.75	0.77	1.07	0.57	0.21	1.13	1.19
Male 3	0.04	0.29	0.25	0.65	0.61	0.24	0.85	0.59	0.30	0.95	1.06

Table 4.8 (continued)

Variable	Foodgrain	Vegetables	Vegetable oil	Animal oil	Pork	Beef and mutton	Poultry meat	Eggs	Aquatic products	Fruits	Sugar
Non-farming 1	0.00	0.24	0.20	0.59	0.53	-0.29	0.39	0.43	0.28	0.62	0.63
Non-farming 2	-0.03	0.18	0.05	0.35	0.75	-0.13	0.59	0.16	0.27	0.66	0.41
Non-farming 3	0.03	0.24	0.17	0.60	0.60	0.22	0.83	0.43	0.25	1.21	0.90
Farming 1	-0.02	0.25	0.32	0.54	0.60	0.36	0.53	0.73	0.14	0.90	0.93
Farming 2	0.08	0.34	0.38	1.05	0.93	0.33	1.72	0.97	0.46	2.32	1.29
Farming 3	0.03	0.16	0.15	0.56	0.46	0.31	0.77	0.45	0.28	0.50	0.85
Tax and fees 1	0.05	0.35	0.59	0.78	0.46	0.73	1.11	0.83	0.25	1.07	1.10
Tax and fees 2	0.06	0.33	0.48	0.75	0.50	0.47	0.80	0.65	0.18	0.99	1.08
Tax and fees 3	0.03	0.24	0.18	0.69	0.71	0.30	0.97	0.47	0.31	1.24	1.15
Income 1	0.02	0.17	0.16	0.52	0.51	0.22	0.85	0.49	0.26	0.85	0.76
Income 2	0.04	0.28	0.20	0.74	0.62	0.41	0.82	0.53	0.27	1.22	0.93
Income 3	0.06	0.36	0.30	0.87	0.87	0.49	1.20	0.60	0.58	1.16	1.42

4.4 Concluding Comments

While food expenditure still accounts for a large proportion of total living expenditure, this proportion is declining. The proportion of expenditure on housing, tertiary services and education is on the increase. This trend will continue into the near future for China's rural areas. As such, although the proportion of income spent on food will decline, total expenditure spent on food will continue to rise due to increased consumer income. On the other hand, the market potential for non-food consumer goods will be enormous.

Direct consumption of foodgrains has started to decline in rural China. At the three-province level, the proportion of food expenditure on staple food is declining while that on food consumed away from home has steadily increased. Expenditure on non-staple food declined slightly.

While direct consumption of foodgrains is declining, there is an increase in the indirect consumption of grains, that is, through increased consumption of animal products whose production consumes grains. However, according to the survey data, at the three-province level, the increase in animal product consumption by the Chinese rural residents has been rather slow over the past decade. It implies that unless there are drastic changes (e.g., rapid increase in consumer income), the increase in the consumption of animal products in China's rural areas is likely to be slow.[8]

However, there are significant regional differences in the composition of food consumption. Per capita consumption of aquatic products in Guangdong is much higher than that in Yunnan. Apart from income differences, availability of some foods is a key determinant that leads to different dietary habits in different regions. Unlike the markets in developed economies, many agricultural markets in China are not well integrated and some food items are simply not available in the vast rural areas in China. It may be anticipated that, as the Chinese agricultural markets are further integrated, the total demand for some food items will increase.

Income plays a major role in determining the composition and the level of food consumption. As income increases, the proportion of food expenditure on staple food, chiefly foodgrains, declines, while that on non-staple food and on food consumed away from home increases. This suggests that the composition of their food consumption changes and diversifies when income increases. The consumption level of pork, beef and mutton, milk, poultry meat and eggs, and aquatic products by higher income groups of rural residents is significantly higher than that of those with lower income. Future increase in rural income will have a great impact on food consumption in China.

A family's ability to earn income off-farm has a very strong impact on their income level and hence their consumption patterns. Those families with very high per capita income derive a very small portion of their income from agriculture. Apart from the fact that more family labour working off-farm earns the family higher income, it is also likely that those working off-farm have great exposure to external influences and subsequently influence home food consumption. As such, increased rural-urban exchanges and urbanisation will impact on China's rural food consumption.

References

Baltagi, B.H. (1995), *Econometric Analysis of Panel Data*, Wiley, Chichester.
Blundell, R. (1988), 'Consumer behaviour: theory and empirical evidence – A survey', *The Economic Journal*, Vol. 98, pp. 16-65.
Chu, Y.T. (2003), 'An analysis on China's feed market', Ph.D. dissertation, China Agricultural University, Beijing.
Cranfield, J.A.L., Hertel, T.W., Eales, J.S. and Preckel, P.V. (1998), 'Changes in the structure of global food demand', Staff Paper 98-05, GTAP Centre, Purdue University.
Fan, S.G., Wailes, E.J. and Cramer, G.L. (1995), 'Household demand in rural China: a two-stage LES-AIDS model', *American Journal of Agricultural Economics*, Vol. 77, pp. 54-62.
Gould, B.W. (2002), 'Household composition and food expenditure in China', *Agribusiness*, Vol. 18, pp. 387-402.
Guo, X.G., Mroz, T. A. and Popkin, B.M. (2000), 'Structural change in the impact of income on food consumption in China, 1989-1993', *Economic Development and Cultural Change*, Vol. 48, pp. 737-60.
Haines, P.S., Guilkey, D.K. and Popkin, B.M. (1988), 'Modelling food consumption decisions as a two-step process', *American Journal of Agricultural Economics*, Vol. 70, pp. 543-52.
Halbrendt, C. and Tuan, F. (1994), 'Rural Chinese food consumption: the case of Guangdong', *American Journal of Agricultural Economics*, Vol. 76, pp. 794-99.
He, X.R. and Tian, W.M. (2000), 'Livestock consumption: diverse and changing preferences', in Yang, Y.Z. and Tian, W.M. (eds), *China's Agriculture at the Crossroads*, Macmillan Press, London, pp. 78-97.
Huang, J.K. and Rozelle, S. (1998), 'Market development and food demand in rural China', *China Economic Review*, Vol. 9, pp. 25-45.
Jones, E., Akbay, C., Roe, B. and Chern, W.S. (2003), 'Analyses of consumers' dietary behaviour: an application of the AIDS model to supermarket scanner data', *Agribusiness*, Vol. 19, pp. 203-221.
Klevmarken, N.A. (1989), 'Panel studies: what can we learn from them?' Introduction, *European Economic Review*, Vol. 33, pp. 523-29.
Regmi, A., Deepak, M.S., Seale, J.L. and Bernstein, J (2001), 'Cross-country analysis of food consumption patterns', in Regmi, A. (ed.), *Changing Structure of Global Food Consumption and Trade*, ERS WRS No. 01-1, USDA, Washington, D.C.
Sakong, Y. and Hayes, D.J. (1993), 'Testing the stability of preferences: a nonparametric approach', *American Journal of Agricultural Economics*, Vol. 75, pp. 269-77.
Shono, C., Suzuki, N. and Kaiser, H.M. (2000), 'Will China's diet follow western diets?' *Agribusiness*, Vol. 16, pp. 271-79.
SSB (State Statistical Bureau), *China Statistical Yearbook*, various issues, China Statistical Press, Beijing.
Wan, G.H. (1998), 'Nonparametric measurement of preference changes: the case of food demand in rural China', *Applied Economics Letters*, Vol. 5, pp. 433-36.
Wu, Y.R. and Li, E. (1995), 'Food consumption in urban China: an empirical analysis', *Applied Economics*, Vol. 27, pp. 509-15.
Wu, Y.R. (1999), *China's Consumer Revolution,* Edward Elgar, Cheltenham.
Yuan, X.G. (2001), 'A study on the consumption of animal products in China', Ph.D. dissertation, Chinese Academy of Agricultural Sciences, Beijing.
Zhou, J.L. (2001), 'A study on the dairy market in China', Ph.D. dissertation, China Agricultural University, Beijing.

Zhou, Z.Y., Tian, W.M., Liu, X.A. and Wan, G.H. (2003), 'Studying China's feedgrain demand and supply: research methodological issues', in Zhou, Z.Y. and Tian, W.M. (eds), *China's Regional Feedgrain Markets: Developments and Prospects*, Grains Research and Development Corporation, Canberra.

Notes

[1]   Note that these three provinces are located in southern and central China. We were unable to include a northern province due to limited data access. Consumption patterns differ between southern and northern China.

[2]   In 1996, one further category was added: no family business operations. Currently, the number of families without any business operations is small.

[3]   In 1995, the poverty line for rural residents in China was 530 yuan (US$1 = ¥8.351 in 1995). In 1999, this was raised to be 625 yuan (US$1 = ¥8.278 in 1999). The poverty line set by the United Nations for developing countries is US$31.67 per capita per month, or roughly US$1 per day. Village-level per capita income data show that in Village 3 of Yunnan province many households live near or under the poverty line as set by the Chinese government. Most worrisome is that the per capita income in this village sometimes declines excessively.

[4]   Tax and fee burden affects net income. We examine this factor separately because we are interested in finding out whether the higher proportion of tax and fees paid by the lower income group of people negatively affect their food consumption.

[5]   1) and 2) are related. Family type will affect the size of the family, and may affect food consumption patterns, e.g., a larger family is more likely to have children and elderly members and to have to cater for their needs.

[6]   5) and 6) are also related and both are also related to income. Generally, if they are higher, we can expect that the family has higher per capita income. However, they can be used as proxies to capture the influence of two other factors on consumption, i.e., urbanisation and influence of outside culture. With more labour engaged in non-farming/non-rural work, these people are more exposed to influences from elsewhere which in turn will affect their family consumption patterns.

[7]   The details of the estimated parameters are available upon request.

[8]   It is noted that faster increase in the consumption of some animal products took place in the early 1990s, largely attributable to a faster increase in income. However, there has been a slowing down in consumer income increase in rural areas in the past several years. During 1997-2001, per capita income growth in rural areas was 3.2%, down from 25.2% during 1992-96.

Chapter 5

Urban Foodgrain Consumption

Wei-Ming Tian and Zhang-Yue Zhou

5.1 Describing Urban Foodgrain Consumption

Data used to describe urban foodgrain consumption are primarily from China's State Statistical Bureau. Since the late 1970s, the availability of diverse foods to urban residents has been significantly improved, thanks to the rural economic reforms. As a result of their increased income, urban residents can now increase their consumption of various foods, and their expenditure on food has been increasing. However, due to a faster increase in their disposable income, the actual share of food expenditure out of total living expenditure, or the Engel coefficient, has been declining over the past two decades (see Figure 5.1). The Engel coefficient declined from 57.5% in 1978 to 37.7% in 2002.

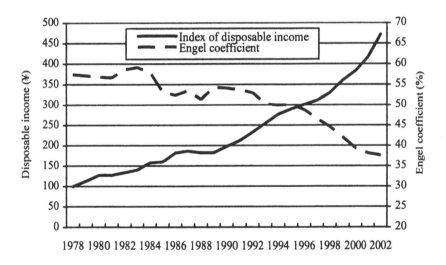

Figure 5.1 Index of disposable income and Engel coefficients, urban China, 1978-2002

Source: SSB 2003a and previous issues.

Table 5.1 Changes in expenditures on staple food, non-staple food and away-from-home consumption

Year	Total living expenditure (¥)	Expenditure (¥) on										
		All foods	Foodgrain	Oil	Meats	Eggs	Aquatic products	Vegetables	Sugar	Fresh fruits	Dairy products	Away-from-home consumption
1992	1672	884	104	33	207	40	59	100	12	61	18	70
1993	2111	1058	130	41	250	47	71	118	14	69	20	92
1994	2851	1422	202	68	335	58	96	152	19	89	26	120
1995	3538	1766	261	73	416	70	121	190	24	112	31	161
1996	3919	1905	272	69	439	79	132	207	25	118	37	186
1997	4186	1943	238	71	460	74	141	204	24	127	41	203
1998	4332	1927	227	75	431	67	142	197	24	121	48	227
1999	4616	1932	215	74	409	66	144	195	23	130	56	250
2000	4998	1958	189	66	411	57	144	192	24	128	69	288
2001	5309	2014	188	59	414	57	152	194	25	131	80	314
2002	6030	2272	190	64	455	59	170	213	25	168	104	414
% increase (2002/1992)	261	157	82	98	120	47	186	115	108	173	495	488

Table 5.1 (continued)

Year	Total living expenditure (¥)	Share of total living expenditure (%)										
		All foods	Foodgrain	Oil	Meats	Eggs	Aquatic products	Vegetables	Sugar	Fresh fruits	Dairy products	Away-from-home consumption
1992	1672	52.9	6.2	1.9	12.4	2.4	3.5	6.0	0.7	3.7	1.0	4.2
1993	2111	50.1	6.2	2.0	11.9	2.2	3.4	5.6	0.7	3.3	0.9	4.3
1994	2851	49.9	7.1	2.4	11.8	2.0	3.4	5.3	0.6	3.1	0.9	4.2
1995	3538	49.9	7.4	2.1	11.8	2.0	3.4	5.4	0.7	3.2	0.9	4.5
1996	3919	48.6	6.9	1.8	11.2	2.0	3.4	5.3	0.6	3.0	0.9	4.8
1997	4186	46.4	5.7	1.7	11.0	1.8	3.4	4.9	0.6	3.0	1.0	4.9
1998	4332	44.5	5.2	1.7	10.0	1.5	3.3	4.5	0.6	2.8	1.1	5.2
1999	4616	41.9	4.7	1.6	8.9	1.4	3.1	4.2	0.5	2.8	1.2	5.4
2000	4998	39.2	3.8	1.3	8.2	1.1	2.9	3.8	0.5	2.6	1.4	5.8
2001	5309	37.9	3.5	1.1	7.8	1.1	2.9	3.7	0.5	2.5	1.5	5.9
2002	6030	37.7	3.2	1.1	7.5	1.0	2.8	3.5	0.4	2.8	1.7	6.9

Source: SSB 2003a and previous issues.

Food expenditure no longer accounts for a major portion of total living expenditure in China's urban areas. An increasing proportion of the total living expenditure is spent on other items, such as housing, education, tertiary services, and cultural activities and entertainment.

Table 5.1 shows that the proportion of expenditure on staple food, chiefly foodgrains, has declined, dropping from 6.2% in 1992 to 3.2% in 2002. The occasional increase in the proportion in 1994 and 1995 was largely due to the double-digit inflation at that time. Expenditure on major non-staple food has also declined from 31.7% in 1992 to 20.9% in 2002. However, the expenditure share on away-from-home consumption has increased steadily from 4.2% in 1992 to 6.9% in 2002.[1]

Table 5.1 also shows that in the current price term, the expenditure on all food items has increased. Eggs had the slowest increase (47%) while dairy products had the highest increase (495%). For all the major non-staple food items except for vegetables and sugar, the per capita consumption in quantity terms has increased (see Table 5.2).

Table 5.2 Changes in per capita consumption of major food items, urban China (kg)

Food item	1985	1990	1995	2000	2001	2002	2003
Foodgrain	134.8	130.7	97.0	82.3	79.7	78.5	79.5
Fresh vegetables	144.4	138.7	116.5	114.7	115.9	116.5	118.3
Vegetable oil	5.8	6.4	7.1	8.2	8.1	8.5	9.2
Pork	16.7	18.5	17.2	16.7	16.0	20.3	20.4
Beef and mutton	2.0	3.3	2.4	3.3	3.2	3.0	3.3
Poultry	3.2	3.4	4.0	5.4	5.3	9.2	9.2
Fresh eggs	6.8	7.3	9.7	11.2	10.4	10.6	11.2
Aquatic products	7.1	7.7	9.2	9.9	10.3	13.2	13.4
Sugar	2.5	2.1	1.7	1.7	1.7	n.a.	n.a.

Source: SSB 2003a and previous issues.

Reduced sugar consumption is probably due to health concerns. On the other hand, reduced vegetable consumption is likely due to substitution by other items such as fresh fruits or to increased consumption in restaurants. One other factor that may have contributed to the reduced consumption of vegetables as shown in the statistics is change in market channels and marketing methods. More and more vegetables are sold through supermarkets and sold in semi-processed form or with inedible parts removed. Thus, although the amount of vegetables purchased is reduced, the actual intake may have not been reduced. While the increase in expenditure on eggs is the smallest, the per capita consumption of eggs has increased quite rapidly. Rapid development in intensive egg farming in recent years is probably responsible for a reduction in the price of eggs. Table 5.2 shows that, in general, the consumption of foods of animal origin is increasing. The consumption of poultry eggs and aquatic products has increased most rapidly. It is noted, however, that although the expenditure on foodgrains has increased by 82%, in quantity terms it has declined (see Table 5.2).

The level of food consumption varies significantly between regions in urban China; however, the variation in the composition of food consumption seems to be relatively small. Table 5.3 shows that the level of food consumption expenditure in some urban centres (such as Beijing and Shanghai) is twice that of some others (e.g., Shanxi and Guizhou). While regional price differences are partially responsible for such variation, differences in the level of disposable income between regions is the key factor affecting the level of consumption. On the other hand, the composition of food consumption expenditures is quite comparable across regions, as shown in Table 5.3. In those economically less developed regions, a higher proportion of the expenditure is spent on foodgrains (e.g., Shanxi, Qinghai and Henan). In south-east coastal regions (such as Zhejiang, Fujian, and Hainan), a higher proportion of the living expenditure is spent on aquatic products.

Income level plays a major role in determining the composition of food consumption. Table 5.4 clearly shows that, as income increases, the consumption of foodgrains declines while that of non-staple food increases, with a few exceptions. One exception is cooking oil: its consumption increases first when income increases then it declines. All other food items exhibit a clear increasing trend when income increases. It is noted, however, that the increase in the consumption of beef and mutton tends to slow down when income reaches a certain level. On the other hand, the consumption of poultry meat, aquatic products and dairy products increases greatly. The consumption of fruits and melons also increases greatly when the income level increases.

With regard to foodgrain consumption, another phenomenon is worth noting. That is, when their income increases, consumers tend to buy more processed or semi-processed foodgrain products, especially wheat flour and wheat-based products. Data from SSB (SSB 2002, pp. 135-36) show that the purchase of wheat flour is negatively related to income, while the purchase of wheat-based flour products is positively related to income. When their income increases, consumers tend to buy more processed wheat-based products, such as steamed bread and noodles, to save time when preparing food. Also, while coarse grains had been commonly regarded as inferior cereals, their consumption has increased in recent years, due to increased understanding of their nutritional value. The SSB survey data indicate that urban residents with higher incomes tend to consume more coarse grains, although the total amount is relatively small. On the other hand, there do not appear to be any major differences in patterns of rice purchase among different income groups.

Table 5.3 Composition of regional food consumption, urban China, 2002

Region	Total living expenditure (¥)	Share in total living expenditure (%)								
		Food	Foodgrain	Oil	Meats	Eggs	Aquatic pr.	Vegetables	Sugar	Fruits
National total	6029.9	37.7	3.2	1.1	7.5	1.0	2.8	3.5	0.4	2.8
Beijing	10284.6	33.8	2.2	0.6	5.5	0.7	1.6	2.4	0.4	3.0
Tianjin	7192.0	36.2	2.8	0.8	5.9	1.2	3.2	2.9	0.3	3.0
Hebei	5069.3	35.4	3.5	1.5	6.5	1.5	1.9	4.1	0.6	3.0
Shanxi	4711.0	32.5	4.6	1.0	4.8	1.4	0.8	3.6	0.4	2.5
Inner Mongolia	4859.9	31.5	4.1	0.8	6.3	0.9	0.8	2.9	0.3	2.7
Liaoning	5342.6	38.8	3.9	1.1	7.2	1.4	3.2	4.0	0.5	3.8
Jilin	4973.9	36.4	3.9	1.1	6.7	1.1	2.0	4.0	0.5	3.9
Heilongjiang	4462.1	35.5	4.4	1.3	6.8	1.3	1.8	3.5	0.5	3.3
Shanghai	10464.0	39.4	2.3	0.7	6.1	0.7	5.7	3.2	0.5	2.8
Jiangsu	6042.6	40.4	2.8	1.0	8.2	1.1	4.0	3.7	0.4	2.5
Zhejiang	8713.1	39.9	2.0	0.6	5.2	0.5	6.3	3.7	0.3	2.7
Anhui	4736.5	43.2	3.4	1.5	8.8	1.7	2.2	3.9	0.5	2.1
Fujian	6631.7	43.4	3.5	1.0	9.2	1.0	8.2	3.7	0.3	3.0
Jiangxi	4549.3	40.5	3.7	2.0	9.2	1.1	2.4	5.2	0.4	3.0
Shandong	5596.3	34.4	3.1	0.7	5.9	1.3	2.2	2.8	0.3	2.9
Henan	4504.7	33.7	4.3	1.1	6.5	1.4	0.8	3.7	0.3	2.4
Hubei	5608.9	37.2	3.2	1.4	7.0	0.9	2.0	4.0	0.4	2.1
Hunan	5574.7	35.6	3.2	1.4	7.8	0.8	1.8	3.8	0.5	3.1
Guangdong	8988.5	38.5	2.6	0.8	9.5	0.5	4.1	3.1	0.4	2.4
Guangxi	5413.4	40.7	2.9	1.2	12.7	0.7	3.4	3.6	0.4	3.0
Hainan	5459.6	44.6	3.1	1.3	12.0	0.5	6.5	4.2	0.4	2.3
Chongqing	6360.2	38.0	2.6	1.4	9.0	1.0	1.5	3.8	0.5	2.4
Sichuan	5413.1	39.8	3.3	1.5	9.8	1.1	1.3	3.9	0.5	2.7

Table 5.3 (continued)

Region	Total living expenditure (¥)	Share in total living expenditure (%)								
		Food	Foodgrain	Oil	Meats	Eggs	Aquatic pr.	Vegetables	Sugar	Fruits
Guizhou	4598.3	38.9	3.2	1.3	9.4	0.9	0.9	4.3	0.7	2.9
Yunnan	5827.9	41.6	3.3	0.9	8.1	0.8	1.2	4.3	0.4	2.7
Tibet	6952.4	40.8	3.8	1.5	8.7	0.7	0.9	4.5	1.4	2.9
Shaanxi	5378.0	34.1	3.4	1.1	4.7	0.9	0.9	3.1	0.4	2.6
Gansu	5064.2	35.4	3.7	1.3	5.4	0.9	0.8	4.0	0.3	3.0
Qinghai	5042.5	36.7	4.5	1.1	7.6	0.8	1.0	3.4	0.4	2.5
Ningxia	5104.9	34.8	3.6	1.3	6.0	0.7	0.8	3.7	0.4	3.1
Xinjiang	5636.4	33.9	3.3	0.9	7.5	0.8	1.0	2.9	0.5	3.2

Source: calculations based on SSB (2003a, pp. 356-58).

Table 5.4 Income level and the composition of food consumption, urban China, 2002 (kg)

Food item	Average	Lowest income	Very low income	Low income	Lower middle	Middle income	Upper middle	High income	Highest income
Foodgrains	78.5	84.2	83.3	82.3	79.6	77.7	77.8	76.8	71.4
Vegetable oil	8.5	7.8	8.2	8.8	8.8	8.7	8.5	8.5	7.8
Edible animal oil	0.5	0.7	0.7	0.6	0.5	0.5	0.4	0.3	0.2
Pork	20.3	14.7	15.7	18.3	20.0	20.8	21.6	22.8	22.4
Beef	1.9	1.1	1.2	1.6	1.8	2.1	2.2	2.2	2.2
Mutton	1.1	0.6	0.7	0.8	1.1	1.3	1.4	1.3	1.2
Poultry	9.2	4.4	5.2	7.0	8.1	9.2	10.4	11.9	13.3
Fresh eggs	10.6	7.9	8.4	9.8	10.5	10.7	11.1	11.6	11.1
Aquatic products	10.9	5.4	6.1	7.7	9.0	10.7	12.4	14.8	17.2
Fresh vegetables	116.5	100.3	102.7	109.1	112.7	116.1	122.0	127.2	126.6
Fresh fruits and melons	56.5	27.0	31.7	44.5	51.0	57.9	64.2	70.7	74.7
Fresh dairy products	15.7	3.6	4.8	8.4	11.8	15.8	20.0	23.6	26.5
Milk powder	0.6	0.3	0.3	0.4	0.6	0.6	0.6	0.7	0.7
Yoghurt	1.8	0.3	0.5	1.0	1.4	1.8	2.3	2.7	3.3

Source: SSB 2003a, p. 353.

5.2 Modelling Urban Foodgrain Consumption

A number of empirical studies have attempted to model the behaviour of urban foodgrain consumption using either the single equation approach (e.g., Wang and Davis 2000) or demand systems (e.g., Lewis and Andrews 1989; Tian 1990; Wang and Chern 1992; Chern and Wang 1994; Shi et al. 1995; Liu and Chern 2001, 2003). Most of these studies use data from SSB urban household surveys. The SSB's survey sample is drawn using a two-stage stratified systematic random sampling scheme and covers about 30,000 households in all provinces. The survey indicators, as well as their definitions and recording methods, have been revised several times since the survey was first started in 1981. Currently, data collected cover both quantities and expenditures of over 300 food and non-food items purchased in a calendar year. The survey also collects a wide range of household characteristics, such as household size, age, gender and education level of each household member, living conditions, and durables owned (SSB 2001). SSB generally does not release the survey data at the household level, instead making available to the public only aggregated data in the form of national averages, regional averages or income group averages. Nonetheless, in recent years, limited survey data at the household level have been made available to some researchers.

Some earlier studies have been summarised in Table 5.5. The magnitude of the estimated parameters of demand for foodgrains has varied greatly among different studies. Expenditure elasticities have varied from -0.03 to 1.30. In particular, some recent studies obtained unusually large income/expenditure elasticities, for instance, Liu and Chern (2001, 2003) and Zhang and Wang (2003).

Most studies try to derive expenditure or income elasticity of demand for foodgrains by studying foodgrains in conjunction with other food items. It is generally expected that the demand for foodgrains would be less income elastic than for many other food items. While some early studies (e.g., Tian 1990 and Huang 1997) tend to confirm that expenditure or income elasticities of demand for foodgrains are smaller than those for other foods, some recent studies have produced contrary results (e.g., Liu and Chern 2001; Zhang and Wang 2003; see Table 5.6).

Due to the use of different data sources, modelling techniques, and underlining assumptions, discrepancies between findings of different studies are not unexpected. Nonetheless, earlier studies did indeed provide some parameters that are valuable for understanding urban foodgrain consumption. Using existing data to carry out another modelling exercise is unlikely to produce another set of parameters that are drastically different from, or superior to, those obtained by existing studies. As such, no attempt is made in this chapter to conduct another empirical study. Instead, efforts are devoted to reviewing several key factors that affect the modelling of urban foodgrain consumption; this may prove to be more valuable to future studies in this important area when better data become available.

Table 5.5 Selected estimates on income and price elasticities of demand for foodgrains, urban China

Study	Data used	Specification of model	Item [a]	Estimated elasticities		
				Expenditure	Income	Own price
Lewis and Andrews (1989)	1982-85 income group data	ELES	GN	0.34	0.31	-0.26
Tian (1990)[b]	1984-88 income group data	LA/AIDS	GN_1	0.39		-0.29
			GN_2	0.46		-1.46
Shi et al. (1995)[c]	1983-93	LA/AIDS	GN_1	0.17		-1.35
			GN_2	-0.03		-1.11
Huang (1997)[d]	1989 and 1991 provincial averages	LA/AIDS	GN_1	0.07		-0.43
			GN_2	0.09		-0.43
Wu (1999)	1990, 33 cities, group averages	Two-stage budgeting procedure: AIDS, SUR	RI	0.98	0.37	-0.70
Wang and Davis (2000)	1952-95 national averages	Single demand equation	GN	0.32		-0.30
Gould and Sabates (2001)	1995-97 household survey data from three provinces	Expenditure share equation system with demographic variables	GN			-0.14
Liu and Chern (2001)	1992-96 provincial averages	LA/AIDS	GN	1.30		-0.38
		AIDS	GN	1.04		-0.05
		LES	GN	0.20		-0.18
		QES	GN	0.32		-0.10
Mu (2001)	1995-99 provincial averages	AIDS	GN	0.61		-0.44

Table 5.5 (continued)

Study	Data used	Specification of model	Item [a]	Estimated elasticities Expenditure	Income	Own price
Ma (2003)	2001 household survey data from five cities	ELES with demographic variables	GN		0.45	-0.39
Liu and Chern (2003)	1998 household survey data from three provinces	Censored QAIDS with demographic variables	RI	0.75		-0.86
			WF	0.72		-0.95
			CG	0.60		-0.93
Zhang and Wang (2003)	1998 household data from a sub-sample of 3500 households covering all provinces	LA/AIDS	GN	1.18	0.38	-0.75
			RI	1.17	0.44	-1.26
			WF	1.45	0.55	-1.90
			PWP	0.38	0.14	-0.77
			OG	0.54	0.20	-0.53

[a] GN, RI, WF, CG, PWP and OG refer to all grains, rice, wheat flour, coarse grains, processed wheat products, and other grains, respectively.
[b] Subscript 1 and 2 stand for models with and without taking into account the food rationing system.
[c] Subscript 1 and 2 stand for elasticities at simple mean and at income-share weighted means.
[d] Subscript 1 and 2 stand for small cities and provincial capital cities, respectively.

Table 5.6 Expenditure elasticities of selected food items

Study	Grains	Pork	Vegetables	Oils and fat
Tian (1990)[a]	0.39	1.04	0.80	0.81
	0.46	1.04	0.73	0.33
Huang (1997), small cities	0.07	0.93[c]	2.25	0.70
Huang (1997), provincial capital cities	0.09	0.97[c]	2.24	0.72
Wu (1999)	0.98[b]	1.17	1.19	-
Liu and Chern (2001)	1.30	0.49	1.17	1.21
Zhang and Wang (2003)	1.18	0.83[c]	1.11	0.99

[a] Estimates in the first row are from models that take into account the food rationing system and those in the second row are from models that do not.
[b] Rice only.
[c] All meats.
- Not available.

5.2.1 Data Accessibility and Related Problems

Data accessibility has been the major constraint that limits the modelling of consumption behaviour in China. Official statistical publications often only report data at the national or regional aggregate levels, and sometimes at the income group level. This often results in an insufficient number of observations for modelling work. To deal with the problem of the small number of observations, many earlier studies tried to use such aggregate data to form pooled time-series and cross-sectional datasets for their econometric modelling (e.g., Tian 1990, income-group data for 1984-88; Huang 1997, provincial averages for 1989 and 1991; Liu and Chern 2001, provincial averages for 1992-96).

However, such an approach is not without problems. When data sorted by income groups are used, researchers often calculate the required price information by dividing the expenditure by the quantity purchased to obtain the unit value of the good. Price information derived in such a way is likely to be inadequate in most cases. Variations in the unit value of the good are caused by food outlet differences and food quality differences. This error-in-variable problem would often lead to biased and inconsistent parameter estimates. When data aggregated at the regional level are used, a major issue that arises is whether consumption behaviours of the urban consumers are uniform throughout China. Dummies are often used to capture regional differences. However, this is unlikely to be sufficient to reflect varied responses to income and prices between regions.

Some recent studies were able to use household level data (e.g., Gould and Sabates 2001; Ma 2003; Liu and Chern 2003). Again, researchers have to use the "unit value of the good" as a price surrogate, and thus the problem regarding the adequacy of price information still exists. In fact it has become even more problematic at the household level as there are often drastic variations in the "unit value of the good" based on household-level survey data. Further, representation of the data is another concern. SSB only makes data of certain regions available to researchers without due considerations for representation of the data. In addition, misreporting of quantities purchased is also an issue. Experience has shown that households often record expenditures more accurately than quantities purchased of a food. Inaccurate household records may cause more problems for econometric modelling in studies using the household-level data than those using the data at more aggregate levels. Household survey data sometimes also present problems of abnormal observations and zero-consumption of certain foods. Nonetheless, thanks to improved access to some household survey data, researchers are able to estimate demand systems at disaggregated levels as well as to include valuable demographic variables in their modelling work.

Formulating panel datasets at the household level is ideal for analysing consumer behaviours, but it is difficult to do using the SSB survey data. SSB has a rolling sample: no household is retained for more than four years. Thus the longest time span would be four years only, even though it would be very costly to make such a four-year panel. The definitions of indicators are also subject to frequent changes, resulting in discontinuity or incompatibility of the data.

In general, modelling with time series data reflects mainly short-term responses to changes in incomes and price, while the cross-sectional data give adjustment of behaviours in the long term. Parameters derived from two types of datasets may also deviate notably. Researchers need to judge what kinds of data they need to use according to the nature of the issue they wish to investigate.

5.2.2 Model Specification

The specification of demand models is also to a great extent dictated by the availability of data. As shown in Table 5.5, various demand models have been used. Many studies by scholars within China tend to use the ELES model (Extended Linear Expenditure System) for its simplicity in estimation under the assumption that there is no price variation among observations. When the number of observations is sufficiently large, more complicated models, such as AIDS (Almost Ideal Demand System), are used. Underlying assumptions of demand behaviours or utility functions for various demand models are different. As such, the estimates obtained are conditional on model specifications.

How model specification would affect the results has been addressed in some recent studies. One example is the study by Liu and Chern (2001), which tests four different functional forms of demand system specification, namely LES, QES, LA/AIDS and AIDS. They estimate demand systems for 12 aggregate food items using the provincial-level data for the period of 1991-96 and then make *ex ante* forecasts using the same type of data for the period of 1997-99. They find that the expenditure elasticities vary under different functional forms (see Table 5.5). This is particularly evident for foodgrains, for which the expenditure elasticities range from 0.199 under LES to 1.302 under LA/AIDS. The derived own-price elasticities vary notably as well from -0.049 under AIDS to -0.383 under LA/AIDS. The *ex ante* forecasts on foodgrain demand for the period of 1997-99 are consistently higher than the level in 1996, while the observed demand had actually declined notably since 1996. Liu and Chern (2001) suggest that model selection should depend on the purpose of the study. The findings in Liu and Chern (2001) suggest that model specification is a very important issue for analysis of demand behaviours.

5.2.3 Chinese Characteristics of Consumption and Econometric Modelling

Available popular demand models are primarily based on neoclassic economics. China's economy is still in a process of transition and the consumer market is not mature but developing. The characteristics of Chinese consumption call for special attention when applying those popular models to China's consumption situation. Attention needs to be given to the following key aspects when modelling China's urban consumption.

Peculiar market situations Before the mid-1990s, urban foodgrain supply in China was subject to rationing. Studies by Tian (1990), Wang and Chern (1992) and Gao et al. (1996) find that rations of foodgrains do have impacts on consumption of other food items. Thus, models that use survey data of earlier years but do not take into account foodgrain rationing may generate biased estimates of parameters.

Dynamic consumption behaviours Unlike those more mature markets in developed countries that are relatively stable, the Chinese consumer market is developing and changing rapidly, as a result of rapid consumer income increase. Such a fast change in consumption behaviour requires the models to accommodate the possible effects resulting from structural changes in consumption. When the standard popular demand models are used, such effects cannot be captured but would be attributed wholly to changes in income. This overestimates the role of income change. To date, few studies have been carried out to verify if there exist any effects resulting from structural changes in consumption behaviours. Related to the fast change in consumption, estimates obtained by models using data several years old may not reflect current scenarios and hence would have limited value for policy purposes and marketing activities.

Data accuracy problem Data inaccuracy often causes tremendous problems in econometric modelling. The problem may originate in part from entry errors but sometimes also from deliberately providing inaccurate entries. This is especially the case when reporting income. Some urban residents obtain grey income or in-kind payments. There is strong tendency for people to under-report or not to report such income at all. Detecting such inaccuracy is almost impossible. How to cope with the data accuracy problem remains a challenge for researchers.

Multi markets versus uniform market Food consumption behaviours vary distinctly between regions in China, making it highly risky to extrapolate the results of modelling based on regional datasets to the whole country. Liu and Chern (2003) argue that China should be treated as several markets instead of just one uniform market.

5.2.4 Selection of Modelling Techniques

What estimation methods are used and how elasticities are calculated also affect the results. Researchers vary in their preferences and often adopt different methods to derive their results. Communications between researchers about their econometric results would be enhanced if details of their estimation techniques were adequately given in their study. However, compared with data and model specification problems, the selection of modelling techniques is a minor issue.

5.3 Rural and Urban Foodgrain Consumption Compared

The previous two sections clearly indicate that foodgrain consumption in urban China has been declining and, on the other hand, that the consumption of most other foods has been increasing. Findings from existing modelling work confirm that when urban residents' incomes increase, the scope for them to increase foodgrain consumption is small but the increase in their consumption of many other food items is promising. In this section, we compare foodgrain consumption in China's rural and urban areas.

In general, in both rural and urban areas, the proportion of consumers' spending on food out of total living expenditure has declined. As expected, this proportion is higher for rural residents than for their urban counterparts. Table 5.7 shows that the Engel coefficients for rural residents are generally about 5 percentage points higher when rural-urban income disparity is smaller, or about 10 percentage points higher when rural-urban income disparity is increased. Compared to 1978, Engel coefficients for both rural and urban residents have declined by about 20 percentage points by 2002 (see Table 5.7).

While the proportion of expenditure on all foods out of total living expenditure has declined, the proportion of expenditure on staple food, chiefly foodgrains, has also declined in both rural and urban areas. In urban areas, the percentage of expenditure on foodgrains is minimal, being only 3.2% in 2002 at the national level (see Table 5.4). The variation across regions is also relatively small, from 2.2% (the lowest in Beijing) to 4.6% (the highest in Shanxi). Detailed data comparable to Table 5.4 for rural residents are not available. However, the percentage of expenditure on staple food (foodgrains) based on a three-province average (sample data used in Chapter 4) is much higher, compared with their urban counterparts, being 20.2% in 2002. This percentage is lower in economically more developed regions (being 16.2% in Guangdong) and is higher in poorer regions (being 24.3% in Yunnan). On the other hand, it is clear from the discussions in Chapters 4 and 5 that consumption of non-staple food, especially foods of animal origin, has been on the increase in the past years. In addition, away-from-home consumption has also been increasing.

In terms of the actual quantity of foodgrains consumed, at the national level, it was about 168 kg per capita (224 kg unmilled) for rural residents in 2003 and was only 80 kg per capita for urban residents (Table 5.8). However, the level of consumption of non-grain food is much higher by urban residents than by rural residents.

Consumption patterns differ significantly across regions in both rural and urban China. Urban differences in consumption have been highlighted in Table 5.4. Unfortunately, similar data for rural residents are again not available. Findings based on the three-province sample data in Chapter 4 provide some useful observation on regional consumption differences. Table 5.9 has been compiled to provide a more complete picture about the consumption differences across all the provinces in rural China.

Table 5.7 Changes in per capita income and Engel coefficients in China

Year	Per capital annual income (¥)			Engel Coefficient		
	Rural residents	*Urban residents*	*Urban-rural ratio*	*Rural residents*	*Urban residents*	*Urban-rural difference*
1978	134	343	2.6	67.7	57.5	10.2
1980	191	478	2.5	61.8	56.9	4.9
1985	398	739	1.9	57.8	53.3	4.5
1990	686	1510	2.2	58.8	54.2	4.6
1991	709	1701	2.4	57.6	53.8	3.8
1992	784	2027	2.6	57.6	52.9	4.7
1993	922	2577	2.8	58.1	50.1	8.0
1994	1221	3496	2.9	58.9	49.9	9.0
1995	1578	4283	2.7	58.6	49.9	8.7
1996	1926	4839	2.5	56.3	48.6	7.7
1997	2090	5160	2.5	55.1	46.4	8.7
1998	2162	5425	2.5	53.4	44.5	8.9
1999	2210	5854	2.6	52.6	41.9	10.7
2000	2253	6280	2.8	49.1	39.2	9.9
2001	2366	6860	2.9	47.7	37.9	9.8
2002	2476	7703	3.1	46.2	37.7	8.5

Source: SSB (2003a, p. 344).

While there are clear differences between rural regions in their consumption of those non-staple foods, the difference in their consumption pattern of staple foods is most distinct. That is, in the northern provinces, wheat is the chief staple food while in the southern provinces rice is the staple food. Note that Table 5.9 displays the actual amount of food items consumed for rural residents while Table 5.4 reports the expenditure on each of the major food items.

In both rural and urban areas, the income level is the major determinant that affects the composition and the level of food consumption. Data in Table 5.10, which are similar to those presented in Table 5.4 for urban residents, suggest that when rural residents' income increases, their consumption level of foods increases. The very high foodgrain consumption by the highest income group is somewhat surprising. While the trend in Table 5.10 is largely in agreement with that shown in

Table 4.6, which is based on data of three provinces, the higher foodgrain consumption by higher income groups is an exception. This may be partially due to the fact that a larger portion of the higher income population is concentrated in southern China where rice is the staple foodgrain. However, the milling rate of rice is lower than that of wheat.

Table 5.8 Changes in per capita consumption of major food items (kg)

Food item	1985	1990	1995	2000	2001	2002	2003
				Urban residents			
Foodgrain	134.8	130.7	97.0	82.3	79.7	78.5	79.5
Vegetables	144.4	138.7	116.5	114.7	115.9	116.5	118.3
Vegetable oil	5.8	6.4	7.1	8.2	8.1	8.5	9.2
Pork	16.7	18.5	17.2	16.7	16.0	20.3	20.4
Beef and mutton	2.0	3.3	2.4	3.3	3.2	3.0	3.3
Poultry	3.2	3.4	4.0	5.4	5.3	9.2	9.2
Fresh eggs	6.8	7.3	9.7	11.2	10.4	10.6	11.2
Aquatic products	7.1	7.7	9.2	9.9	10.3	13.2	13.4
Sugar	2.5	2.1	1.7	1.7	1.7	n.a.	n.a.
				Rural residents			
Foodgrain (unmilled)	257.5	262.1	258.9	249.5	238.0	236.5	223.7
Vegetables	131.1	134.0	104.6	112.0	109.3	110.2	107.4
Vegetable oil	2.6	3.5	4.3	5.5	5.5	5.8	6.3
Pork	10.3	10.5	10.6	13.4	13.4	13.7	15.0*
Beef and mutton	0.7	0.8	0.7	1.1	1.2	1.2	
Poultry	1.0	1.3	1.8	2.9	2.9	2.9	3.2
Fresh eggs	2.0	2.4	3.2	5.0	4.7	4.7	4.8
Aquatic products	1.6	2.1	3.4	3.9	4.1	4.4	4.7
Sugar	1.5	1.5	1.3	1.3	1.4	n.a.	n.a.

* Includes beef and mutton.

Source: SSB 2003a and previous issues.

5.4 Concluding Comments

Analyses in Chapters 4 and 5 confirm that rapid structural changes in food consumption have been taking place in China in the past two decades. Foodgrain consumption has declined, first in urban areas and later in rural areas. On the other hand, the consumption of many other foods has increased. The increase in the consumption of foods of animal origin has been especially notable. Income has been found to be the most influential factor affecting the dynamics of food consumption. As such, it is not surprising to find that rural consumption is lagging behind urban consumption due to lower level income in the rural areas. Rural consumption is expected to largely follow the pattern of urban consumption.

Table 5.9 Per capita consumption of major food items, rural China, 2002 (kg)

Region	All foodgrains	Cereals and tubers				Beans and products	
		Wheat	Rice	Corn	Tubers	All beans	Soybeans
National	235	76	123	18	8	5.8	2.2
Beijing	143	83	34	16	4	7.5	0.7
Tianjin	159	100	40	16	2	4.8	0.4
Hebei	209	156	13	25	3	3.2	1.8
Shanxi	230	138	9	22	15	5.7	2.3
Inner Mongolia	220	85	41	30	14	6.2	4.0
Liaoning	211	29	103	43	10	9.5	5.5
Jilin	208	23	120	46	17	13.2	7.8
Heilongjiang	222	51	88	63	17	13.2	11.1
Shanghai	231	7	192	1	0	12.6	0.3
Jiangsu	264	59	183	15	4	7.5	2.5
Zhejiang	224	7	208	1	4	8.3	1.1
Anhui	241	83	148	3	4	7.4	2.4
Fujian	230	7	198	0	19	6.3	0.9
Jiangxi	276	2	257	0	7	4.6	2.0
Shandong	235	184	4	35	5	5.8	2.6
Henan	238	200	16	16	4	3.3	1.5
Hubei	274	30	207	15	13	7.3	3.0
Hunan	269	2	259	1	2	3.9	0.9
Guangdong	235	2	217	1	13	4.8	1.5
Guangxi	218	2	200	12	4	3.5	1.5
Hainan	335	1	318	0	14	1.6	0.3

Table 5.9 (continued)

Region	All foodgrains	Cereals and tubers				Beans and products	
		Wheat	Rice	Corn	Tubers	All beans	Soybeans
Chongqing	229	18	190	7	11	3.6	0.8
Sichuan	235	29	178	13	11	3.4	1.4
Guizhou	206	14	145	34	9	7.3	2.5
Yunnan	221	15	147	41	14	8.3	1.7
Tibet	276	78	52	1	16	17.4	0.4
Shaanxi	201	146	21	15	6	5.2	2.3
Gansu	249	213	4	12	11	3.2	0.2
Qinghai	229	191	3	0	20	1.5	0.0
Ningxia	235	168	49	1	8	1.1	0.0
Xinjiang	249	200	16	31	0	1.1	0.3

Region	Vegetables	Edible oil	Pork	Beef	Mutton	Poultry	Eggs	Dairy pr.	Aquatic pr.	Sugar	Fruits
National	111	7.5	13.7	0.5	0.7	2.9	0.6	4.7	1.2	4.4	1.6
Beijing	104	11.9	11.1	0.9	3.1	3.6	6.4	9.7	10.5	4.2	2.6
Tianjin	91	11.7	8.9	0.6	1.1	0.7	0.9	10.0	1.3	7.1	2.0
Hebei	59	6.9	6.9	0.3	0.2	0.4	0.7	5.6	0.4	2.2	1.0
Shanxi	81	6.4	4.9	0.1	0.3	0.2	0.5	6.1	1.3	0.6	1.8
Inner Mongolia	75	4.5	15.0	0.4	3.2	1.2	0.2	3.5	3.1	1.5	1.4
Liaoning	199	7.8	14.6	0.3	0.2	1.7	0.7	8.8	0.7	4.6	0.8
Jilin	117	7.1	10.7	1.3	0.1	2.1	0.5	7.7	0.2	3.7	1.2
Heilongjiang	104	7.7	7.3	0.3	0.1	2.5	0.5	6.5	0.5	3.6	1.0
Shanghai	87	8.7	15.9	0.4	0.6	8.3	3.0	10.7	2.4	16.4	3.4
Jiangsu	108	9.7	11.5	0.5	0.3	4.2	1.0	6.2	1.0	8.5	1.4
Zhejiang	87	5.9	15.3	0.5	0.3	5.5	1.4	4.9	1.8	14.0	2.4

Table 5.9 (continued)

Region	Vegetables	Edible oil	Pork	Beef	Mutton	Poultry	Eggs	Dairy pr.	Aquatic pr.	Sugar	Fruits
Anhui	82	7.8	9.0	0.3	0.1	3.9	0.5	4.7	0.2	4.6	2.1
Fujian	113	5.7	17.9	0.2	0.1	5.3	1.2	3.5	1.1	12.6	3.5
Jiangxi	141	9.5	12.6	0.2	0.0	2.5	0.3	2.9	0.2	4.4	1.3
Shandong	108	7.2	7.6	0.2	0.2	2.6	1.8	11.5	1.6	3.9	1.2
Henan	155	5.8	10.9	0.8	0.4	1.8	0.2	9.3	0.3	1.1	2.1
Hubei	151	10.8	18.1	0.2	0.1	2.1	0.2	3.5	0.1	7.3	2.1
Hunan	170	9.3	19.0	0.3	0.1	3.9	0.1	3.4	0.1	6.0	1.4
Guangdong	121	7.1	21.2	0.3	0.1	9.0	2.0	2.7	0.1	12.0	2.4
Guangxi	118	6.3	14.1	0.2	0.0	7.0	0.5	1.1	0.0	3.6	1.3
Hainan	68	19.5	13.6	1.2	0.3	8.3	0.0	0.6	0.2	16.3	1.7
Chongqing	157	6.7	25.7	0.1	0.1	2.3	0.3	4.6	0.3	1.8	4.4
Sichuan	147	6.8	25.0	0.3	0.1	2.8	0.4	3.6	1.1	1.6	1.5
Guizhou	126	4.7	27.2	0.6	0.1	1.1	0.0	1.2	0.1	0.3	0.9
Yunnan	102	5.4	23.6	0.4	0.1	2.4	0.2	1.7	-	1.3	1.4
Tibet	24	8.4	2.4	4.9	4.7	0.0	0.0	0.6	15.2	0.0	3.2
Shaanxi	54	6.5	6.4	0.1	0.2	0.3	0.2	2.1	1.1	0.3	1.0
Gansu	41	6.3	8.5	0.2	0.6	1.0	0.1	2.3	0.7	0.2	0.8
Qinghai	43	9.2	9.4	4.2	6.7	0.5	0.1	0.7	16.9	0.5	1.3
Ningxia	75	7.9	8.0	1.0	2.0	2.7	0.1	2.7	1.4	0.8	1.8
Xinjiang	88	10.4	1.3	2.4	7.3	1.4	0.0	1.1	3.9	0.4	0.4

Source: SSB 2003b, pp. 255–59.

Table 5.10 Per capita food consumption by income group, rural China, 2002 (kg)

Food item	Lowest income	Low income	Medium income	High income	Highest income
Foodgrain (unmilled)	215.0	230.0	244.0	244.0	249.0
Vegetables	86.0	105.0	116.0	125.0	127.0
Edible oil	5.9	7.0	8.3	8.0	8.9
Sugar	1.2	1.4	1.6	1.8	2.4
Fruits	12.1	15.0	17.8	22.0	29.6
Pork	11.0	12.5	13.5	14.9	17.8
Beef and mutton	1.0	1.0	1.0	1.1	1.8
Dairy products	1.0	0.8	1.0	0.9	2.5
Poultry	1.4	2.1	2.7	3.5	5.4
Eggs	2.7	3.8	4.8	5.6	7.1
Aquatic products	1.6	2.8	3.7	5.3	9.7
Net income (¥)	857.0	1548.0	2164.0	3030.0	5896.0

Source: SSB 2003b, pp. 255-59.

Consumer income will further increase as China's economy continues to grow strongly. Hence, in the near future, foodgrain consumption may decline further, especially in rural areas. The consumption of foods of animal origin may continue to increase. As a result, the demand for grains as animal feeds will continue to increase. In this regard, it is imperative to examine the consumption trends of animal product consumption in China to shed light on the likely potential demand for feedgrains. This is the subject of the next chapter.

References

Chern, W.S. and Wang, G. (1994), 'The Engel function and complete food demand system for Chinese urban households', *China Economic Reviews*, Vol. 5, pp. 35-57.

Gao, X.M., Wailes, E. and Cramer, L. (1996), 'Partial rationing and Chinese urban household food demand analysis', *Journal of Comparative Economics*, Vol. 22, pp. 43-62.

Gould, B. W. and Sabates, R. (2001), 'The structure of food demand in urban China: a demand system approach', paper presented at the AAEA (American Agricultural Economics Association) Annual Meeting, Chicago, 2-8 August, 2001.

Huang, J.K. (1997), 'Social development, urbanisation and food demand', in Institute of Agricultural Economics (CAAS), *Annual Report on Economic and Technological Development in Agriculture*, China Agricultural Press, Beijing, pp. 36-66.

Lewis, P. and Andrews, N. (1989), 'Household demand in China', *Applied Economics*, Vol. 21, pp. 793-807.

Liu, K.E. and Chern, W.S. (2001), 'Impacts of income changes and model specification on food demand in urban China', paper presented at the AAEA Annual Meeting, Chicago, 5-8 August, 2001.

Liu, K.E. and Chern, W.S. (2003), 'Food demand in urban China: an application of a multi-stage censored demand system', paper presented at the AAEA Annual Meeting, Montreal, Canada, 27-30 July, 2003.

Ma, J. (2003), 'Comparative study on the food consumption structure of different households in China', unpublished master thesis, China Agricultural University.

Mu, Y.Y. (2001), 'AIDS models of demand systems for China's urban and rural residents', *Economic Problems*, Vol. 8, pp. 25-28.

Shi, H.Q., Mitterlhammer, R., and Wahl, T.I. (1995), 'Aggregate food demand analysis for a transitional economy: an application to Chinese household expenditure data', *Journal of Food Distribution Research*, Vol. 26, pp. 20-27.

SSB (State Statistical Bureau of China) (2001), 'Instructions on urban household surveys', State Statistical Bureau, Beijing.

SSB (2002), *China Statistical Yearbook of Price and Urban Household Survey - 2002* (and previous issues), China Statistical Press, Beijing.

SSB (2003a), *China Statistical Yearbook 2003* (and previous issues), China Statistical Press, Beijing.

SSB (2003b), *Rural Household Survey Yearbook 2003*, China Statistical Press, Beijing.

Tian, W.M. (1990), 'Relationship between demand for agricultural products and prices for urban and rural residents', project report, Institute of Agricultural Economics, Chinese Academy of Agricultural Sciences, Beijing.

Wang, L.M. and Davis, J. (2000), *China's Grain Economy: the Challenge of Feeding more than a Billion*, Ashgate Publishing Ltd, Aldershot.

Wang, Z. and Chern, W.S. (1992), 'Effects of rationing on the consumption behaviour of Chinese urban households during 1981-87', *Journal of Comparative Economics*, Vol. 16, pp. 1-26.

Wu, Y.R. (1999), *China's Consumer Revolution*, Edward Elgar, Cheltenham.

Zhang, W. and Wang, Q.B. (2003), 'Changes in China's urban food consumption and implications for trade', paper presented at the AAEA Annual Meeting, Montreal, Canada, 27-30 July, 2003.

Note

[1] It is generally held that the SSB data tend to underestimate away-from-home consumption.

Chapter 6

Animal Product Consumption

Ji-Min Wang and Zhang-Yue Zhou

Chapters 4 and 5 confirm that in both rural and urban China consumption of foodgrain has been declining while that of other foods, especially animal products, has been increasing. Increased consumption of animal products requires more feedgrains to produce extra animals. Indeed, it has been increasingly recognised that feedgrain demand in China will become the major component of China's total grain demand. Many believe that any future increase in total grain demand in China will be mainly caused by an increasing demand for feedgrains (for example, Garnaut and Ma 1992; Findlay 1998, p. 32; Zhou and Tian 2003).

As a derived demand, the demand for feedgrains is closely related to the demand for animal products. As such, an understanding of animal product consumption trends in China is invaluable. It is imperative to gain reliable information about the current level of animal product consumption, as this is fundamental to predicting the likely consumption of animal products and hence to shed light on likely demand for feedgrains.

What, then, is the current consumption level of animal products in China? According to China's State Statistical Bureau (SSB), in 2002 per capita meat consumption in rural areas was 17.7 kg, per capita egg consumption was 4.7 kg, and per capita aquatic products was 4.4 kg. The corresponding figures for urban areas were 32.5 kg, 10.6 kg, and 13.2 kg, respectively (SSB 2003, pp. 352, 374). While these represent significant increases in consumption compared to the levels of 20 years ago, the per capita consumption data provided by SSB are most likely lower than the actual consumption levels. For example, based on a weighted average, per capita meat consumption in China was 23.5 kg in 2002. However, per capita meat output in 2002 was 51.3 kg. Considering the small amount of China's meat export, the existing gap between production and consumption needs investigating. In fact, since 1994, the SSB's consumption data can only explain an average of about 42% of the production (the lowest being 37.3% in 1995).

Some researchers believe that the output level of China's animal products is inflated. Zhong (1997) believes China's meat production statistics could have been inflated by 50% or even more. Lu (1998) believes output of meat, poultry eggs and aquatic products for 1981-95 could have been inflated by at least 40%. Aubert (1999), Colby et al. (1999), and Fuller et al. (2000) also believe that China's official meat production statistics have been overstated. However, Yuan (1999) disagrees with these claims and argues that the level of inflation for meat output is significantly below 40%. Jia (1999) even believes that the previously published meat production statistics are reasonable and there is little inflation.

On the other hand, some researchers may have underestimated the Chinese consumption of animal products, for example, Huang and Bouis (1996), Liang (1998), Fuller et al. (2000), and the SSB surveys. In many studies, away-from-home consumption and retail processed animal products, which have become an increasingly important part of total animal product consumption, are often overlooked.

In response to the increasing gap between production and consumption data and aided by the 1996 national agricultural census findings, the Chinese government adjusted downwards the output level of animal products for 1996. Yuan (1999) believes that, after the adjustments, pork, beef and mutton output figures since 1996 are now reasonable, although poultry and egg output remain inflated to some extent. Keeping this fact in mind, the gap still present between production and consumption levels in recent years suggests that it is most likely that consumption level was seriously underestimated.

Reliable information about animal product consumption in China is very important. Without it, any attempt to project consumption trends of animal product into the future, and hence the likely future feedgrain demand, may be futile. In this chapter, we estimate a set of animal product consumption levels for China at present and in the near future. We first, however, will look into China's animal product consumption over time.

6.1 Long-term Trends in Animal Product Consumption

Since the People's Republic of China was founded in 1949, China's animal product consumption has experienced three main stages according to changing diet patterns. During the first stage (1949-78), foodgrain was the main component of the diet for the Chinese. In the second stage (1979-85), changes in the Chinese dietary structure took place and livestock product consumption started to increase rapidly. In the third stage (1986 to present), foodgrain consumption began to decrease while livestock product consumption continued to grow steadily (see Table 6.1).

6.1.1 Low Level of Animal Product Consumption, 1949-1978

Food shortage was severe at the time when the People's Republic of China was founded in 1949. Following the land reforms in the early 1950s, agricultural supply increased rapidly and per capita consumption of food, chiefly foodgrains, started to increase. At that time, having enough food (chiefly cereal food) was the priority and limited effort could be devoted to the production of animal food. The increase in agricultural supply, however, was shortly reversed. Starting in 1958, the so-called Great Leap Forward movement caused serious damage to agricultural production and this was further aggravated by adverse weather conditions during 1960-62. Having enough food of plant origin, let alone of animal origin, had become a great challenge during 1960-63. Some recovery in agricultural production occurred in 1964-65, but in 1966 another political movement, the Cultural Revolution, started and lasted for ten years, resulting in overall economic slowdown. The agricultural sector managed to increase slowly, but due to a faster growth in population, per capita availability of food remained low. The Cultural Revolution ended in 1976 and agricultural production slightly increased in 1977-78, resulting in slightly improved per capita availability of food.

Table 6.1 Per capita consumption of foodgrain, livestock products, and aquatic products, selected years (kg)

Year	Foodgrain [a]	Red meat	Pork	Beef and mutton	Poultry meat	Poultry eggs	Milk	Aquatic products
1952	227	6.84	5.92	0.92	0.43	1.02	-	2.67
1957	233	6.19	5.08	1.11	0.50	1.26	-	4.34
1960	164	2.56	1.53	1.03	0.36	0.49	-	-
1965	210	7.31	6.29	1.02	0.36	1.42	-	3.33
1978	225	8.42	7.67	0.75	0.44	1.97	-	3.50
1980	246	11.99	11.16	0.83	0.80	2.27	-	3.41
1985	239	12.81	11.83	0.98	1.55	3.19	-	2.93
1990	239	14.09	12.63	1.45	1.82	3.69	-	3.60
1995	222	13.73	12.51	1.21	2.45	5.11	-	5.06
1999	206	15.76	14.00	1.76	3.23	6.33	3.10	5.83
2000	199	16.46	14.53	1.93	3.76	7.10	4.28	6.07
2001	189	16.24	14.33	1.91	3.79	6.86	5.23	6.46
2002 [b]	185	18.16	16.27	1.89	5.38	6.97	6.87	7.82

[a] Foodgrain is unmilled raw grain. Consumption data for 1952-80 are obtained directly from SSB publications. Those for 1985-2002 are weighted averages based on SSB statistics for urban and rural residents. There was severe food shortage at the time when the People's Republic of China was founded. Following the land reforms in the early 1950s, agricultural supply increased rapidly and per capita consumption of food, chiefly foodgrains, started to increase. There was a drop in per capita consumption of foodgrains in 1960 as shown in this table. This was the consequence of the damage to agricultural production resulting from the so-called Great Leap Forward movement in the late 1950s followed by further natural disasters in the early 1960s. From the mid-1960s, agricultural supply started to recover.
[b] The sudden jump in per capita consumption of red meat in 2002 was due to an irregular increase in urban per capita pork consumption, together with poultry and aquatic product consumption. The government official publications offered no explanations. There was no such jump for rural consumption. In this study, red meat includes pork, beef and mutton.

Source: SSB, *China Statistical Yearbook*, various issues.

Without substantial increase in cereal food supply during 1949-78, cereal production was paramount, and few resources could be spared to produce animal products. Not surprisingly, the level of animal product consumption by the Chinese was very low and the increase in absolute terms was only nominal. From 1952 to 1978, as shown in Table 6.1, per capita consumption of meat (including pork, beef, mutton, and poultry meat) increased only marginally, from 7.3 kg to 8.9 kg, that of poultry eggs increased from 1 kg to about 2 kg, and that of aquatic products increased from 2.7 kg to 3.5 kg. In terms of calorie intake, 90% came from food of plant origin, and only a very small portion from food of animal origin.

6.1.2 Rapid Increase of Animal Product Consumption, 1979-85

Rural economic reforms that started in the late 1970s greatly motivated farmers to work their land to increase agricultural supply. Grain production increased rapidly. As a result, for the first time in recent history, the Chinese had enough foodgrain to eat. The consecutive bumper harvests of foodgrains in the early 1980s enabled farmers to spare some grains to feed more animals, resulting in increased supply of animal products to the market. Improved agricultural supply coupled with increased consumer income led to changes in the Chinese people's dietary structure, with increased consumption of animal products. Although the consumption of foodgrain was also increasing, the rate of growth was much slower than the increase in the consumption of animal products. According to Table 6.1, from 1978 to 1985, the increase in the consumption of foodgrain was 14 kg, an increase of 6.2%. However, for the same time period, the increase in meat consumption and egg consumption was 5.5 kg (62.1%) and 1.22 kg (61.9%), respectively.

6.1.3 Continuing Increase in Animal Product Consumption, 1986–present

During this stage China's GDP has been growing at a high speed. In the meantime, China's livestock sector has also expanded dramatically. Animal products have become widely available in the market. Higher consumer income has led to further increased consumption of animal products. On the other hand, consumption of foodgrains has started to decline. Comparing 2002 to 1985, consumption of foodgrains has dropped to 185 kg from 239 kg, while the consumption of animal products has increased. For example, the increase in consumption of aquatic products, milk, eggs, and poultry meat has more than doubled. The consumption of beef and mutton, though still very low in absolute terms, has also almost doubled. However, the consumption of pork seems to have slowed down and its rate of increase is the lowest, being about 38%.

Examination of the long-term consumption trends of animal products in China in the past five decades clearly shows that changes have taken place in the dietary structure of the Chinese consumer, largely since the late 1970s, as a consequence of the rural economic reforms. Since the mid-1980s, consumption of animal product has increased much faster in the Chinese diet.

6.2 Current Level of Animal Product Consumption: Adjusted Estimates

As noted earlier, there has been a gap between China's production and consumption of animal products since the mid-1980s. This is clearly shown in

Table 6.2. Indeed, the SSB's consumption data can only explain an average of about 42% of the production since 1994, the lowest being 37.3% in 1995. The gap between consumption and production remained sizeable despite the fact that in 1997 the government adjusted its inflated production data for 1996, and that output data since the adjustments have been believed to be largely reliable.

Table 6.2 Discrepancies between meat consumption and production data, 1983 to 2002

Year	Per capita meat consumption (kg)	Per capita meat output * (kg)	Consumption of production (%)
1983	13.33	13.62	97.9
1984	13.92	16.19	85.9
1985	14.37	18.20	79.0
1986	15.97	19.65	81.3
1987	15.84	20.27	78.1
1988	15.07	22.33	67.5
1989	15.39	23.32	66.0
1990	15.93	24.99	63.7
1991	16.98	27.15	62.6
1992	16.97	29.28	58.0
1993	16.48	32.41	50.8
1994	15.98	37.54	42.6
1995	16.21	43.43	37.3
1996	17.35	37.45	46.3
1997	18.24	42.62	42.8
1998	18.50	45.86	40.3
1999	18.89	46.23	40.9
2000	20.40	48.39	42.2
2001	20.03	49.63	40.4
2002	23.54	51.28	45.9

* Carcass weight.

Source: SSB, *China Statistical Yearbook*, various issues.

It is noted that the consumption data are based on retail weight. From carcass weight to retail weight, weight losses of varying degrees occur for different animal products. However, even taking this fact into consideration, the gap still cannot be closed. Hence, most likely the SSB consumption data are underestimates. Three factors may have contributed to the underestimation. (1) In the SSB household surveys, away-from-home consumption of animal products was largely overlooked. (2) Only fresh and frozen animal products were included. Retail processed animal products and foods with animal product ingredients were neglected. (3) The SSB surveys pay only a very small amount of money to those surveyed households to compensate their time for maintaining household records, thus offering very limited incentives for wealthier households to participate in the survey. Hence, the samples are likely to be biased in favour of lower income households.

In this section, we present two sets of estimates of the current consumption level of animal products by the Chinese consumers. One set is based on a household survey that attempts to estimate the consumption level in 1998 and the other is based on a balance-sheet approach to estimate the consumption level in 2000.

6.2.1 Quantity and Composition of Animal Product Consumption in 1998

To verify the likely underestimation by the SSB survey data, in 1999 the Ministry of Agriculture in Beijing funded a research project, for which one of the authors was the project leader. The project was chiefly designed to collect household consumption data in order to compare with those provided by SSB and also to gather more detailed consumption data that SSB is unable to provide. Based on carefully planned sampling procedures,[1] household surveys were conducted in capital cities, towns and rural villages in six provinces of China, namely, Jilin, Inner Mongolia, Shandong, Jiangsu, Sichuan, and Guangdong. The surveys were conducted simultaneously in the six provinces in June 1999, collecting household animal product consumption data for 1998. Most of the interviewers were researchers specialising in livestock economics and a few were postgraduate research students. Before the surveys, pilot surveys were carried out to test the questionnaires, and all the interviewers were trained.

In each province 110 households were surveyed. Three hundred and fifty-nine valid questionnaires were obtained from urban surveys and 274 from rural surveys, resulting in 633 valid questionnaires in total. The surveyed families were sufficiently diverse, covering those engaged in various careers in cities, towns and villages. Key characteristics of both the urban and rural samples were compared with the national averages to ascertain how representative the samples were. Most of the sample features are comparable to the national averages. However, per capita income level is somewhat higher in the samples than in the national averages, especially in the rural sample (¥6218 in the urban sample, compared with ¥5952 of the national urban average; ¥3015 in the rural sample, compared with ¥2554 of the national rural average). Two major reasons are probably responsible for this higher sample income: (1) non-inclusion of any of the poorest provinces in the survey, such as Yunnan, Guizhou, Gansu and Shaanxi; and (2) the proportion of households falling into higher income groups in the samples is slightly higher, especially in the rural sample. Given that consumer income is generally regarded as the key factor affecting the consumption level of animal products, the estimates of animal product consumption from our surveys are probably biased slightly upwards.

Given that the surveys by the State Statistical Bureau only include the quantity purchased by households for at-home consumption, in our surveys, we tried to overcome this shortcoming by modifying the survey instrument in the following ways:

- For urban households, animal product consumption includes at-home and away-from-home consumption.

- At-home-consumption includes not only the purchased quantity but also that given by employers as staff welfare and that given by friends and relatives as gifts.

- Away-from-home consumption comprises all food containing animal products eaten outside the house, including breakfast, lunch and dinner.

- For rural residents, animal product consumption includes the quantity consumed from self-produced products, the quantity purchased, and the quantity consumed away from home.

With these modifications to our survey instrument, we believe that our survey can cover the majority of animal products consumed by households in both rural and urban China. In what follows, we report the findings on animal product consumption by households in the surveyed provinces.

Animal product consumption in China has reached a higher level Based on the survey, per capita meat consumption in 1998 was 33.73 kg at the all-China level (see Table 6.3). This figure is composed of pork (22.54 kg), beef and mutton (4.73 kg), and poultry (6.54 kg). This weight does not include the amount consumed of animal heads, hoof and paws, tails and offal, and was calculated at the retail weight. The per capita consumption of eggs, which does not include eggs contained in retail processed foods, was 9.68 kg. Dairy products, converted into fresh milk, were 6.31 kg and fish was 8.97 kg.

Table 6.3 Per capita and total animal product consumption in China, 1998

Animal food items	Per capita consumption				Total consumption				
	Urban (kg)	Rural (kg)	All China (kg)	Urban-rural ratio	Urban		Rural		All China
					mt	% All China	mt	% All China	mt
Total meat	49.81	26.83	33.73	1.9:1	18.9	44.9	23.2	55.1	42.1
Pork	30.72	19.04	22.54	1.6:1	11.7	41.4	16.5	58.6	28.1
Beef and mutton	8.86	2.96	4.73	3.0:1	3.4	56.9	2.5	43.1	5.9
Poultry	10.24	4.83	6.45	2.1:1	3.9	48.3	4.2	51.7	8.1
Eggs	15.84	7.04	9.68	2.3:1	6.0	49.7	6.1	50.3	12.1
Dairy products	13.96	3.04	6.31	4.6:1	5.3	67.3	2.6	32.7	7.9
Aquatic products	16.10	5.65	8.79	2.8:1	6.1	55.7	4.9	44.3	11.0

Source: Based on the 1999 CAAS survey.

Using the information in Table 6.3, it is calculated that in 1998 total meat consumption in China was 42.1 million tonnes, of which pork accounted for 28.1 million tonnes, beef and mutton accounted for 5.9 million tonnes, and poultry

8.1 million tonnes. Eggs, milk and fish consumption was 12.1, 7.9 and 10.9 million tonnes respectively (see Table 6.3).

The survey reveals that pork consumption still accounts for a major portion in total meat consumption, being 67%. Beef and mutton together account for about 14% while poultry accounts for 19% (see Table 6.4). In rural areas, the proportion of pork consumption is even higher, being over 70%. However, beef and mutton consumption is lower. Urban residents tend to consume more poultry meat.

Table 6.4 Composition of meat consumption, 1998

	Urban	Rural	All China
Per capita consumption (kg)			
Pork	30.72	19.04	22.54
Beef and mutton	8.86	2.96	4.73
Poultry	10.24	4.83	6.45
Total meat	49.81	26.83	33.73
% of total meat consumption			
Pork	62	71	67
Beef and mutton	18	11	14
Poultry	21	18	19
Total meat	100	100	100

Source: Based on the 1999 CAAS survey.

Another observation emerging from the survey results is that the consumption of animal products in China has reached a much higher level than previously calculated by the government. The amount of various animal products consumed by Chinese consumers is clearly much higher than the reported amount from the SSB surveys (see Table 6.5). Therefore, the SSB household surveys significantly underestimate the consumption level of animal products by residents in both rural and urban China. Nonetheless, the SSB survey confirms that the consumption level of animal products by urban residents is higher than that of rural residents, and the urban-rural ratio is largely comparable to that revealed by the current survey (Table 6.5).

Table 6.5 Comparison of per capita animal product consumption between this study and SSB, 1998

Animal food items	Per capita consumption (this survey)			Per capita consumption (SSB survey)			Underestimation by SSB			
	Urban (kg)	Rural (kg)	Urban–rural ratio	Urban (kg)	Rural (kg)	Urban-rural ratio	Urban		Rural	
							Quantity	%	Quantity	%
Total meat	49.81	26.83	1.9:1	23.90	15.50	1.5:1	-25.91	-52	-11.33	-42
Pork	30.72	19.04	1.6:1	15.88	13.20	1.2:1	-14.84	-48	-5.84	-31
Beef and mutton	8.86	2.96	3.0:1	3.34	*	n.a.	-5.52	-62	n.a.	n.a.
Poultry meat	10.24	4.83	2.1:1	4.65	2.33	2.0:1	-5.59	-55	-2.50	-52
Poultry eggs	15.84	7.04	2.3:1	10.76	4.11	2.6:1	-5.08	-32	-2.93	-42
Dairy products	13.96	3.04	4.6:1	n.a.	n.a.	n.a.	n.a.	n.a.	n.a.	n.a.
Aquatic products	16.10	5.65	2.8:1	9.84	3.31	3.0:1	-6.26	-39	-2.34	-41

* Included in pork

n.a.: not available.

Sources: Based on the 1999 CAAS survey; SSB (1999), *China Statistical Yearbook*, pp. 322, 346.

The consumption gap between rural and urban residents is still very large Both this survey and the SSB surveys show that the per capita consumption level of animal products by urban residents is higher than that by rural residents. In some cases, the level may be 3 to 4 times higher (e.g., for beef and mutton, and for dairy products). However, the consumption gap between more traditional animal products is smaller (e.g., pork and poultry meat), tending to suggest that income increase and urbanisation are likely to affect the composition of animal product consumption.

At the aggregate level, urban residents consume almost the same amount of animal products as do rural residents, and in some cases this proportion is much higher (e.g., beef and mutton, dairy products and aquatic products, see Table 6.3). However, China's urban population is less than 30% of the total population and the rest is rural. This further shows that the consumption gap between the urban and the rural populations is still very large.

The low per capita consumption level in rural areas suggests that there is greater potential for rural areas to increase consumption of animal products in the future. This is simply because the rural population base is huge. When rural income increases, demand for animal products will increase. A small per capita increase in animal product consumption by the large rural population will result in a huge increase in total quantity demanded.

Away-from-home consumption is on the increase Table 6.6 shows that away-from-home consumption of animal products now accounts for an important portion of total consumption. About 21% of meat, 30% of aquatic products, 15% of dairy products and 13% of eggs are consumed outside the home. Among all the meats, the consumption of poultry meat away from home has the highest portion, being 32.2%, followed by beef and mutton, 28%. Pork has the lowest proportion, being 17%. A possible reason for a lower proportion of pork and eggs being consumed away from home could be that their consumption by urban residents has reached a plateau and that cooking them at home is relatively easy.

Table 6.6 also shows that, compared with their rural counterparts, urban households have a much higher away-from-home consumption for most animal products. The only exception is dairy consumption, because some farm family members who work in urban areas are influenced by urban people and tend to consume some dairy products. But, on the other hand, dairy consumption by rural households is too low. When combined, this produces a higher proportion for away-from-home consumption of dairy products by rural households.

Table 6.6 At-home and away-from-home consumption of animal products in China

	Per capita at-home consumption		Per capita away-from-home consumption		% away-from-home consump. by urban residents	% away-from-home consump. by rural residents
	kg	% of total consump.	kg	% of total consump.		
Total meat	26.54	78.7	7.19	21.3	33.6	11.5
Pork	18.77	83.3	3.77	16.7	26.6	9.9
Beef and mutton	3.39	71.6	1.34	28.4	37.5	16.7
Poultry	4.37	67.8	2.08	32.2	51.3	14.8
Eggs	8.40	86.8	1.28	13.2	13.0	13.4
Dairy products	5.38	85.2	0.93	14.8	4.2	35.5
Aquatic products	6.16	70.1	2.63	29.9	43.5	13.3

Source: Based on the 1999 CAAS survey.

Consumption of fatty meats is on the decrease but that of lean meats is on the increase Some 20 years ago, many Chinese people, particularly rural people, liked to buy very fatty meats – the fatter, the better. This seems to have changed significantly. The survey results in Table 6.7 indicate that the consumption of fatty meats by both urban and rural residents accounts for only a very small portion of their meat consumption, being 2.3% and 7%, respectively. On the other hand, the consumption of lean meat accounts for an important proportion, 53.1% for urban residents and 34.7% for rural residents. In rural areas, there is still a significant preference for meats that are not very fatty but not very lean either (44.5%). This is perhaps because rural workers still require some fats in the body so as to perform heavy manual work, and also because rural people are perhaps less aware of potential problems that animal fats may cause to health. It seems the Chinese consumers more readily accept the head, claws, tails and offal of pigs than of cattle and sheep (Table 6.7).

Consumption of retail processed meat products is relatively low According to the extent of meat product processing, meat products may be put into three categories: raw, semi-processed, and processed. In Table 6.8, semi-processed products are treated as part of the raw products. Table 6.8 suggests that the consumption of processed meat products by Chinese urban residents is generally low, being only about 10%. Almost 90% of meat products consumed at home is unprocessed. The proportion of semi-processed products is very low. While these results tend to suggest that there is potential to develop the semi-processed and processed animal product market, they also reflect the fact that many Chinese consumers' incomes are not yet high enough to afford a large portion of semi-processed or processed meat products. Future consumer income increase may lead to increased consumption of such processed products.

Table 6.7 Composition of various animal parts consumed by urban and rural residents (%)

Resident	Animal	Head, foot and claws, tails and offal	Ribs	Fatty meat	Lean meat	Fatty and lean meat	Total
Urban	Pig	7.4	22.1	4.0	33.7	32.8	100
	Cattle	1.2	1.5	0.3	87.0	10.1	100
	Sheep	1.6	6.0	0.1	70.2	22.1	100
	Average	6.0	14.1	2.3	53.1	24.5	100
Rural	Pig	6.6	10.6	9.4	24.9	48.5	100
	Cattle	0.8	1.8	0.6	88.5	8.3	100
	Sheep	1.4	5.4	1.3	43.0	48.9	100
	Average	5.1	8.7	7.0	34.7	44.5	100

Source: Based on the 1999 CAAS survey.

Table 6.8 Proportion of processed and unprocessed animal products consumed at home by urban residents (%)

Food item	Raw	*% semi-processed, raw*	Processed	Total
Pork	90.5	1.2	9.5	100
Beef	79.4	1.1	20.6	100
Mutton	92.5	2.5	7.5	100
Poultry	81.0	1.9	19.0	100
Aquatic products	96.6	2.3	3.4	100
Average	89.6	1.7	10.4	100

Source: Based on the 1999 CAAS survey.

Among different kinds of processed products, beef has a higher proportion consumed at home by urban residents (20.6%), followed by poultry meats (19.0%) (see Table 6.8). This may be partially attributable to (1) the fact that beef is not traditionally consumed by most Chinese consumers and they may lack the skills to cook beef dishes at home, and (2) some specially cooked poultry products cannot be prepared at home. On the other hand, Chinese people are well used to cooking pork at home. As for mutton (or lamb), the popular way of preparing it in China in recent years is by the "hot pot" method – sliced lamb is quickly dipped into the boiling soup in the "hot pot" and then consumed by mixing with other seasonings and side dishes. In this case, raw meat must be used. Chinese people do not like buying too many pre-cooked aquatic products, preferring instead to use fresh raw materials for cooking.

6.2.2 Adjusted Animal Product Consumption Level in 2000

In this part, we derive a balance sheet for China's animal product consumption and production in 2000. This allows us to estimate the per capita consumption level in 2000 that can be used to crosscheck the 1998 estimates and also be used as a foundation to project the likely consumption level in 2010. The balance sheet approach is a useful alternative, vis-à-vis household surveys, to estimate the consumption level of animal products for China. In addition, due to the lack of quality data, it is also unrealistic to employ more sophisticated techniques to estimate China's animal production consumption levels.

The derivation of a balance sheet between production and consumption is based on the assumption that the production data are largely accurate. As noted earlier, the inflated production figure for 1996 was adjusted downwards. Since then, there has been no exceptional growth of animal product between years and many have argued that the production data are relatively accurate. Hence, the official animal production data are used without further adjustments.

Since the consumption estimates from this balance sheet will be used as the baseline to project future consumptions, it is necessary to avoid yearly fluctuations. To this end, a three-year average (1999-2001) is used. Three-year averages are calculated for total output, net export, and SSB consumption estimates; the last of these for comparison with the consumption estimates from this balance sheet.

The balance sheet on China's animal product production and consumption for 2000 is presented in Table 6.9. In retail weight, China's per capita meat consumption in 2000 had reached 37.7 kg (including 24.23 kg of pork, 4.99 kg of beef and mutton, and 8.5 kg of poultry meat). This figure is much higher than the consumption level of 19.75 kg as published by SSB. Based on the balance sheet, egg consumption in 2000 was 16.8 kg and milk consumption was about 7.5 kg. The consumption that falls into the categories of "home cooked", "away-from-home" and "processed products" is also given in Table 6.9.

We also calculated the consumption growth rates between 1998 and 2000 using two sets of data: (1) the consumption data by SSB for 2000 and 1998; and (2) the 2000 consumption level derived in the above balance sheet and the 1998 level as reported in Section 6.2.1. The growth rates from the two sets of data for various categories of animal products are also largely comparable (see Table 6.10), except for eggs due to data complication (see note b to Table 6.9). The comparability in the growth rates from the two set of data lends support to the findings regarding the 1998 consumption level based on the survey. It also suggests that the consumption levels of various animal products derived for 2000 using the balance-sheet method are, in the main, reasonable. Hence, it would be reasonably safe to use these estimates as baseline to project the likely consumption levels of animal products by the Chinese in the near future.

Grains of China

Table 6.9 Adjusted estimates of animal product consumption in 2000 (three-year average 1999-2001)

Data item	Total meat	Red meat	Pork	Beef	Mutton	Poultry meat	Milk	Eggs
Total output (mt)[a]	60.16	48.38	40.36	5.29	2.73	11.78	9.50	22.38
Net export (mt)[a]	0.59	0.15	0.12	0.03	0.004	0.44	0.04	0.04
Domestic consumption (mt)	59.57	48.23	40.24	5.26	2.726	11.34	9.46	22.34
Per capita availability (kg)	47.01	38.06	31.76	4.15	2.15	8.95	7.47	17.63[b]
Carcass: retail loss rate (%)[c]			23.7	26.0	11.0	5.0		5.0
Per capita consumption, retail weight (kg)	37.72	29.22	24.23	3.07	1.92	8.50	7.47	16.75[b]
of which:								
away-from-home consumption (%)[d]			17.0	29	29.0	33.0	15.0	14.0
(kg)	8.37	5.57	4.12	0.89	0.56	2.81	1.12	2.34
consumption of processed products (%)[e]			6.5	14.0	5.1	12.9		20.0
(kg)	3.19	2.09	1.57	0.43	0.10	1.10		3.35
consumption of home-cooked food (kg)	26.16	21.56	18.55	1.75	1.26	4.60	6.35	11.05
Per capita consumption, SSB data (kg)[a]	19.75	16.15	14.29	1.87		3.59	4.20	6.77

[a] Output, net export, and SSB per capita consumption are three-year averages (1999-2001). Output and per capita consumption data are from SSB *China Statistical Yearbook*, various issues. Red meat includes pork, beef and mutton in this study and total meat includes red meat and poultry meat. Net export data are from the production, supply and distribution (PS&D database), ERS, USDA.

[b] In China, conventionally, seed eggs are included in total egg production. There is no reliable information about the proportion of total egg output used to hatch chicks, and hence it is difficult to deduct the seed eggs from the total output. Subsequently, the per capita availability of eggs, and thus the per capita egg consumption, is likely to be slightly higher than the actual.

[c] Carcass retail weight-loss parameters are based on Putnam and Allshouse (1996). Due to the lack of a conversion ratio to account for milk retail loss, per capita milk consumption remains the same as per capita availability.

[d] Away-from-home consumption proportion was based on Table 6.6.

[e] The consumption proportion of processed products is based on the assumption that rural residents consume half the amount consumed by urban residents. The consumption proportion of processed products is based on Table 6.8.

Table 6.10 Annual growth rates of animal product consumption based on SSB data and adjusted estimates

Data source	Total meat	Red meat	Pork [a]	Beef and mutton [a]	Poultry meat	Poultry eggs
SSB 1998 (kg)	18.1	15.1			3.0	6.1
SSB 2000 (kg)	20.2	16.5	14.5	1.9	3.8	7.1
Annual growth (%)	5.7	4.4			12.0	7.9
Survey, 1998 (kg)	33.7	27.2	22.5	4.7	6.5	9.7
Balance sheet 2000 (kg)	37.7	29.2	24.2	5.0	8.5	16.8
Annual growth (%)	5.8	3.6	3.8	3.0	14.4	31.4 [b]
Underestimation 1998	46.3	44.5			53.8	37.1
Underestimation 2000	46.4	43.7	40.0	61.3	55.8	57.6 [b]

[a] In 1998, there were no separate statistics for pork, beef and mutton. All were placed into one category: pork, beef and mutton, which is treated as red meat in this study. Total meat includes red meat plus poultry meat.
[b] This is not comparable: see note b to Table 6.9 for details.

6.3 Possible Scenarios of China's Animal Product Consumption in 2010

Based on the 2000 per capita consumption level derived above, we now turn to project the likely consumption level of animal products by the Chinese consumers in 2010. In making projections, it has been popular to employ structural equations (such as partial equilibrium systems or general equilibrium systems) or time-series auto-regression equations. For consumption research, many have opted to use demand system equations. Due to the lack of necessary data coupled with poor data quality, no attempt is made to use some sophisticated econometric techniques for our projections. Instead, we use some conventional simpler methods. To "compensate" the inability to use more complex econometric methods, we use three conventional methods to project China's demand for animal product in 2010, allowing us to carry out cross-checking and comparison of the results of different methods. These three methods are trend extrapolation, analogies method, and income elasticity method.

6.3.1 Trend Extrapolation

From the mid-1980s, China experienced a period of very fast increase in animal product consumption. Given that the 1985 per capita consumption data by SSB show only minimal underestimation, using the adjusted 2000 per capita consumption data in Table 6.9, the annual growth rate of consumption between 1985 and 2000 is 4.9% for pork, 11.5% for beef and mutton, 12% for poultry meat, and 11.7% for eggs, respectively. Because the growth rate of consumer income has slowed down significantly in recent years, it is reasonable to assume that these high growth rates of animal product will not continue into the future.

In fact, given that China's import and export of animal products is so small, the production is largely equal to the consumption. In this sense, the slower growth rate of animal production in recent years also reflects a slower growth rate of animal consumption. During 1996-2000, the annual growth rate was 7.5% (8.2% during 1985-1996) for meat production, 3.3% (18.9% during 1985-1996) for poultry meat and 3.4% for eggs (12.6% during 1985-1996). The growth rates for poultry meat and egg production dropped by a greater amount.

Based on the above, we assume that the consumption growth rate during 2001-2010 will be 3% for pork, 6% for beef and mutton, 6% for poultry meat, 2.5% for eggs and 7% for milk. The projected consumption level in 2010 is given in Table 6.11.

Based on the trend extrapolation, by 2010, per capita meat consumption in China will be 56.7 kg, comprising 32.6 kg of pork, 8.9 kg of beef and mutton and 15.2 kg of poultry meat. Egg consumption will be 21.4 kg and milk consumption will reach about 15 kg.

Table 6.11 Per capita animal product consumption in 2010 (kg)

Method	Total meat	Pork	Beef and mutton	Poultry meat	Eggs	Milk
Baseline (2000)	37.72	24.23	4.99	8.50	16.75	7.47
Trend extrapolation	56.72	32.56	8.94	15.22	21.44	14.69
Analogies method	56.50	33.90	9.60	13.00	21.50	14.26
Income elasticity method	60.36	36.07	8.10	16.18	26.31	17.06
Range	56-60	32-36	8-10	13-16	21-26	14-17

6.3.2 Analogies Method

By comparing consumption and income levels of China and some other "Chinese communities" such as Taiwan, Hong Kong and Singapore, Garnaut and Ma (1992, pp. 23-37) found that there is a strong relationship between the income level and the consumption level of meat consumption among the "Chinese communities". This, however, is subject to the multiplication of the mainland China per capita GDP by a factor of 2 to 3, due to the likely underestimation of GDP in China. In 2000, for example, mainland China's meat consumption was 37.7 kg (based on our adjusted estimates) and thus equal to Taiwan's average consumption in 1978 and 1979; at that time Taiwan's per capita GDP was about US$1700 (Xiao 1993), a figure twice that of the mainland's per capita GDP in 2000, i.e., US$855 (7078 yuan, SSB 2001).

This finding provides a useful way to predict animal product consumption in China by comparing the income levels between China and other "Chinese communities". This approach also possesses another advantage: changes in consumer tastes and preferences have been "built in" in the predication – when consumer income rises, their tastes and preferences may change in a similar way due to the similarities in their ethnic background. The following assumptions are made when using this "analogies method":

1. Consumers in mainland China and other "Chinese communities" have similar tastes and preference in meat consumption.[2]
2. China's per capita GDP will grow at an annual rate of 7% from 2000 to 2010. China's GDP annual growth rate was 12.0% during 1991-1995, and 8.3% during 1996-2000. Many believe that China's GDP will increase at an annual growth rate of about 8% from 2000 to 2010 (Li 1999; Lin 1999; Xu 2002). At the same time, population growth rate is slightly less than 1%. Thus, per capita GDP will grow at about 7%.
3. The amount of meat consumption in mainland China is equal to the consumption in other Chinese communities such as Taiwan, Hong Kong and Singapore at the same income level when China's per capita GDP is multiplied by 2. However, the composition of meat will follow China's own pattern as exhibited in the past few decades.

China's per capita GDP in 2000 was 7078 yuan. At an annual rate of 7%, it will reach 13924 yuan (US$1682, constant price in 2000) by 2010. Based on Assumption 3 above, China's per capita meat consumption will be equal to the consumption of Taiwan at its income level of US$3364 (US$1682 × 2). Taiwan's per capita GDP was about US$3364 in 1985-86 and at that time its per capita meat consumption was 56.5 kg. As a result, per capita meat consumption in mainland China is likely to reach 56.5 kg by 2010.

In the past decade, the share of pork consumption in China's total meat consumption has decreased from almost 80% in 1990 to 64% in 2000. Beef and mutton's share increased from 9% to 13%, and the share of poultry meat increased from 11% to 22%. Based on our judgement, we believe that the share of pork will continue to decline but that of beef and mutton will increase because beef and mutton are likely to become more popular with the Chinese, particularly in the emergence of new cooking methods. On the other hand, the fast increase in poultry meat consumption is unlikely to continue. Hence, we assume that by 2010, the share of pork, beef and mutton, and poultry meat out of total meat consumption will be 60%, 17% and 23%, respectively. Subsequently, per capital pork, beef and mutton, and poultry meat consumption will be 33.9 kg, 9.6 kg and 13 kg, respectively (see Table 6.11). As such, the consumption of beef and mutton in 2010 will be higher than Taiwan's (2.5 kg) in the mid-1980s, while poultry meat will be lower than Taiwan's (20 kg) in the mid-1980s.

6.3.3 Income Elasticity Method

This method depends heavily on an important parameter: income elasticity of demand for animal products. The accuracy of this parameter is crucial. However, as shown in Table 6.12, available elasticity estimates for China vary greatly. Hence, an average is used and its calculation is explained in the note to Table 6.12.[3] As for the "analogies method", we assume China's per capita GDP will increase at an annual rate of 7% from 2000 to 2010. Based on the income elasticity method, by 2010, total meat consumption will be 60.4 kg per capita, which includes 36.1 kg of pork, 8.10 kg of beef and mutton, and 18.2 kg of poultry meat. Egg consumption will be 26.3 kg while that of milk will be 17.1 kg (see Table 6.11).

Examining the results presented in Table 6.11 that are derived from three different methods, we note that the differences in projection by different methods are relatively small. The differences in projections between the income elasticities approach and other two methods are slightly larger, but the magnitude should be quite acceptable. The differences between the results from the trend extrapolation and analogies method are only nominal although those for beef and mutton and poultry are slightly greater. This lends us confidence in accepting these projections.

According to the results in Table 6.11, consumption of animal products in China will continue to increase. Per capita total meat consumption will increase from 37.7 kg in 2000 to about 56-60 kg in 2010. Per capita egg consumption will increase from 16.8 kg in 2000 to 21-26 kg in 2010, and per capita milk consumption will increase from 7.5 kg in 2000 to 14-17 kg in 2010. While the consumption of all animal products will increase, the rate of increase among different animal products differs. The annual growth rate of milk consumption of 7.6% is the fastest, followed by beef and mutton (6.1%) and poultry meat (5.5%). The increase in pork and eggs will be relatively slower, at 3.4% for both.

6.4 Conclusions

In this chapter, we first examined China's long-term animal product consumption trends, which shows that since the early 1950s the consumption level has increased significantly, especially since the mid-1980s. We then estimated the current levels of animal product consumption. These estimates laid the foundation for us to project the consumption levels of animal product consumption by 2010.

Our estimation reveals that the current consumption of animal products in China has reached a much higher level than previously held. The SSB household surveys significantly underestimate the consumption level of animal products by the Chinese consumers. Take 2000 as an example. For all meat, the underestimation is 46.4%. For red meat and poultry meat, it is 43.7% and 55.8%, respectively. The estimates derived in this chapter offer a valuable understanding of the current level of animal product consumption in China.

Projections by three different methods indicate that the consumption level of animal products in China will continue to increase. While the consumption of all animal products will increase, the rate of increase among different animal products differs. The increase in milk consumption will be the fastest, followed by beef and mutton and poultry meat. The increase in pork and eggs will be relatively slower.

Hence, the analyses in this chapter confirm that China's animal product consumption will continue to increase, which will subsequently lead to increased demand for more feedgrains. Will China be able to meet the increased demand for feedgrains with its domestic supply or will China need to import feedgrains? Or, will China choose to import animal products? These questions will be dealt with in the following chapters.

Table 6.12 Estimates of income elasticities of demand for animal products in China

Rural or urban	Year, or income level	Income elasticities of demand for						
		Meat	*Pork*	*Beef and mutton*	*Poultry*	*Eggs*	*Milk*	*Fish*
Zhu et al. (1991) [a]			0.57	0.57	1.46	0.66		1.34
Pinstrum-Anderson et al. (1991) [a]		0.63	1.23	1.16	1.18	1.71	0.86
RGCFDS (1993, p. 14) [b]								
	1995	0.580				0.936	1.400	0.468
	2000	0.540				0.673	1.189	0.606
	2020	0.426				0.553	1.100	0.472
Huang and Rozelle (1998, p. 245)								
Rural	1999-2000	0.757	0.765	0.343	0.854	0.512	1.557	1.053
Rural	2000-2010	0.835	0.782	0.789	0.985	0.455	1.637	1.244
Rural	2010-2020	0.835	0.782	0.789	0.985	0.455	1.637	1.244
Urban	1999-2000	0.835	0.782	0.689	0.985	0.455	1.637	1.244
Urban	2000-2010	0.870	0.797	0.686	1.064	0.491	1.912	1.290
Urban	2010-2020	0.870	0.797	0.686	1.064	0.491	1.912	1.290
Cai et al. (1999, p. 155) [c]								
	Low income	1.102	0.610		1.392			
	Medium income	1.756	0.627		0.541			
	High income	1.482	0.731		0.710			
Wang and Fan (1999) [d]								
Rural	1998		0.25	0.57	0.22	0.36	0.32	0.37
Urban	1998		0.32	0.49	0.48	0.26	0.49	0.51
Average [e]		0.928	0.583	0.712	0.954	0.661	1.225	0.879
Huang (1996), USA estimates		0.66	0.39 [f]	0.08	0.29	0.12		

[a] Quoted from Garnaut and Ma (1992, p.72).
[b] Numbers in the 'Fish' column are for aquatic products; no separate estimates for individual meat.
[c] Expenditure elasticities for three income groups; numbers in 'Meat' column are for ruminant meat. Based on a small sample.
[d] Numbers in the 'Fish' column are for aquatic products.
[e] These averages are calculated from those estimates that are largely based on consumption data in the 1990s and those estimates beyond 2000 are not included. They will be used to project future consumption levels using the income elasticity method.
[f] For beef only.

Source: Adapted from Zhou et al. (2003); Huang (1996).

References

Aubert, C. (1999), 'Food consumption and food production in China: statistical uncertainties, educated guesses, and reasoned optimism', *Chinese Rural Economy*, No.12, pp. 16-21.

Cai, H.O., Brown, C., Longworth, J. and Wan, G.H. (1999), 'A demand analysis of ruminant-meat, pork and poultry-meat by Chinese households segmented by three income strata', in Zhou, Z.Y., Chudleigh, J., Wan, G.H. and MacAulay, G. (eds), *Chinese Economy towards 21st Century*, Vol. 1, The University of Sydney, pp.145-159.

Colby, H., Zhong, F.N. and Giordano, M. (1999), 'A review of China's meat production', *Agriculture in China and OECD Countries: Past Policies and Future Challenges*, OECD Proceedings, Paris, France, pp.185-213.

Findlay, C. (ed.) (1998), *Grain Market Reform in China: Global Implications*, ACIAR Technical Report No. 43, Australian Centre for International Agricultural Research, Canberra.

Fuller, F., Hayes, D. and Smith, D. (2000), 'Reconciling Chinese meat production and consumption data', *Economic Development and Cultural Change*, Vol. 49, pp. 23-43.

Garnaut, R. and Ma, G. (1992), *Grain in China*, East Asia Analytical Unit, Department of Foreign Affairs and Trade, Commonwealth of Australia.

Huang, J.K. and Bouis, H. (1996), *Structural changes in the demand for food in Asia*, Agriculture and the Environmental Discussion Paper No.11, International Food Policy Research Institute, Washington, DC.

Huang, J.K. and Rozelle, S. (1998), *China's grain economy to the twenty-first century*, China Agricultural Press, Beijing.

Huang, K.S. (1996), 'Nutrient elasticities in a complete food demand system', *American Journal of Agricultural Economics*, Vol. 78, pp. 21-29.

Jia, Y.L. (1999), 'Factors constraining China's animal husbandry development and their macro adjustments', *Chinese Rural Economy*, No. 1, pp. 40-45.

Li, J.W. (1999), 'Analysis of China's economy and its prospects', in Zhang, Z.Y., *Economists Review of China's Economy in the 21 Century*, Henan People's Press, pp. 100-115.

Liang, Z.H. (1998), 'Demand for livestock products in China', in Zhu, X.G., *Annual Report on Economic and Technological Development in Agriculture*, China Agriculture Press, pp. 158-169.

Lin, Y.F. (1999), 'Outlook of China's economy in the New Millionaire', in Zhang, Z.Y., *Economists Review of China's Economy in the 21 Century*, Henan People's Press, pp. 31-37.

Lu, F. (1998), 'On discrepancies between production and consumption data of China's agricultural products and artificial inflation in production statistics', *Chinese Rural Economy*, No. 10, pp. 47-53, 71.

Pinstrum-Anderson, P. et al. (1991), 'Changes in incomes, expenditures, and food consumption among rural and urban households in China during the period of 1978-88', in proceedings of International Conference on Food, Nutrition, and Social-Economic Development, Beijing. Quoted from Garnaut, R. and Ma, G. (1992), *Grain in China*, East Asia Analytical Unit, Department of Foreign Affairs and Trade, Commonwealth of Australia.

Putnam, J.J. and Allshouse, J.E. (1996), *Food Consumption, Price, and Expenditures, 1970-95*, Statistical Bulletin Number 939, ERS, USDA.

RGCFDS (Research Group for China's Medium- and Long-term Food Development Strategies) (1993), *China's Medium- and Long-term Food Development Strategies*, China Agricultural Press, Beijing.

SSB (State Statistical Bureau), *China Statistical Yearbook*, various issues, Beijing, China.

Wang, J.M. and Fan, Y.L. (1999), 'A study on animal product consumption by rural and urban residents in China', Research Report for a project commissioned by the Ministry of Agriculture, Chinese Academy of Agricultural Sciences, Beijing.

Xiao, Q.R. (1993), 'Demand and consumption composition of agricultural products in Taiwan', in Niu, R.F., *China Agricultural Development Symposium,* China People's University Press, pp. 122-37.

Xu, C.X. (2002), 'China economic growth in the future and its position outlook in the world', *Journal of Economic Research*, No.3, p. 27.

Yuan, X.G. (1999), 'Are China's animal product output figures inflated?' in Wang, J.M. and Fan, Y.L., *A Study on Animal Product Consumption by Rural and Urban Residents in China*, Research Report, Chinese Academy of Agricultural Sciences, Beijing.

Zhong, F.N. (1997), 'An analysis of the level of artificial inflation in China's meat output statistics and the causes of inflation', *Chinese Rural Economy*, No. 10, pp. 63-66.

Zhou, Z.Y. and Tian, W.M. (2003), *China's Regional Feedgrain Markets: Developments and Prospects*, Grains Research and Development Corporation, Canberra.

Zhou, Z.Y., Tian, W.M., Liu, X.A. and Wan, G.H. (2003), 'Research methodological issues in projecting China's feedgrains demand and supply', *Chinese Agricultural Economic Review*, Vol. 1, pp. 54-74.

Zhu et al. (1991), 'Food consumption and food acquisition behaviour among rural households in China, in proceedings of International Conference on Food, Nutrition, and Social-Economic Development, Beijing. Cited from Garnaut, R. and Ma, G. (1992), *Grain in China*, East Asia Analytical Unit, Department of Foreign Affairs and Trade, Commonwealth of Australia.

Notes

[1] Full details will be made available from the authors on request.

[2] However, it is noted that there are some differences in the composition of meat demanded and also the consumption level of eggs, milk and aquatic products. For example, at a comparable level of income, consumers in Taiwan seem to consume more poultry meat than those in the mainland while the latter seem to consume more beef and mutton than the former. On the other hand, egg consumption level in the mainland tends to be higher but that of milk is much lower than that of Taiwan. Further, per capita aquatic product consumption in the mainland is also much lower, partly perhaps due to the lower per capita production of aquatic products.

[3] The average reported in Table 6.12 suggests that the income elasticities for all the animal products in China are greater than those in more mature markets (such as the United States, see the last row in Table 6.12). This indicates that if the consumer income continues to increase, there will be scope for the increase in animal product consumption in China, which is confirmed by various projections in this section.

Chapter 7

China's Feedgrain:
Production and Consumption

Xian Xin, Zhen-Hai Yang and Zhang-Yue Zhou

It has been shown in earlier chapters that in China direct consumption of grains by humans has declined but, through increased use of grains as feed to produce more animal products, indirect consumption of grains has increased. In this chapter, we examine China's feedgrain production and consumption. Section 7.1 addresses feedgrain production while Section 7.2 discusses feedgrain consumption. In Section 7.3 we highlight feedgrain demand and supply imbalances between regions. Finally, in Section 7.4, we briefly touch on the prospects for China's feedgrain production and consumption.

7.1 Feedgrain Production

In China, 'feedgrain' mainly refers to coarse grains, including corn, sorghum, millet, barley, oats and some other minor cereal crops.[1] It is estimated that some 80% of corn is used for feed purposes (National Grain and Oil Information Centre 2000). While rice and wheat are treated as fine grains, a certain amount is also used for feed.

Farmers in southern China feed their livestock with rice of inferior quality, chiefly early-crop indica rice. Early-crop indica rice does not taste good but has higher yields and a longer storage life than late-crop indica rice, wheat or corn. According to a survey by the Research Centre for Rural Economy of the Ministry of Agriculture in 1993, it was common for farmers in Jiangsu, Zhejiang, Jiangxi, Hunan, Hubei, Guangdong, Guangxi and Sichuan to feed livestock with rice. In some areas (for example, Hunan and Jiangxi), rice accounts for about 50% of total feedgrain consumption. In addition, the government grain policy in the 1990s unintentionally encouraged farmers in southern China to grow and sell early-crop indica rice to fulfil their rice quota obligation to the government (see Chapter 2 for details). However, with increased income, consumers have turned away from low quality rice and they now demand better, tastier grains. As a consequence, government grain bureaus end up storing early-crop indica rice for several years, then selling it at low prices for feed.

Wheat is also sometimes used as feed. Wheat products are traditionally the staple diet in northern China, with farmers often retaining enough stock from their harvests for their own consumption. As in the case of rice, farmers tended to deliver lower quality wheat to the government to fulfil their quota, which also led to lower quality wheat being accumulated in the government's storage. About 7.5 million tonnes of inferior quality wheat are reported to be in stock, accounting for nearly one-third of China's 26 million tonnes of wheat stocks. As the quality of such wheat deteriorates further over time, it is likely to end up as feed. In addition, some major wheat-producing provinces, such as Shandong, regularly allocate about 20% of their wheat harvest for feed (USDA 2000, p. 9).

Nationwide, it is estimated that, annually, about 6% of rice and 1% of wheat were used as feedgrain in China in the late 1990s and the proportions are projected to rise (MOA 2002a). In this regard, feedgrain also includes rice and wheat as a part. The rest of this chapter, however, focuses on coarse grains, and particularly corn.

China's coarse grain production is concentrated in northern China, the main production area for corn, sorghum and millets. The climatic conditions in the south-east and southern China are not very favourable for corn production and barley is often planted as a winter crop in these regions. Coarse grain production has increased in the past decade in response to the increased demand for feedgrains (see Table 7.1). Total output of coarse grains reached 148 million tonnes in 1998, accounting for 32% of China's total cereal output. Coarse grain output in the following years declined, partly due to weather conditions and partly due to lower prices.

Table 7.1 Sown area (m ha) and output (mt) of coarse grain in China

Year	Corn		Coarse grain		Corn/ grain*		Corn/ cereal*		Corn/ coarse*		Coarse/ cereal*	
	Area	Output	Area	Output	Area	Output	Area	Output	Area	Output	Area	Output
1991	21.6	99	30.5	116	19.2	22.7	22.9	25.0	70.7	85.2	32.5	29.3
1992	21.0	95	29.9	114	19.0	21.5	22.7	23.7	70.3	83.8	32.4	28.4
1993	20.7	103	28.3	121	18.7	22.5	23.3	25.3	73.1	84.7	31.9	29.9
1994	21.2	99	28.4	119	19.3	22.3	24.2	25.2	74.5	83.7	32.4	30.1
1995	22.8	112	29.7	129	20.7	24.0	25.5	26.9	76.7	87.0	33.3	30.9
1996	24.5	127	31.2	146	21.8	25.3	26.6	28.2	78.5	87.5	33.8	32.3
1997	23.8	104	30.1	119	21.1	21.1	25.9	23.5	78.9	87.3	32.8	26.9
1998	25.2	133	31.1	148	22.2	26.0	27.4	29.1	81.1	90.0	33.8	32.4
1999	25.9	128	31.4	141	22.9	25.2	28.3	28.3	82.5	91.1	34.3	31.0
2000	23.0	106	29.1	118	21.2	22.9	27.0	26.2	79.0	89.8	34.1	29.1
2001	24.3	114	29.1	125	22.9	25.2	29.3	28.8	83.4	91.3	35.2	31.5
2002	24.6	121	29.4	133	23.7	26.5	30.2	30.4	83.7	91.0	36.1	33.4
2003	24.1	116	28.3	127	24.2	26.9	31.3	30.9	85.0	91.2	36.9	33.9

* Ratios of sown area or output.

Sources: Calculations based on SSBb, *China Rural Statistical Yearbook*, various issues.

Grains in China

Table 7.1 clearly shows that corn is the major coarse grain crop, with a share increasing from about 85% in 1991 to 90% in recent years. China's corn output reached 130 million tonnes in the late 1990s, making China the world's second largest corn producer after the USA. The following factors are probably responsible for China's rapid expansion in corn production: (1) corn can be relatively cheaply produced with high yield; (2) improvements have occurred in technology; and (3) corn is the preferred cereal for feeding animals.

Corn production is very widely spread across China, covering almost all seasons and all regions. Spring corn is mainly grown in north-east China and in mountainous, high altitude arid climate zones in north-west China. Summer corn is mainly produced in Huang-Huai-Hai Plain in central China, and autumn corn is produced in southern coastal provinces and inland mountainous areas, such as Zhejiang, Jiangxi, Guangxi and Sichuan. Winter corn can be found in Yunnan, Guangxi and Hainan.

Although corn production is widespread in China, the major corn-producing provinces only include Shandong, Henan, Hebei, Jilin, Liaoning, Heilongjiang, Inner Mongolia and Sichuan, which together contributed over 70% of the national output in most of the 1990s. Geographically, these regions are located from the north-east to the south-west, an area known as China's "Corn Belt" (see Map 7.1).

Table 7.2 Changes in corn production

Year	Area sown (m ha)			Output (mt)				
	Total	*Corn Belt*	*North-east**	*Total*	*Corn Belt*		*North-east**	
					Output	National share (%)	Output	National share (%)
1985	17.7	12.0	4.9	63.8	45.4	71.2	18.1	28.4
1986	19.1	13.2	5.5	70.9	51.7	72.9	24.5	34.6
1987	20.2	14.0	6.1	79.2	59.1	74.6	28.2	35.6
1988	19.7	13.6	5.8	77.4	59.7	77.1	29.0	37.5
1989	20.4	14.0	5.9	78.9	57.2	72.5	24.1	30.5
1990	21.4	14.9	6.5	96.8	75.1	77.6	37.9	39.2
1991	21.6	15.0	6.7	98.8	76.7	77.6	38.5	39.0
1992	21.0	14.6	6.6	95.3	73.4	77.0	39.1	41.0
1993	20.7	14.2	6.0	102.7	75.5	73.5	37.1	36.1
1994	21.2	14.5	6.4	99.3	74.6	75.1	37.2	37.5
1995	22.8	15.9	7.3	112.0	83.5	74.6	40.3	36.0
1996	24.5	17.1	7.8	127.5	94.5	74.1	49.2	38.6
1997	23.8	16.1	7.9	104.3	72.8	69.8	37.7	36.1
1998	25.2	16.9	6.5	133.0	95.5	71.8	42.5	32.0
1999	25.9	17.3	6.7	128.1	91.1	71.1	39.1	30.5
2000	23.0	15.6	5.4	106.0	72.5	68.4	23.4	22.1
2001	24.3	16.3	6.3	114.1	84.0	67.1	29.7	25.9
2002	24.6	16.5	6.3	121.3	83.6	68.9	34.7	28.6
2003	24.1			115.8				

* North-east refers to Liaoning, Jilin and Heilongjiang provinces.

Sources: Calculations based on SSBb, *China Rural Statistical Yearbook*, various issues.

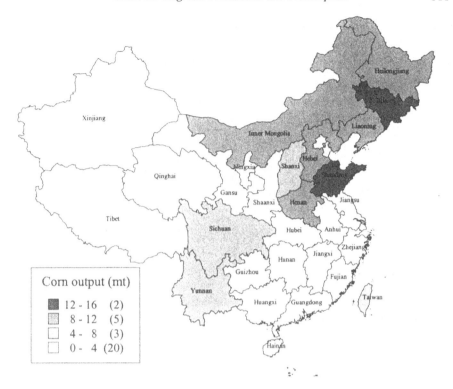

Map 7.1 Corn output in China, 2002

Source: SSBb, *China Rural Statistical Yearbook 2003*, p. 152.

Along the Belt, the North-east Plain has the highest competitive advantages in corn production, followed by the Northern China Plain.

In the 1980s and 1990s, the Corn Belt produced over 70% of China's corn (Table 7.2). In most years since the mid-1980s, the three northeast provinces (Jilin, Liaoning and Heilongjiang) produced more than 30% of the national corn output, with the highest being 41% in 1992 (see Table 7.2). The year 2000 was an exception when the total sown area in these three provinces dropped by 17%. This exceptional drop may have been caused by drought or by depressed corn prices due to over-supply in the preceding years and the subsequent shift of sown area to other crops.

The cost of corn production varies significantly among different provinces (Figure 7.1). Production costs are generally lower in northern China than in southern China. Data show that in 2002 the production cost in the three north-east provinces (Jilin, Liaoning and Heilongjiang) was relatively lower, being below 0.6 ¥/kg, while in Guangxi it was more than 1.0 ¥/kg, and highest in Guizhou, at 1.16 ¥/kg (State Planning Commission 2003, pp. 107-10, see Figure 7.1).

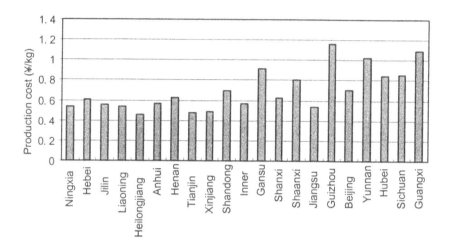

Figure 7.1 Corn production cost, 2002

Source: State Planning Commission 2003, pp. 107-10.

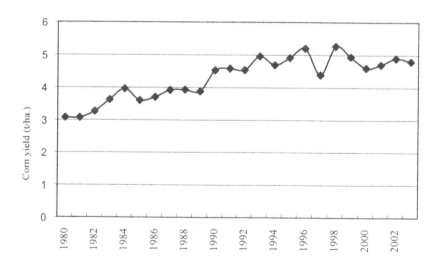

Figure 7.2 Corn yield, 1980-2003

Source: SSBa 2002, p. 117; SSBb, *China Rural Statistical Yearbook 2003*, pp. 140, 152.

The improvement in coarse grain yield contributed to the growth of feedgrain output in China in the past two decades. Corn yield increased from a little over 3 tonnes/ha in the early 1980s to over 5 tonnes/ha in the late 1990s (Figure 7.2). In 1998, the yield reached 5.3 tonnes/ha. It dropped to a little under 5 tonnes/ha after 1999 due to unfavourable weather conditions in several provinces and lower prices.

The major reason for improvement in corn yield has been the adoption of new technologies in corn production, such as using hybrid varieties, coating the land with a plastic membrane, increased use of dense-leaf corn, and increased use of modern inputs. Dense-leaf corn is characterised by dense planting with 60-70 thousand units per hectare, which is 30%-50% more than the planting density of ordinary corn. The area planted to dense-leaf corn accounted for 28% in 1997. Moreover, according to official statistics, the yield of hybrid corn was 23% higher than that of conventional varieties in 1998, while it was 39% higher in 1999. In China, a very large share of total corn area, 88%, was planted to hybrid corn in the late 1990s. At the same time, the plastic film-covered area also increased from 31500 hectares in 1985 to about 1.2 million hectares in the late 1990s. Plastic film extends the growth·period in areas with cool weather conditions, which is critical to the increase in yield in the north-east.

While coarse grains (chiefly corn) are mainly used for feed purposes, their output may not be the best approximation for feedgrains that are available to the livestock industries. This is due to the complications as pointed out earlier, that some coarse grains are used directly for human consumption and some fine grains (rice and wheat) are also used for animal feed. What, then, is the likely level of feedgrain production in China? Unfortunately, there are no reliable statistics. This is because feedgrain production has not become an independent industry, and no separate data are collected about it. In 1993, the government made an effort to change China's crop production from the dual "grain – cashcrop" production pattern to a "grain – feed – cashcrop" production pattern. The motive was to let feed production become an independent industry. The government also wished to have production statistics of feed crops separately reported (State Council 1993). So far, progress has been slow.

In the absence of official statistics on the amount of feedgrains produced, attempts have been made to estimate the supply of China's feedgrains: further details are given in Chapter 8. In this book, we have also made an effort to estimate feedgrain supply at the regional level (see Chapter 10). Based on various sources, the amount of feedgrains supplied in the early 2000s would be around 160 million tonnes.

7.2 Feedgrain Consumption

As with the production of feedgrains, there is a lack of reliable data on the consumption of feedgrains. Similarly, estimates have been made. According to the Ministry of Agriculture, in the late 1990s China used about one-third of grains produced in the country as feedgrains (MOA 2002b, pp. 47). Yang (2003) provides a set of estimates that largely align with this assertion (see Table 7.3).

Grains in China

Table 7.3 Feedgrain consumption in China

Year	Feedgrain consumption (mt)	Total grain output (mt)	Feedgrain use as % of total grain output
1996	147.8	504.5	29.3
1997	149.2	494.2	30.2
1998	159.8	512.3	31.2
1999	162.7	508.4	32.0
2000	155.9	462.2	33.7
2001	156.2	452.6	34.5
2002	160.0	457.1	35.0
2003	163.7	430.7	38.0

Source: Adapted from Yang (2003).

It is hard to estimate the proportion of the feedgrain that is used by each of the major feeding practices, due to a lack of reliable information. There are three kinds of major animal raising practices: (1) very small-scale traditional household backyard animal raising; (2) specialised animal raising households; and (3) larger-scale animal feedlots. The first two occupy an important share: for example, in 1998, about 95% of China's pork was produced by these two animal-raising practices. Backyard animal raising alone produced some 80% of total pork production (Qi 1999, p. 2). In general, the proportion of feedgrain used in the total feed ration varies among the three different practices. The proportion would be higher for the feedlot feeding regime, lower for backyard animal raising, and medium for the specialised practice. In major feedgrain-producing provinces such as those in China's north-east (e.g., Jilin), the proportion of feedgrain use in the total feed ration is also relatively high (Zhou et al. 2003).

The different animal raising practices also vary in the way they feed grain to the animals. According to a survey of household animal raising practices in various provinces (Zhou et al. 2003), backyard-raising practices sometimes cook raw grains (mostly ground) and mix them with other feed items. They also buy industrial processed feed, especially concentrated feed. Specialised households often process the grains and mix them with other components by themselves to reduce cost, or, in other cases, buy industrial processed feed. For feedlotters, feedgrains are generally processed and mixed with other ingredients.

Industrial processed feed is gaining popularity and its use has increased very rapidly in recent years (Qin and Yin 2003). China has now become the second largest industrial feed producer, after the United States, and may surpass the United States in the near future. Feedgrain accounts for a significant portion in industrial feed (see Table 7.4). However, this proportion has been declining over the years, from 59.3% in 1996 to 47.4% in 2003. The following factors have contributed to this declining proportion:

- The proportion of concentrate feed and additive premix feed has been increasing relative to total industrial feed in recent years: producing these feeds uses less feedgrains.

- The output of feed for aquatic production is on the increase: this feed is based mainly (more than 50%) on protein.
- In industrial feed, the use of non-conventional feed ingredients such as DDGS (distillers dried grains with solubles) and micro-organisms is increasing.

The proportion of feedgrains used for industrial feed production out of total feedgrain consumption is around 22% to 25% in recent years (Table 7.4). As China's animal husbandry industry gradually moves away from small-scale backyard raising, the demand for industrial processed feed is expected to increase (Zhou et al. 2003).

Table 7.4 Industrial feed production and the use of feedgrain in industrial feed

Year	Industrial feed production (mt)	Feedgrain use in industrial feed (mt)	% of feedgrain in industrial feed (%)	Total feedgrain use (mt)	Feedgrain used in industrial feed as % of total feedgrain use
1996	56.1	33.3	59.3	147.8	22.5
1997	63.0	35.6	56.5	149.2	23.8
1998	66.0	36.2	54.9	159.8	22.7
1999	68.7	36.1	52.5	162.7	22.2
2000	74.3	38.4	51.7	155.9	24.6
2001	78.1	39.6	50.7	156.2	25.3
2002	83.2	40.6	48.8	160.0	25.4
2003	87.8	41.6	47.4	163.7	25.4

Source: National Feed Industry Statistical Data from 1995 to 2004.

Major feedgrain users include the following provinces: Shandong, Guangdong, Sichuan, Hebei, Hunan, Henan, Liaoning, Heilongjiang, Hubei, Jiangsu, Zhejiang, Jiangxi, Fujian, Shaanxi, and Jilin. The majority of these provinces are located in southern coastal provinces, central and north-east China. As with feedgrain production, there is a lack of data on feedgrain consumption at the regional level. In this book, we have attempted to estimate feedgrain consumption at the regional level: this is reported in Chapter 10.

7.3 Regional Imbalances

As noted in the earlier sections, China's corn production is concentrated in the north, while corn consumption is concentrated in deficit south-east, east, south-west regions and the cities of Beijing, Tianjin and Shanghai. In recent years, provinces with a major corn surplus include Jilin, Heilongjiang, Liaoning and Inner Mongolia. These provinces provided 60% to 70% of commercial corn. Hunan,

Guangdong, Sichuan, Chongqing, Jiangsu, Hubei, Fujian, Guangxi and Zhejiang are the major provinces with a corn deficit. These provinces are located in central and southern China and are major pork producers. These provinces use more feedgrains than they can produce locally.

Pork production in some southern provinces has been declining and animal production is gradually shifting to northern parts of the country. Sichuan, the single largest pig-producing province, produced over 17% of China's pork in 1991, but the share had dropped to 13% in the late 1990s. The seven provinces along the middle and lower sections of the Yangtze River used to produce nearly 60% of China's pork 10 years ago. This percentage has fallen to about 50% in recent years.

The relocation of livestock production from the south to the north is a gradual process and has only marginally altered the existing patterns of livestock production and feedgrain consumption. A large share of pork output is still from Sichuan, Hunan, Hubei, Guangdong, Jiangsu and Jiangxi, although production in Shandong, Hebei and Liaoning has been on the increase in recent years. Generally speaking, the fifteen provinces north of the Yangtze River produce more than 77% of China's corn. The 15 provinces south of the Yangtze River produce only 23% of China's corn, yet they use over 50% of China's total corn production. It seems that *bei liang nan yun* – transporting feedgrains from the north to the south – has become a reality in China in the past decade. (Prior to the 1990s, *nan liang bei diao* – transporting foodgrains from the south to the north – was the basic pattern of inter-regional grain shipment.) Some claim that the distance that corn was shipped from the north to the south could be as much as 3000 kilometres or more (Liu 2000).

Long-distance shipment of coarse grains is expensive and resource-intensive, placing significant strain on China's already stretched transport infrastructure. However, China restricted corn imports for years before its accession to the WTO at the end of 2001 (see Chapter 2). As a result, southern provinces had to rely on domestic supply by either promoting local production at high cost or purchasing from northern provinces and bearing the high transport cost.

Due to the cost of shipment coupled with import restrictions, the corn price gap between major corn-surplus and corn-deficit regions is large. The prices on the rural markets of two northern provinces, Jilin and Shandong, and two southern provinces, Sichuan and Guangdong, are shown in Figure 7.3. The prices in Jilin and Shandong are much lower than those in Sichuan and Guangdong in almost all months between January 1987 and December 2000.

In northern and north-east China, corn constitutes a large share of total grain stocks. The corn stocks of the three northeast provinces take up some 70% of national corn stocks. In the past few years, more corn dryers have been constructed at grain stations, grain depots, and major railway terminals. Much of China's north-east corn can be stored in temporary wicker-walled, thatched-roof bins, because autumn and winter weather is cold and dry.

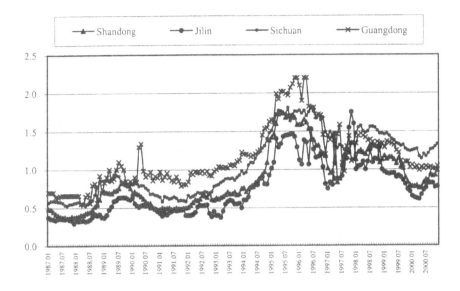

Figure 7.3 Monthly free market corn prices, rural areas, selected provinces (¥)

Source: Research Centre for Rural Economy, Ministry of Agriculture, Price Database.

7.4 Prospects of Feedgrain Production and Consumption

China's potential to increase feedgrain supply is very important. If China's future supply cannot satisfy its demand for increased feedgrains, the imports that may be required would have an important impact on the international market. Some researchers argue that there is still potential for China to increase its feedgrain production, not so much through increased sown area but primarily through higher yields. They believe that grain yields can be raised significantly with technological improvements (MOA 1999; Lin et al. 1996, pp. 136-43). Currently, China's corn yield of around 5 tonnes per hectare is a little above the world average (4.3 t/ha); however, it is well below that of the USA (around 8.5 t/ha) and France (around 9 t/ha). The fact that China's cultivated land is under-reported also allows China to raise yield.[2] To assess this potential, Tian and Wan (2000) used a frontier production function to measure regional technical efficiency based on the production cost data during 1983-96. They found that technical inefficiency does exist in corn production. However, all the major producing regions are relatively efficient except Sichuan, a south-west inland province. Other inefficient producers include Zhejiang, Hubei, Hunan, Guangxi, Guizhou and Yunnan: all are south of the Yangtze River. Their results also suggest that there is potential to increase corn yield in the few major corn-producing regions in northern China.

In order to increase supply of feedgrain, particularly in southern China, the Chinese government has proposed a wide range of measures (Chen et al. 1996; MOA 1999). For instance, conversion of paddy land to corn production has been encouraged in some southern provinces. Feed rice production bases are planned for Hunan, Jiangsu, Hubei and Sichuan, and feed sugarcane production bases for Guangdong, Guangxi and Fujian (MOA 1999).[3] All these measures suggest that the Chinese government is attempting to use its domestic resources to ensure a basic supply of feedgrains. Whether such an approach is economically viable in the long term, or even practical, particularly given that China is now a member of the WTO, is yet to be seen.

The central government has also tried to exercise stricter control over the conversion of cultivated land for non-agricultural purposes. Efforts are being made to improve agricultural infrastructure for the purpose of raising land productivity. China is endeavouring to maintain appropriate growth of coarse grain production in the next decade, particularly if world prices begin to rise.

For acceptance to the WTO, China committed to opening up its domestic agricultural markets. With respect to corn, a major feedgrain item, China committed to setting an initial import quota of 5.85 million tonnes on accession, and increasing this to 7.2 million tonnes by 2004. This import quota of 7.2 million tonnes is significantly smaller than future imports as predicted by many studies, such as Garnaut and Ma (1992); Crook and Colby (1996); Findlay (1998); USDA (1998); and Tang and Zheng (2000, p. 209). On the other hand, since being accepted into the WTO in late 2001, China has been net exporting corn to the world market.

China's domestic grain price was much higher than the world price during 1998-2000 but now the gap has narrowed due to both a decline in domestic price and an increase in the world price. In the meantime, China's grain reserve stocks have been reduced as a result of consecutive lower grain output along with net export during the past few years (2000-03). This has to some extent contributed to the price rises since September 2003. In the longer term, domestic prices will be increasingly linked to the world price. As a result, it is likely that southern provinces may shift gradually to using imported feedgrains, instead of purchasing from major producers in northern China. This change will place great pressure on corn producers in northern regions, especially in the north-east provinces.

On the other hand, private grain traders are likely to play an increasing role in grain import and export. In China's agreement to join the WTO, a provision was included that China's private sector would initially receive 25% of corn import quota, rising to 40% by 2004, with all unused quota by state trading companies (STC) being reallocated in later months of a year. With such a quota reallocation clause, the Chinese government will gradually lose its major instrument to intervene in trade. This is because, under such an arrangement, it will be to the advantage of both the STCs and private traders to import at full quota as long as the domestic market price is sufficiently higher than the world price. This may lead to lower domestic prices, which in turn will discourage feedgrain production but encourage feedgrain consumption.

China's future feedgrain consumption will also be affected by how GMO policy will evolve in China and how agricultural subsidy policy in developed countries will respond to WTO negotiations. It will also be affected by whether China can increase its animal product export to the rest of the world and whether imported animal products can take a significant share in the Chinese market: the former will increase China's demand for feedgrains, while the latter will work in the opposite direction.

China's feedgrain production and consumption is a very complex issue and is affected by many factors. In the next chapter, we will address such factors in more detail and develop a framework that will enable us to better examine China's feedgrain issues.

References

Chen, Y.B, Zhu, J. and Li, L. (eds) (1996), *The Ninth Five-Year Plan and 2010 Long-term Program for the Rural Economic Development*, China United Industry and Commercial Publishing House, Beijing.

Crook, F.W. and Colby, W.H. (1996), 'The future of China's grain market', USDA *Agricultural Information Bulletin*, No. 730, Washington D.C.

Findlay, C. (ed.) (1998), *Grain Market Reform in China: Global Implications*, ACIAR Technical Report No. 43, Australian Centre for International Agricultural Research, Canberra.

Garnaut, R. and Ma, G.N. (1992), *Grain in China*, East Asia Analytical Unit, Department of Foreign Affairs and Trade, Canberra.

Li, A.D. and Zou, Q.L. (1999), 'China's total arable land is 1951 million *mu*', *People's Daily*, 4 November 1999, p. 1.

Lin, Y.F., Shen, M.G. and Zhou, H. (1996), *Prioritising China's Agriculture Research*, Chinese Agricultural Press, Beijing.

Liu, X.R. (2000), 'WTO accession on China's corn production and marketing', *Chinese Grain Economy*, No. 8, pp. 6-9.

MOA (Ministry of Agriculture) (1999), *Agriculture Action Plan for China's Agenda 21* (English version), China Agricultural Press, Beijing.

MOA (2002a), Measures to promote a sustainable and healthy development of feed industry, obtained from http://www.agri.gov.cn.

MOA (2002b), Development of feed industry: targets for the tenth Five-Year plan and outlook of 2015, in *Outlook of China's Agriculture in the New Century*, pp. 66-75, China Agricultural Press, Beijing.

National Feed Industry Statistical Data, Ministry of Agriculture, Beijing.

National Grain and Oil Information Centre (2000), *Agricultural Market Forecasting*, Vol.16, pp. 3-4.

Piao, X.S., Zhang, D.F. and Creswell, D. (2003), 'Brown rice is a better energy source than corn', *Asian Pork Magazine*, October/November 2003, pp. 2-4.

Qi, J.F. (ed.) (1999), *Yearbook of China Animal Husbandry Industry 1999*, China Agricultural Press, Beijing.

Qin, F. and Yin, J.H. (2003), 'China's feed industry: developments and trends', in Zhou, Z.Y. and Tian, W.M., *China's Regional Feedgrain Markets: Developments and Prospects*, full report, Grains Research and Development Corporation, Canberra.

Research Centre of Rural Economy, Price Database, Ministry of Agriculture, Beijing.

SSBa (State Statistical Bureau), *China Statistical Yearbook,* various issues, China Statistical Press, Beijing.

SSBb, *China Rural Statistical Yearbook,* various issues, China Statistical Press, Beijing.

State Council (1993), 'Guiding principles for China's dietary structural reforms and development in the 1990s', State Council of PRC, Beijing.

State Planning Commission, *Costs and Benefits of Agricultural Products,* various issues, State Planning Commission, Beijing.

Tang, Z.P. and Zheng, Z.H. (2000), *China's Joining the WTO and the Opening Up of Agricultural Markets*, China Foreign Economy and Trade Press, Beijing.

Tian, W.M. and Wan, G.H. (2000), 'Technical efficiency and its determinants in China's grain production, *Journal of Productivity Analysis.* Vol. 3, pp. 159-174.

USDA (1998), *International Agricultural Baseline Projection into 2007,* Washington D.C.

USDA (2000), *China: Situation and Outlook Series*, International Agriculture and Trade Reports, Washington D.C.

Yang, Z.H. (2003), 'China's feedgrain: production, trade and its usage in the feed industry', in Zhou, Z.Y. and Tian, W.M., *China's Regional Feedgrain Markets: Developments and Prospects*, full report, Grains Research and Development Corporation, Canberra.

Zhou, Z.Y., Tian, W.M., and Liu, X.A. (2003), 'Developments and trends in household animal raising practice in China: a survey report', *China Agricultural Economic Review*, Vol. 1, pp. 477-502.

Notes

[1] Apart from feeding animals, these cereals are also used as foodgrains directly for human consumption or as raw materials for processing food products and alcoholic beverages.

[2] In early November 1999, the Chinese government officially admitted that the total arable land was 130 million hectares (1.951 billion *mu*) (Li and Zou 1999). According to this new figure, China's per capita arable land is 0.105 hectare. Earlier, the officially acknowledged arable land area was about 100 million hectares (1.5 billion *mu*).

[3] Recent trials tend to show that brown rice is a better energy source than corn. Brown rice is paddy rice that has the hull removed and thus contains all the endosperm and the aleurone and bran layers. It is believed that its protein content is comparable with corn but its price is relatively low in southern China, often being equal or lower than that of corn. This makes brown rice a potential replacement for corn (Piao et al. 2003).

Chapter 8

Projecting China's Feedgrain Demand and Supply: What Matters?

Zhang-Yue Zhou, Wei-Ming Tian, Xi-An Liu and Guang-Hua Wan

Discussions in earlier chapters suggest that feedgrain demand in China will become the major component of China's total grain demand in the future. Any future increase in total grain demand in China will be mainly caused by an increasing demand for feedgrains. On the other hand, some researchers hold that China will not be able to meet the increased demand for feedgrains with its domestic supply (Garnaut and Ma 1992, p. 71; RGCFDS 1993, p. 26; Crook and Colby 1996; Findlay 1998, p. 32; Tian and Chudleigh 1999).

Due to the importance of this issue for China and the world, an increasing number of studies have attempted to project China's feedgrain demand and supply. Researchers have attempted to make projections from various angles using different approaches and, not unexpectedly, obtaining different findings. A survey of the available literature on China's feedgrain demand and supply will help to (1) gain an overview of the major influences that affect China's feedgrain demand and supply; (2) understand why earlier projections differ; and (3) identify areas where future research attention should be focused to produce more plausible projections.

In the next section, we first address some conceptual considerations applicable to projecting China's feedgrain demand and supply. In Section 8.2, we examine China's feedgrain demand and supply in the past two decades, which helps to identify the discrepancies between the actual realised observations and some projections. Some existing projections are then highlighted in Section 8.3. Section 8.4 is devoted to addressing possible reasons why some projections differ from each other and why some deviate significantly from realised observations. We then in Section 8.5 address some other difficulties and uncertainties that researchers may encounter in their attempts to project China's feedgrain demand and supply. The last section points out some areas that deserve future research priority which will be dealt with in our modelling work in later chapters of this book.

8.1 Conceptual Considerations

Before addressing conceptual issues concerning projections of China's feedgrain demand and supply, it is useful to trace the emergence of China's feedgrain demand and supply as a topical issue and ascertain the nature of the issue.

Before the 1980s, feedgrain was not an 'issue' in China. Until the late 1970s, China had great difficulties in producing sufficient foodgrain to feed its huge population, and moderate imports of foodgrain were required. Little grain could be spared to feed animals. Almost all pigs, which were the major source of China's meat supply, were raised with very limited feedgrains. Large working animals were, likewise, raised with minimum feedgrains. In many cases, the primary purpose of raising pigs was for producing manure and for consuming table scraps. Consequently, the animal husbandry industry was only a small part of China's agricultural economy (varying between 6% and 15% of total agricultural output value, MOA 1983, p. 63). Not surprisingly, few researchers and policy-makers bothered to pay attention to the feedgrain issue.

Feedgrain emerged as an issue only after several consecutive years of good harvests in the early 1980s, which resulted in difficulties in selling, transporting and storing grains. When human consumption demand had been basically met, some grains could be spared to feed animals. CAAS (1985) and Liu (1988) are among the pioneers who tried to draw people's attention to feedgrain issues and to the development of China's animal husbandry industry. However, many held that grains could be used as feed only after foodgrain needs were met; the use of grains as feed was a way of disposing of grains in excess of direct human consumption. This attitude towards feedgrain is clearly demonstrated in the literature published in the 1980s.

Even in the early 1990s, feedgrain was still not regarded as an 'independent' issue. It continued to be discussed largely in the context of China's overall foodgrain demand and supply. In most cases, projections of China's feedgrain demand and supply were included in projections of China's total grain demand and supply. To a large extent, feedgrain was treated as a residual of China's total grain availability and the need for foodgrain (RGCFDS 1993, pp. 33, 179).

Understanding the importance of foodgrains in China's economy and the nature of feedgrain supply – still regarded as a residual of total grain availability and the need for foodgrain – is crucial for those who are interested in China's feedgrain market, shedding light on changes in the feedgrain market and related government policy changes.

In addition to the special nature of foodgrain and feedgrain in China, there are other social, economic, and cultural conditions peculiar to China that also impact on China's feedgrain demand and supply. It is thus useful to have a framework that depicts these major influences. We now develop such a framework below.

On the supply side, factors such as the prices of outputs and inputs, price expectations, technology, weather, and the number of suppliers are important. Other factors that need to be taken into consideration when addressing China's ability to supply feedgrains include total grain production and government policy choices. As a residual of total grain output and foodgrain, everything else being constant, the higher the total grain output, the greater the supply of feedgrains. Similarly, if government policy favours the production of grains, the supply of feedgrains may also increase.

On the demand side, demand for feedgrains is a derived demand. The more animal products to be produced, *ceteris paribus*, the more feedgrains will be demanded. Holding the demand for animal products constant, the amount of feedgrains demanded will be inversely related to the feed-meat conversion ratio. Any factors that affect the demand for animal products and the conversion ratio will affect the demand for feedgrains.

In addition to the conventional determinants of demand, some other factors must also be taken into account when assessing the demand for animal products in China: i.e., urbanisation, the government's food consumption policy choices, and China's access to the overseas meat market.

As for the conversion ratio, it is primarily determined by a range of technological factors. These include breeds of animals, use of additives, feed compositions, methods of animal raising (backyard, specialised, feedlot), and animal accommodation. However, the conversion ratio also responds to prices of feedgrains and animal products.

The above considerations can be intuitively presented diagrammatically (Figure 8.1).

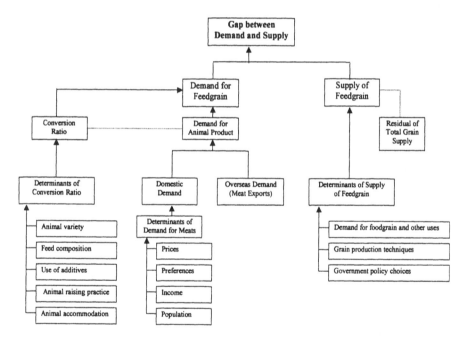

Figure 8.1 Major determinants of demand for and supply of feedgrains in China

Further, unlike the situation in many developed countries, feedgrain is not necessarily the primary source of feed in China's animal feeding. For example, backyard pig-raising is still predominant in China (as high as about 80%, Qi 1999, p. 2). Feed used to raise animals in this kind of practice may include anything that animals eat (such as table scraps, grasses, tree leaves, crop straws), and feedgrains typically account for a much smaller portion (Tian and Chudleigh 1999). Recent surveys in rural China also reveal that some specialised animal-raising households do not feed grains directly to animals. Instead, they use cereals, beans or tubers first for producing other products (e.g., liquors, starch products, bean curd) and then use the residues to feed the animals (Zhou et al. 2003). An increase in non-grain feed will reduce the demand for feedgrain, and the use of such feed inevitably complicates any projection of China's feedgrain demand-supply balance.

8.2 Feedgrain Demand and Supply: Past Experience

Rapid economic growth in China since 1980 has led to a significant increase in the consumption of animal products by both rural and urban residents. In rural areas, per capita meat consumption has increased from 9.4 kg in 1981 to 17.4 kg in 2001. During the same period, per capita egg consumption increased from 1.25 kg to 4.72 kg, and per capita aquatic products from 1.28 kg to 4.12 kg. The corresponding figures for urban areas are 20.5 kg to 24.3 kg, 5.22 kg to 10.41 kg, and 7.26 kg to 10.33 kg, respectively (SSB 2002, pp. 328, 350).[1]

The steady increase in demand for animal products has so far been met by increased domestic supply. The increase in production of animal products in China in the past two decades is most impressive. Total meat production increased from 12 million tonnes in 1980 to 63 million tonnes in 2001. During the same period, milk production increased from 1.4 million tonnes to 11.2 million tonnes while aquatic products increased from 4.5 million tonnes to 44 million tonnes. Poultry eggs increased from 5.3 million tonnes in 1985 to 23.4 million tonnes in 2001 (SSB 2002, pp. 406-408). Among all animal products, the increases in beef, poultry meat, and aquatic products have been the fastest.

The demand for, and the production of, more animal products have generated a strong and growing demand for feedgrains. Surprisingly, in the past two decades China's feedgrain imports have been minimal. In fact, China was a net exporter of feedgrains in most years (Xin et al. 2001). Clearly, China's domestic supply of feedgrains must have also increased. But roughly how much feedgrain has been produced and supplied in recent years? Few researchers have been able to give an accurate estimate.

According to Cheng and Wang (1997), feedgrain has been the main component of animal feed in China in recent years. However, feedgrain production is not an independent industry and there are no reliable statistics about the actual amount of feedgrain supplied and demanded in China. In 1993, the government encouraged the farming community to change from the dual 'grain – cashcrop' production pattern to a 'grain – feed – cashcrop' production pattern (State Council 1993). The motive was to let feed production become an independent industry. The government also wished to have production statistics of feed crops separately reported. So far, progress on this front has been slow.

Nevertheless, there have been attempts to gauge the amount of feedgrains consumed. Two basic approaches have been used: the demand approach and the supply approach. The former estimates the amount of feedgrain demanded and the latter the amount of feedgrain available or supplied. When using the former, feedgrain demand is calculated by multiplying the outputs of animal products by estimated feed-meat conversion ratios (Cheng and Wang 1997). The demand approach, however, encounters a number of difficulties. First, China's animal product output data is unreliable. Second, reliable feed-meat conversion ratios are not available. Further, little information exists on the prevalence of different kinds of animal-raising practices. Finally, for each kind of animal-raising practice, especially traditional backyard animal raising, there is a lack of data on the proportion of feedgrain out of total feed. Because of these limitations, the demand approach is used infrequently and the corresponding results are suspicious. The Ministry of Agriculture used this approach and obtained the results as reported in Table 8.1. The results are rather different from those obtained employing the supply approach – see, for example, the estimation of feedgrain supplied for 1980 to 1994 by Cheng and Wang (1997) given in Table 8.1. Aubert (1999) used the demand approach and officially published meat output data to estimate the amount of feedgrain that would be required for 1985-96. The estimates are unrealistically high, especially for the years after 1991 (see Table 8.1). Aubert argues that it is likely that the meat output statistics have been inflated.

Table 8.1 Estimates of feedgrains consumed (mt)

Year	Feedgrains consumed (demand approach)			Feedgrains consumed (supply approach)
	MOA	*Aubert*		
		Low	High	
1980				59.4
1981				61.8
1982				69.1
1983				77.4
1984				81.1
1985	48.7	106	118	84.6
1986	60.6	112	125	84.6
1987	73.8	114	128	93.6
1988	89.0	124	139	99.4
1989	105.2	127	142	103.4
1990	125.6	143	161	108.9
1991	132.6	151	161	114.8
1992	126.2	151	169	120.9
1993	-	162	182	127.4
1994	169.5	182	205	134.2
1995	143.6	202	227	
1996	225.6	225	254	

Sources: Garnaut and Ma (1992, p. 75) for demand approach estimates 1985-89; MOA, *Statistics of China's Animal Husbandry* (various issues) for demand approach estimates 1990-96; Aubert (1999) for demand approach estimates 1985-96; Cheng and Wang (1997) for supply approach estimates 1980-94.

The supply approach, on the other hand, involves deducting human consumption, seeds, industry usage, storage wastage and so on from total grain output. The residual is treated as total feedgrain supply. Some believe that this approach is more appropriate for China (Garnaut and Ma 1992, p. 77; Cheng and Wang 1997). Using this method, RGCFDS (1993, p. 180) estimated the amount of feedgrain available in 1987 at 86 million tonnes, accounting for 21% of total grain output. Cheng and Wang (1997) provided estimates of feedgrain supplied for 1980 to 1994 (included in Table 8.1). Their estimate of feedgrain supply was 59 million tonnes in 1980 and 134 million tonnes in 1994, implying an annual growth rate of 6%. According to their results, feedgrain represented 18.5% of total grain output in 1980, and this increased to 30% in 1994. Garnaut and Ma (1992, p. 77) believe this same proportion was 22% (92 million tonnes) in 1987 and 25% (115 million tonnes) in 1990.

Proponents of the supply approach have obtained similar results (see Table 8.2). Taking 1987 as an example, the estimate of Cheng and Wang (1997) was slightly higher than those of Garnaut and Ma (1992) and RGCFDS (1993). This could be attributed to the fact that, in addition to the usual deductions from human consumption, Garnaut and Ma (1992) deduct the grains used for producing Chinese spirits. RGCFDS (1993) goes even one step further by deducting the amount of grains consumed by the unregistered population.

The proportion of feedgrains out of total grains and the total feedgrains supplied as suggested by the above authors seem to be reasonable estimates. According to a recent interview with an expert at China's Ministry of Agriculture, the proportion of feedgrains out of total grains was around 33% in 1999 (which means a supply of 168 million tonnes of feedgrains in 1999). According to the same expert, this proportion has been increasing by about one percentage point each year. If this judgement is plausible, the proportion in 1990 would be about 24%, which is close to the estimates of Garnaut and Ma (1992) and Cheng and Wang (1997) (see Table 8.2). In 2000, total grain output dropped to 462 million tonnes from 508 million tonnes in 1999. Using this lower grain output and assuming 34% of it was used for feedgrain purposes, the feedgrain supply in 2000 would be at least 157 million tonnes.

Table 8.2 Comparison of the estimates of feedgrains consumed obtained by the supply approach

Author	For the year	Feedgrains consumed (mt)	Proportion out of total grains produced (%)
RGCFDS (1993, p. 180)	1987	86	21
Garnaut and Ma (1992, p. 77)	1987	92	22
	1990	115	25
Cheng and Wang (1997)	1980	59	19
	1987	94	23
	1990	109	24
	1994	132	30

8.3 Feedgrain Demand and Supply: the Projections

Liu (1988) was the first to attempt to forecast feedgrains to be demanded and supplied in 1990 and 2000. Since then, there has been increased interest in projecting China's feedgrain demand and supply. However, the research frameworks of some of the available studies, especially those published in Chinese journals, seem to lack rigour. While making projections, some authors provide no details about the data and models (e.g., Liu 1988; Zhang 1997). Others seem to just guess based on other research findings (e.g., RGCFMR 1998). In this survey, only representative projections are included for discussion and their projections are summarised in Table 8.3.

CAAS (1989), RGCFDS (1993), Cheng et al. (1997), and Guo et al. (2001) are all studies based on large projects funded by Chinese government agencies. These authors all had good access to data and information. CAAS (1989) represents one of the few pioneer grain research projects. However, few details are given about how the projection is carried out. In addition, feed-meat conversion ratios are based on carcass weight rather than animal liveweight which is the case in most other studies. RGCFDS (1993, p. 22) provides projections on feedgrain supply but gives no details on how they are derived.

Cheng et al. (1997) is based on a project on feed demand and supply commissioned by China's Ministry of Agriculture. The study uses both time-series analysis and demand systems to estimate the demand for animal products. The feed-meat conversion ratios used seem reasonable, compared with most others (see Table 8.5 for details). Guo et al. (2001) is based on another project funded by the Ministry of Agriculture conducted in 1996. No details about research methodology were given. Further, they used the same feed-meat conversion ratio (4:1) for pork, beef, mutton and poultry (p. 23), although the conversion ratio for mutton and poultry is generally thought to be lower.

Acknowledging the difficulty in obtaining reliable feed-meat conversion ratios, Zhu (2000) used the 'supply approach' to gauge the likely feedgrains available in 2000, 2010 and 2020. Then he treated such estimates as the amount of feedgrains to be demanded. However, the 'supply approach' takes little account of the possible influence of important factors on the demand side such as consumer income, urbanisation and changes in population structure.

Huang and Rozelle (1998), using econometric techniques, also allow varying growth scenarios (high, medium, and low) for some key variables such as income and population. However, even with high growth scenarios in both population and income, the amount of feedgrains demanded for 2000 is only 117 million tonnes, which is rather low. This could be due to two factors: (1) The income elasticities of demand for animal products they use seem to be too high (Huang and Rozelle 1998, p. 245). For details, see Table 8.5; (2) Per capita consumption of animal products is based on official statistics from the State Statistical Bureau, which, according to Wang, Zhou and Cox (2002), are low estimates. While higher income elasticities will result in higher quantity of animal products demanded, lower per capita consumption of animal products will have a much greater impact on the quantity of animal products demanded due to the huge population base. On balance, this would have yielded a lower quantity of animal products demanded and thus a lower quantity of feedgrains demanded. Further, Huang and Rozelle gave few details about the feed-meat conversion ratios used.

Table 8.3 Projections of China's feedgrain demand and supply

Author	Projection results (mt)			
	Year	*Demand*	*Supply*	*Balance*
Liu (1988)	2000	153.7	125	-28.7
CAAS (1989, p. 45) [a]	2000	242 (I)		
		190 (II)		
		242 (III)		
Garnaut and Ma (1992, p. 98) [b]	2000	162		
	2000	196		
RGCFDS (1993, p. 22)	2000		131	
	2020		194	
Huang and Rozelle (1996)	2000	109		
	2010	158		
	2020	232		
Cheng et al. (1997)	2000	160-170		
Zhang (1997)	2000	222	150	-72
RGCFMR (1998)	2000	150		
Findlay (ed.) (1998, pp. 11, 49) [c]	2000	239	210	-29
	2010	346	282	-64
	2020	466	378	-88
	2000	201	210	9
	2010	311	282	-29
	2020	443	378	-65
Zhu (2000, p. 4)	2000	170		
	2010	220		
	2020	280		
Guo et al. (2001, p. 25) [d]	2000	154		
	2010	223		
	2020	272		

[a] Three scenarios are projected. I. Less cereal but relatively more animal product consumption; II. Relatively more cereal but less animal product consumption; III. Medium level cereal consumption but relatively more animal product consumption. Feedgrain demand for I and III is the same because animal product consumption is assumed to be the same for both scenarios.

[b] Two growth scenarios are assumed. Normal growth scenario (the first row): a per capita GDP growth rate of 6%; high growth scenario (the second row): a per capita GDP growth rate of 7.2%.

[c] Three sets of projections are given in their report with different assumptions. Set 1: low feeding efficiency scenario and income growth by 8%. Set 2: results under low efficiency are scaled down by 25% to reflect some improvement in efficiency. Set 3: high feeding efficiency scenario and income growth by 10%. Only Set 1 and Set 3 are used in this table.

[d] Research conducted in 1996.

Garnaut and Ma (1992) used the 'demand approach' to predict demand for feedgrains, employing minimum feed-meat conversion ratios available at the time of their study. They make use of the similarity of China's food consumption patterns to those of Taiwan in the early 1960s to draw on the experiences of the 1960s in Taiwan. Garnaut and Ma's study is heavily based on a set of assumptions and suffers from the lack of some data.

Findlay (1998) projected feedgrain demand for 2000, 2010, and 2020 as part of the projection of grain demand, conducted by a group of researchers from Australia and China. They take into account changes in feeding efficiency by having two efficiency scenarios: high and low. They also had two growth scenarios: 8% and 10% of GDP growth. According to their results, feedgrain demanded in 2000 would be nearly 240 million tonnes and imports would be nearly 30 million tonnes under the low feeding efficiency scenario. Clearly, this significantly exaggerated China's demand for feedgrains in 2000. However, information on methodology used for the predictions is limited in Findlay (1998).

Clearly, available studies show that there are discrepancies in projections. This is hardly surprising given the differences in assumptions, research methods and data used. Generally speaking, discrepancies in demand projections are greater than those in supply projections. Taking 2000 as an example, the projections for feedgrain demand range from 109 million tonnes to 239 million tonnes. On the supply side, projections range from 125 million tonnes to 210 million tonnes. Given the fact that China's imports of feedgrains were minimal in 2000, actual feedgrain usage should be roughly equal to available domestic supply, unless there was a major drawing from stocks. Based on the discussion in the previous section, the available supply of feedgrain in 2000 is likely to be some 157 million tonnes. If so, all authors underestimate feedgrain supply for the year 2000, except Findlay (1998) who overestimated supply by almost 60 million tonnes. On the other hand, the demand projections by Garnaut and Ma (1992, normal growth scenario) and Cheng et al. (1997) are close to the likely supply.

In short, existing projections indicate that (1) China's demand for feedgrain is increasing and (2) demand for feedgrain is greater than supply and feedgrain imports would be needed. However, there exist substantial discrepancies in demand and supply projections and the quantity of imports required. As projections are meant to guide future policy initiatives and market activities, the reliability of such projections is of utmost importance. Clearly, some of the projections (as for 2000) are far from the actual picture. Then, why are there such discrepancies?

8.4 Why Do Existing Projections Differ?

The conceptual framework discussed in Section 8.1 identifies the many possible factors that may affect China's demand for or supply of feedgrains and thus the projections derived. In this section we will focus on several major variables and examine how they may affect China's feedgrain demand and supply projections.

8.4.1 Demand Side

On the demand side, major factors that may cause differences in feedgrain demand projections include feed-meat conversion ratios, income and income elasticities, and animal feeding methods.

Conversion ratio Which ratios should be used in feedgrain demand projections? There are few commonly accepted ratios. It is believed that insufficient attention has been given to studying feed-meat conversion ratios (Cheng and Wang 1997; Findlay 1998, p. 28). However, feed-meat conversion ratios are indispensable for any feedgrain demand calculations or projections. Consequently, many researchers have tried to calculate the likely conversion ratios for their research work and, not surprisingly, their results vary, sometimes vastly (see Table 8.4). For example, Liu et al. (1988) put forward a conversion ratio for pork at about 8:1, whereas many others use a ratio in the range 3.5-4.0:1 (e.g., Wang and Huo 1996; Cheng et al. 1997; NORHS 1998; Guo et al. 2001). Given the use of such vastly different conversion ratios, the difference in projected feedgrain demand is unavoidable.

Animal feeding practices An important factor that contributes to uncertainty concerning feed conversion ratios is lack of knowledge on different animal feeding practices. These practices are associated with different feed compositions, which, in turn, lead to different feed conversion ratios (Tuan et al. 1998; NORHS 1998; Fang et al. 2000). NORHS (1998) believe that specialised households have a lower feed-meat conversion ratio while backyard animal-raisers have a higher conversion ratio. However, others argue that backyard raising has the smallest conversion ratio because this practice uses less feedgrains (Guo et al. 2001, quoted from Zhang, X.H. 1998). It is especially difficult to estimate conversion ratios that are appropriate for backyard raising conditions. There are millions of rural households practising backyard animal-raising, and animal-raising conditions are also different between regions. To date, few researchers are in a position to suggest ratios that are representative of the three kinds of practices.

Income and income elasticities Income growth and income elasticities are believed to be most important parameters that affect demand projections (Wan 1996a).While the income elasticity is crucial, its estimation, especially in the case of China, is often not an easy task. Due to data problems (see elaboration below) and different modelling techniques, estimated income elasticities of demand for the same product may be quite different (Wan 1996b). It can be seen from Table 8.5 that significantly different income elasticities have been produced. For example, Lewis and Andrews' income elasticity of demand for pork is four times that of Wang and Fan. In the case of aquatic products, their income elasticity is about ten times that of Wang and Fan for rural people and seven times for urban people.

Table 8.4 Estimates of feed-meat conversion ratios in China

Author	Conversion ratio						
	Pork	Beef	Mutton	Poultry	Eggs	Milk	Fish
Liu et al. (1988)	8	10		5	5		
MOA (1988) [a]	5.8			3	3-3.5	1	1.5
Zeng (1988)	4.5			2.2	3.2	0.4	1.5
Lu (1989) [b]	4			2.5	2.5-3		
	5-6			3.5	3-3.5		
Gao (1990) [a]	6-7	3.3		2			1.5
Yu (1991) [a]	5.1	3		3	2.8-3	0.33	2
Food Study Group (1991) [a]	5.5-6.4	4.8		2.5-3.8	3-3.5	3	
Editing Committee of MOA (1991) [a]	4-4.5	2		2.5			2
Zhou (1993)	5			2.2	2.8		
RGCFDS (1993, pp. 182-183)	5.5-6			2.5-3.5	3-3.5		
Wang and Huo (1996) [b]	3.1			1.9	2.7		
	3.5			2.2	3		
Cheng et al. (1997)	3.5	3.2	3.2	2.1	3	1.84	
NORHS (1998) [c]	3.3-3.5						
	3.24	2	1.13	2.36	2.96		
	3.47	4.01	1.34				
Guo et al. (2001, p. 23)	4	4	4	4	2.5	0.3	0.8
Minimum	3.1	2	1.13	1.9	2.5	0.3	1.5
Maximum	8	10	4	5	5	3	2
Average	4.70	4.03	2.42	2.79	3.13	1.15	1.55

[a] Taken from Garnaut and Ma (1992, p.76); beef and mutton together.
[b] Row 1: more efficient feeding practices; Row 2: on average.
[c] Row 1: for feedlots; Row 2: specialised households; Row 3: backyard raising.

These large differences in income elasticities, holding income growth the same, will lead to different estimates of demand for animal products. For example, CAAS (1989, pp. 25, 35), Garnaut and Ma (1992, pp. 96-97), RGCFDS (1993), Huang and Rozelle (1998, p. 23) and Wang and Fan (1999, p. 52) all produced different animal product demand projections. The difference between the latter two is significant. For example, the projection for the year 2005 by Wang and Fan (1999) is even higher than the projection for year 2010 by Huang and Rozelle (1998).[2] If the demand projections for animal products are different, demand projections for feedgrains will be different.

Table 8.5 Estimates of income elasticities of demand for animal products in China

Author	Rural or urban	Year, income level	Meat	Pork	Beef and mutton	Poultry	Eggs	Milk	Aquatic products
						Income elasticities of demand for			
Lewis and Andrews (1989)[a]	Rural	1983-85		1.02		1.95	0.66		3.65
Zhu et al. (1991)[a]	-	-		0.57	0.57	1.46	1.18		1.34
Pinstrum-Anderson et al. (1991)[a]	-	-		0.63	1.23	1.16		1.71	0.86
RGCFDS (1993, p. 14)[b]	-	1995	0.580				0.936	1.400	0.468
	-	2000	0.540				0.673	1.189	0.606
	-	2020	0.426				0.553	1.100	0.472
Huang and Rozelle (1998, p. 245)	Rural	1999-2000	0.757	0.765	0.343	0.854	0.512	1.557	1.053
	Rural	2000-2010	0.835	0.782	0.789	0.985	0.455	1.637	1.244
	Rural	2010-2020	0.835	0.782	0.789	0.985	0.455	1.637	1.244
	Urban	1999-2000	0.835	0.782	0.689	0.985	0.455	1.637	1.244
	Urban	2000-2010	0.870	0.797	0.686	1.064	0.491	1.912	1.290
	Urban	2010-2020	0.870	0.797	0.686	1.064	0.491	1.912	1.290
Cai et al. (1999, p. 155)[c]	-	Low income	1.102	0.610		1.392			
	-	Medium income	1.756	0.627		0.541			
	-	High income	1.482	0.731		0.710			
Wang and Fan (1999)	Rural	1998		0.25	0.57	0.22	0.36	0.32	0.37
	Urban	1998		0.32	0.49	0.48	0.26	0.49	0.51

[a] Quoted from Garnaut and Ma (1992, p.72).
[b] No separate estimates for individual meats.
[c] Expenditure elasticities for three income groups; numbers in 'Meat' column are for ruminant meat. Based on a small sample.

8.4.2 Supply Side

Total grain supply, the adoption of new technologies, and government policy changes are among the major factors that lead to differences in feedgrain supply projections.

Total grain supply As indicated earlier, feedgrain is a residual of total grain supply and non feedgrain usage. Non-feedgrain usage is unlikely to change drastically between years. However, total grain production can be affected by many factors such as weather conditions and input and output prices and thus may vary from year to year. This leads to uncertainty in the projections of feedgrain supply.

New technologies New technologies may increase yield and total grain supply, holding other factors unchanged. For example, since the early 1990s, plastic film has become widely adopted in corn production in China. This practice allows earlier sowing, extends the period of corn growth and as a result raises yield. However, the advent of new technologies, the scope of their adoption and their effects on output may not always be easily anticipated. This makes it difficult to incorporate the impact of new technologies in the prediction of grain production and thus the availability of feedgrains.

Government policy changes When government policy emphasises grain production, as in 1995 with the institution of the so-called 'provincial governor grain-bag responsibility system', total grain supply is likely to increase, although at the expense of other crops. Given the fact that the Chinese government has been so sensitive about grain supply, it is likely that the government will shift its policy attention to increasing grain production whenever deemed necessary. However, it is difficult to anticipate when and to what extent the government may introduce changes to its grain production policy.

8.4.3 Data and Conceptual Problems

Another important aspect that contributes to projection discrepancies is data problems, including data availability, data coverage, data reliability, and conceptual problems.

Data availability Some data are simply not available. For example, the amount of feedgrain available from each year's harvest has not been collected separately. Data on proportions of the three kinds of animal feeding practices are very limited. Detailed information about feed composition for different feeding methods, especially for backyard animal raising, is hardly available. There are no well-studied feed-meat conversion ratios.

Data coverage In some studies, one cannot be sure about the exact data coverage. For example, when referring to feedgrains, exactly what products are covered or included as feedgrains is not clear. Also, in recent years, specialised household animal raising has been fast emerging. What kind of households would be treated as specialised and what is the criterion for separating specialised animal raisers from traditional backyard animal raisers? Again, this is not clear.

Data reliability It has been well known that some Chinese data are unreliable (Wu and Kirke 1994; Wu 1995; Aubert 1999). One typical example is the arable land area in China. In November 1999, the government officially acknowledged that the arable land area in China was more than previously claimed. Accordingly, the government adjusted it from 100 to 128 million hectares. This would affect the reported yield level and the sown area.

Quite often, statistics may be under- or over-reported. Zhong (1997) argues that China's meat production statistics could have been inflated by 50% or more. Lu (1998) indicates that output of meat, poultry eggs and aquatic products for 1981-95 could have been inflated by at least 40%. According to Aubert (1999), Colby et al. (1999), and Fuller et al. (2000), China's official meat production statistics have been overstated. However, Yuan (1999) disagrees with these claims and argues that the level of inflation for meat output is significantly below 40%. Jia (1999) even claims that previously published meat production statistics are reasonable and there is little inflation.

However, the gap between animal production and consumption data had been increasing since the early 1990s and became even larger by 1995 and 1996. In light of this increasing gap, in 1997 the government adjusted 1996 meat output figures downwards but without any due explanation. On the other hand, in 1998, the government adjusted 1997 meat output figures upwards and eggs and milk output downwards. The details of the adjustments of various animal products are given in Table 8.6. The table shows that the 1996 downward adjustment was by 22% for all meat, with beef being the highest, 28%. Egg output for 1996 was adjusted slightly upwards, but for its 1997 output it was adjusted downwards by almost 11%, making total egg output for 1997 lower than that of 1996. After these adjustments, then, how close are the government-published output figures to the real output levels? According to Yuan (1999), for those figures prior to 1996 where no adjustment was applied, pork, beef and mutton output would remain over-estimated by about 20%, while poultry and egg output would remain over-estimated by as much as 45%. However, milk output is believed to be little inflated. Yuan (1999) believes pork, beef and mutton output figures since 1996 are reasonable, although poultry and egg output remain inflated to some extent.

Conceptual problems The above-mentioned data coverage problem is largely related to conceptual definitions. One example is the calculation of feed-meat conversion ratios. While it is commonly held that liveweight should be used when calculating the conversion ratios, CAAS (1989, p. 43) used carcass weight instead. In addition, what feed is used as the numerator to calculate the conversion ratio? Is it all the feed material the animal eats, is it the processed industrial feed (which contains grains), or is it feedgrain only? If feedgrain only is used as the numerator, the derived conversion ratio would be lower (see, for example, CAAS 1989, p. 43).

Table 8.6 Adjustments of output figures of animal products in *China Statistical Yearbook* (mt)

Output for the year	Year of publication of the yearbook	Total meat	Pork	Beef	Mutton	Poultry meat	Poultry eggs	Milk
	1997	59.15	40.38	4.95	2.40	10.75	19.54	7.36
1996	1998	45.95	31.58	3.56	1.81	8.35	19.65	7.36
	Adjustment (%)	-22.3	-21.8	-28.1	-24.6	-22.3	0.6	0.0
	1998	51.52	34.64	4.15	2.10	9.36	21.25	7.75
1997	1999	52.69	35.96	4.41	2.13	9.57	18.95	6.81
	Adjustment (%)	2.3	3.8	6.3	1.4	2.2	-10.8	- 12.1

Sources: SSB, various issues; Yuan (1999).

Given the above data problems, surrogates may be used. In many other cases, data without reliability or data without clear coverage boundaries may be used. When this is the case, deviations in predictions are inevitable.

8.5 Projecting Future Feedgrain Demand and Supply: Other Unknowns

The discussion in Section 8.4 highlighted the difficulty and complexity in projecting China's feedgrain demand and supply. There are other unknowns or challenges that add to this difficulty and complexity, especially for future studies in this area.

8.5.1 Government Policy

If the Chinese can afford to eat more animal products, where would these products come from? Will the Chinese increase domestic animal feed production so as to produce more animal products, import feedgrains, or import animal products? The Chinese government's future policy directions and choices will have an important bearing on the source of animal feed and animal products. It is hard to predict what choices the government will make and such choices are also influenced by many international factors. If the international agricultural trade liberalisation proceeds smoothly under the WTO guidelines, it is likely that China may import more feedgrains to raise animals. However, it is also possible that China may import more animal products should the government give priority to environment protection.

8.5.2 Income Growth and Changes in Income Elasticities

Whether the Chinese will eat more animal products will be heavily influenced by their income growth. If the current rate of income growth is sustained, total demand for animal product will increase. Related to income growth are the likely changes in income elasticities. For animal products these may increase when consumers' incomes increase from a very low level. However, after income has reached a certain high level, income elasticities may decline with further increase in consumers' income. For example, Zhou (2001) reveals that the income elasticity of demand for milk tends to decline when income rises. Shono et al. (2000) also noted that income elasticities decreased as income and consumption levels of some meats increased over time.

8.5.3 Technological Choices

China's future demand for, and supply of, feedgrains can be greatly affected by technological choices. The use of crop residues to feed animals will reduce the demand for feedgrains (Guo and Yang 1997). Many believe that if the feed-meat conversion ratio is improved by a small margin, the potential savings in feedgrains can be enormous (Fan and Agcaoili-Sombilla 1997; Zhang and Lu 1997; and MOA 1998a, pp. 16-17). Many have explored the ways in which this can be achieved; for example, the use of additives, the extension of improved animal breeds, and better accommodation for animals in northern China for the winter season (see, for example, He and Wang 1993; RGCFDS 1993, pp. 44-46; MOA 1998b, pp. 58, 92). On the other hand, with the use of improved technologies, there is also potential to increase feedgrain supply (Qing 1998; Tian and Chudleigh 1999; and Tian and Wan 2000). How fast technologies will become available and to what extent they will be adopted remain to be seen.

8.5.4 Water Availability and Quality

Water introduces more uncertainty into future grain and feedgrain projections. China has 22% of the world's population but only 7% of the world's fresh water (Ryan and Flavin 1995). Per capita water availability is very low, being the second lowest in the world. Over 80% of water is used for agricultural purposes. However, recent years have seen increased water being diverted to meet the needs of rapid industrialisation and urbanisation. Given that a significant portion of China's grain is grown on irrigated land, grain production will be challenged by decreasing water availability (Heilig et al. 2000; Han 2002). In addition, most of China's water is in the south, and northern China is seriously short of water. This will undoubtedly affect regional grain production which has recently attracted much attention from researchers (see, for example, Heilig et al. 2000; Yang and Zehnder 2001). Further, the water shortage problems are exacerbated by the fact that a growing share of the water is polluted. The Chinese government has taken measures to combat the water shortage and quality problems and is planning a huge project to carry water from the Yangtze River to northern China. Future regional grain/feedgrain production will certainly be affected by changes in water quality and its availability to farming.

8.5.5 China's Access to International Markets

If China can export more animal products it will need to import more feedgrains. China's access to international markets is critically dependent upon the acceptance of its products by overseas consumers. At present, China's animal product exports, except for poultry meat, are limited. China has almost no access to the markets of developed countries, due to the lower safety standards of its products (Tian 2002). How fast China can improve the safety standards is uncertain. Further, China's ability to export is also affected by the overall progress of the international trade liberalisation under the WTO arrangements and the willingness of developed countries to reduce or withdraw subsidy to their animal production and export programs.

8.5.6 Regional Differences

Being such a vast country, China has many regional variations that affect feedgrain demand and supply. For example, different climatic conditions affect both cropping patterns (thus the availability of feedgrains) and animal growth (i.e., severe or mild winter, thus affecting feed-meat conversion ratios). The availability of non-grain feed resources in a region affects the composition of feed. Animal raising methods in different regions, especially under backyard practices, may lead to different efficiencies.

These regional factors tend to contribute to different feed-meat conversion ratios. Table 8.7 clearly shows that the grain-pork conversion ratios are different in different regions. Liaoning experiences severe cold winters; the ratio is thus high in that province. On the other hand, in some southern provinces, perhaps due to warmer weather conditions and availability of non-grain feed, the ratios are commonly low, e.g., in Guangdong, Zhejiang and Hunan (it seems Guangdong's ratio was too low to be realistic).

Table 8.7 Grain-pork conversion ratios in different provinces in 1990

Province	Ratio
Guangdong	1.95
Jiangsu	2.53
Zhejiang	2.3
Sichuan	2.4
Hunan	2.26
Anhui	3.5
Henan	3.4
Liaoning	5.8
Shanxi	3.8
Shaanxi	3.0

Source: Zhang and Lu (1997, p. 55).

Consumer preferences for meats vary from region to region. One meat may be preferred over others, or one region may prefer to have more fatty meat than lean meat. These preferences affect the kinds of feed needed and the feed-meat conversion ratios.

A good understanding of regional differences may be difficult and costly to achieve, but it is essential. Without it, real insight into China's feedgrain issues will be difficult to gain. Some have realised the importance of looking into China's regional differences (RGCFMR 1998; Qin and Tian 2000) but few have actually made a serious effort in this regard.

8.5.7 Changes in Tastes and Preferences

If China's economy and consumer income continue to grow as in the past two decades, changes in consumers' tastes and preferences are expected to continue (Wan 1998; He and Tian 2000). Rural consumers and urban low-income consumers are likely to consume less cereal and more animal products (Delgado et al. 1999). Higher-income consumers are likely to consume less ruminant meats but more fruits, dairy and aquatic products (Wang and Fan 1999; Shono et al. 2000). The increase in meat consumption by rural and urban low-income consumers may to some extent be offset by the reduction in red meat consumption by higher income consumers. It is not easy to gauge the speed and the extent of changes in consumers' tastes and preferences and the likely offsetting effect.

8.6 The Way Ahead

The review of existing literature in this chapter tends to confirm that China's domestic feedgrain supply will not be sufficient to meet demand and thus there will be the need for feedgrain imports. However, how much to import remains a puzzle due to the vast discrepancies between projections. Clearly, further research efforts are called for. To ensure research findings are realistic and relevant to policy-making and marketing activities, research efforts should be devoted to the areas as highlighted below.

8.6.1 Areas for Research

Regional focus Only by carefully considering regional characteristics can we gain useful insights into China's feedgrain issues. Previous studies have dealt with China's feedgrain issues largely at the aggregate national level. Studies at the regional level will make significant contributions to understanding China's feedgrain issues. The following regional characteristics are worth looking into:

- Differences between the three kinds of feeding practices across regions.
- Proportion of different feeding practices at the regional level and its change over time.
- Conversion ratios between different feeding practices and across regions.

- Income elasticities of demand for various kinds of animal products at the regional level, for rural and urban consumers, and for different income groups.
- Differences in consumer preferences between rural and urban areas, between regions, and between different income groups.

Away-from-home consumption Dining in restaurants has become increasingly popular in China. One reason that government statistics on per capita animal product consumption are lower is due to the omission of away-from-home consumption. Information on away-from-home consumption will help gain more accurate data on per capita consumption of animal products which in turn helps projection work. However, so far, few serious studies have been conducted in this area. Carefully designed household surveys are necessary.

Feedgrain use in the farming of aquatic products Aquaculture has grown dramatically in the past two decades in China. Grain accounts for an important portion, about 80%, of the feed used for aquatic farming. Currently, very limited attention has been devoted to assessing the demand for feedgrains by the aquatic farming sector.

Rural demand for animal products Given the huge size of the rural population, the potential demand for animal products by rural residents is enormous. A small increase in per capita consumption will translate into a large aggregate demand. More effort needs to be devoted to studying rural demands for animal products.

8.6.2 Priority Needed

While all the research areas discussed above are important, discussions in this chapter tend to suggest that the use of vastly different elasticities and conversion ratios by various studies may have contributed greatly to the different projections. Hence, in future studies, priority should be given to, in order of importance and urgency, (1) the estimation of income elasticities of demand for animal products, and (2) the estimation of feed-meat conversion ratios.

- Estimation of income elasticities using recent data. Earlier we pointed out that income elasticities may decrease as income and consumption levels of meats increase. Hence, new estimates of income elasticities with recent data are needed for projection work; otherwise, the future demand will be overstated. Income elasticities need to be estimated for different income groups and for different regions. Data may be collected through researchers' own household surveys. However, such exercises have become increasingly expensive in China. One alternative is to obtain household survey data from China's State Statistical Bureau, which conducts annual urban and rural household surveys. The Research Centre for Rural Economy of the Ministry of Agriculture also conducts an annual household survey but covers rural households only.

- Estimation of feed-meat conversion ratios. It is suspected that feed-meat conversion ratios may have declined in recent years due to, for example, improved feed diet composition and better feeding practices. Surveys may be conducted on a regional basis to collect data and to interview animal producers.

In this book, although it is not possible for us to tackle all the important research areas as identified in the above, we are nonetheless able to look into several of the most important ones. More specifically, we will examine how the economic growth, income elasticities of demand for animal products, feed-meat conversion ratios, feedgrain production technological improvements, and the export growth of animal products will affect China's feedgrain demand, supply and trade flows at the regional level. We will also examine how agricultural trade reforms in China and internationally will affect China's regional feedgrain trade and China's needs for feedgrain imports. The findings are reported in Chapters 10 and 11.

References

Aubert, C. (1999), 'Food consumption and food production in China: statistical uncertainties, educated guesses, and reasoned optimism', *Chinese Rural Economy*, No.12, pp. 16-21.

Cai, H.O., Brown, C., Longworth, J. and Wan, G.H. (1999), 'A demand analysis of ruminant-meat, pork and poultry-meat by Chinese households segmented by three income strata', in Zhou, Z.Y., Chudleigh, J., Wan, G.H. and MacAulay, G. (eds), *Chinese Economy towards 21st Century,* Vol. 1, The University of Sydney, Sydney, pp. 145-59.

Cheng, G.Q. and Wang, J.M. (1997), 'An estimation of feed demand and supply in China', in Zhu, X.G. (ed.), *A Study of China's Grain Issues*, China Agricultural Press, Beijing, pp. 114-24.

Cheng, G.Q., Zhou, Y.H., Wang, J.M. and Shi, Z.L. (1997), 'Feed demand and supply in China', *Problems of Agricultural Economics*, No. 5, pp. 25-29.

CAAS (Chinese Academy of Agricultural Sciences) (1985), *Study of the Development of Grain and Cash Crop Production in China*, Vol. 4, CAAS, Beijing.

CAAS (1989), *Research on China's Grains,* China Agricultural Science Press, Beijing.

Colby, H., Zhong, F.N. and Giordano, M. (1999), 'A review of China's meat production', *Agriculture in China and OECD countries: Past Policies and Future Challenges*, OECD Proceedings, pp.185-213, Paris, France.

Crompton, P. and Phillips, B. (1993), 'Effects on feed grains of China's rising demand for livestock products', *Agricultural and Resource Quarterly*, Vol. 5, pp. 242-53.

Crook, F.W. and Colby, W.H. (1996), *The Future of China's Grain Market,* USDA Agriculture Information Bulletin No. 730, Washington, D.C.

Delgado, C., Rosegrant, M., Steinfeld, H., Ehui, S. and Courbois, C. (1999), 'Livestock to 2020: the next food revolution', Food, Agriculture, and the Environment Discussion Paper 28, International Food Policy Research Institute, Washington, D.C.

Editing Committee of MOA (1991), *Proceedings of International Symposium on Food, Nutrition and Social Economic Development*, China's Science and Technology Press, Beijing.

Fan, S.G. and Agcaoili-Sombilla, M. 1997, 'Why projections on China's future food supply and demand differ' *Australian Journal of Agricultural and Resource Economics*, Vol. 41, pp. 169-90.

Fang, C., Fuller, F., Lopez, M. and Tuan, F.C. (2000), 'Livestock production slowly evolving from sideline to principal occupation', in USDA International Agriculture and Trade Reports, *China*, Situation and Outlook Series, WRS-99-4, March 2000, Washington D.C., pp. 24-28.

Findlay, C. (ed.) (1998), *Grain Market Reform in China: Global Implications*, ACIAR Technical Report No. 43, Australian Centre for International Agricultural Research, Canberra.

Food Study Group (1991), *A Study of Medium- and Long-term Strategies for China's Food Development*, Food Study Group, Beijing.

Fuller, F., Hayes, D. and Smith, D. (2000), 'Reconciling Chinese meat production and consumption data', *Economic Development and Cultural Change*, Vol. 49, pp. 23-43.

Gao, R. (ed) (1990), *Symposium of China's Fishery Economy*, China Agricultural Press, Beijing.

Garnaut, R. and Ma, G.N. (1992), *Grain in China*, East Asia Analytical Unit, Department of Foreign Affairs and Trade, Canberra.

Guo, Q.F., Liu, X.A., Teng, H.Y. and Wang, L. (2001), 'Household animal raising behaviour in China's feedgrain surplus regions: the case of Jilin', AARC Working Paper No.17, the University of Sydney.

Guo, S.T., Huang, P.M., Yu, J.B., Wu, T.X., Zhu, P.R., Zhang, T., Tang, Y.L. and Liu, L.Y. (2001), 'China's grain demand and supply, 2000-2030', in Du. Y. (ed.), *China's Food Security Issues*, China Agricultural Press, Beijing, pp. 18-37.

Guo, S.T. and Yang, Z. H. (1997), 'New developments in livestock systems based on crop residues in China', paper presented to the Second FAO Electronic Conference on "Livestock Feed Resources within Integrated Farming Systems", 9 September 1996 - 28 February 1997, available at http://www.fao.org/livestock/AGAP/FRG/conf96.htm/guo.htm.

Han, H.Y. (2002), 'Chinese agricultural water resource utilisation in the 21st century', paper presented to the 46th Annual Conference of the Australian Agricultural and Resource Economics Society, 13-15 February, Canberra, Australia.

He, C.M. and Wang, J.M. (1993), 'Reflections on animal husbandry development in the three provinces of north-east China', *Problems of Agricultural Economics*, No. 2, pp. 44-48.

He, X.R. and Tian, W.M. (2000), 'Livestock consumption: diverse and changing preferences', in Yang, Y.Z. and Tian, W.M. (eds), *China's Agriculture at the Crossroads*, Macmillan Press, London, pp. 98-117.

Heilig, G.K., Fischer, G. and van Velthuizen, H. (2000), 'Can China feed itself? An analysis of China's food prospects with special reference to water resources', *International Journal of Sustainable Development & World Ecology*, Vol. 7, pp. 153-72.

Huang, J.K. and Rozelle, S. (1996), 'China's grain at the turning point to the twenty-first century: retrospect and prospect', *Problems of Agricultural Economics*, No. 1, pp. 17-24.

Huang, J.K. and Rozelle, S. (1998), *China's Grain Economy to the Twenty-First Century*, China Agricultural Press, Beijing.

Jia, Y.L. (1999), 'Factors constraining China's animal husbandry development and their macro adjustments', *Chinese Rural Economy*, No. 1, pp.40-45.

Lewis, P. and Andrews, N. (1989), 'Household demand in China', *Applied Economics*, No. 21, pp. 793-807.

Liu, J. (1988), 'Strategic issues for the development of animal husbandry', *Chinese Rural Economy*, No. 2, pp. 5-12.

Liu, S.B., Chang, J.W. and Yang, T.K. (1988), 'What strategies should China adopt to develop its animal husbandry industries?' *Chinese Rural Economy*, No. 1, pp. 31-33.

Lu, F. (1998), 'On discrepancies between production and consumption data of China's agricultural products and artificial inflation in production statistics', *Chinese Rural Economy*, No. 10, pp. 47-53, 71.

Lu, X.J. (1989), 'Strategic choice for the development of animal husbandry in China: improving productivity of individual production entities', *Problems of Agricultural Economy*, No. 6, pp. 40-42.

MOA (Ministry of Agriculture) (1983), *Agricultural Economy Statistics*, Ministry of Agriculture, Beijing.

MOA (ed.) (1988), *Development Strategies of China's Animal Husbandry Industries*, China Outlook Press, Beijing.

MOA, *Statistics of China's Animal Husbandry Industry*, various issues, China Economic Press, Beijing.

MOA (1998a), *Agriculture Action Plan for China's Agenda in the Twenty-First Century*, China Agricultural Press, Beijing.

MOA (1998b), *Development Report of China's Agriculture 1998*, China Agricultural Press, Beijing.

NORHS (National Office for Rural Household Surveys) (1998), 'A comparative study of production efficiency and profitability of various animal raising practices', *Reference Materials for Rural Economic Research*, No. 8, pp. 20-25.

Pinstrum-Anderson, P. et al. (1991), 'Changes in incomes, expenditures, and food consumption among rural and urban households in China during the period of 1978-88', in proceedings of International Conference on Food, Nutrition, and Social-Economic Development, Beijing.

Qi, J.F. (ed.) (1999), *Yearbook of China Animal Husbandry Industry 1999*, China Agricultural Press, Beijing.

Qin, F. and Tian, W.M. (2000), 'Feeding the livestock: technological choice, trade policy and efficiency', in Yang, Y.Z. and Tian, W.M. (eds), *China's Agriculture at the Crossroads*, Macmillan Press, London, pp. 78-97.

Qing, X.G. (1998), 'Attention should be paid to the development of feed rice', *Chinese Rural Economy*, No. 8, pp.28-32.

RGCFDS (Research Group for China's Medium- and Long-term Food Development Strategies) (1993), *China's Medium- and Long-term Food Development Strategies*, China Agricultural Press, Beijing.

RGCFMR (Research Group for China's Feedgrain Marketing Reforms – *Siliaoliang liutong tizhigaige yanjiu ketizu*) (1998), 'A study on the reform of China's feedgrain marketing system', *Chinese Rural Economy*, No. 8, pp. 33-40.

Ryan, M. and Flavin, C. (1995), 'Facing China's limits', in L.R. Brown et al. (eds), *State of the World 1995*, Earthscan, London, pp. 113-31.

Shono, C., Suzuki, N. and Kaiser, H.M. (2000), "Will China's diet follow western diets?' *Agribusiness*, Vol. 16, pp. 271-79.

State Council (1993), 'Guiding principles for China's dietary structural reforms and development in the 1990s', State Council of PRC, Beijing.

SSB (State Statistical Bureau of China), *China Statistical Yearbook*, various issues, China Statistical Press, Beijing.

Tian, W.M. (2002), 'Development in China's animal husbandry industry', paper presented to the International Workshop on "China's Regional Feedgrains Market", University of Sydney, Orange, 19 July 2002.

Tian, W.M. and Chudleigh, J. (1999), 'China's feedgrain market: development and prospects', *Agribusiness: An International Journal*, Vol. 15, No. 3, pp. 393-409.

Tian, W.M. and Wan, G.H. (2000), 'Technical efficiency and its determinants in China's grain production', *Journal of Productivity Analysis*, Vol.13, pp. 159-74.

Tuan, F.C., Zhang, X.H. and Wailes, E. (1998), 'China's pork economy: production, marketing, foreign trade, and consumption', in USDA International Agriculture and Trade Reports, *China*, Situation and Outlook Series, WRS-98-3, July 1998, Washington D.C., pp. 17-25.

Wan, G.H. (1996a), 'Income elasticities of household demand in rural China: estimates from cross-sectional survey data', *Journal of Economic Studies*, Vol. 23, pp. 18-34.

Wan, G.H. (1996b), 'Using panel data to estimate Engel functions: food consumption in China', *Applied Economics Letters*, Vol. 3, pp. 621-24.

Wan, G.H. (1998), 'Nonparametric measurement of preference changes: the case of food demand in rural China', *Applied Economics Letters*, Vol. 5, pp. 433-36.

Wang, H. and Huo, Q.G. (1996), 'China's grain and animal product production' *China Feed*, No. 10, pp. 6-8.

Wang, J.M. and Fan, Y.L. (1999), 'A study on animal product consumption by rural and urban residents in China', Chinese Academy of Agricultural Sciences, Research Report for a project commissioned by the Ministry of Agriculture, Beijing.

Wang, J.M., Zhou, Z.Y. and Cox, R. (2002), 'Animal product consumption trends in China', paper presented at the Agribusiness Forum, 2002 Australian Agribusiness Congress, 12-13 November 2002, Sydney, Australia.

Wu, Z.P. and Kirke, A.W. (1994), 'An assessment of some key Chinese agricultural statistics', *China Information*, IX, pp. 42-76.

Wu, Z.P. (1995), *An Econometric Analysis of Supply Response for the Main Grain Crops in China, with Particular Emphasis on the Impact of Reforms since 1979*, unpublished Ph.D. thesis, Queen's University Belfast.

Xin, X., Tian, W.M. and Zhou, Z.Y. (2001), 'Changing patterns of feedgrain production and marketing in China', *Australian Agribusiness Perspectives*, paper 47.

Yang, H. and Zehnder, A. (2001), 'China's regional water scarcity and implications for grain supply and trade', *Environment & Planning A*, Vol. 33, pp. 79-95.

Yuan, X.G. (1999), 'Are China's animal product output figures inflated?' in Wang, J.M. and Fan, Y.L. 1999, 'A study on animal product consumption by rural and urban residents in China', Chinese Academy of Agricultural Sciences, Research Report, Beijing.

Yu, J. (ed) (1991), *Study on Rationalisation of China's Food Structure*, Research Institute of Aerospace Ministry, Beijing.

Zeng, Q.L. (1988), 'On issues of livestock production', *Problems of Agricultural Economy*, No. 12, pp. 27-28.

Zhang, H. (1997), 'Relationships between grain production and the development of livestock industry in China', *Reference Materials for Rural Economic Research*, No.7, pp. 43-48.

Zhang, X.H. (1998), 'An analysis of household pig raising situation and economic return in China', *Chinese Rural Survey*, No. 1, pp. 53-61.

Zhang, X.H. and Lu, M. (1997), 'Pig production scale and feed conversion ratios', *Chinese Rural Economy*, No.5, pp. 53-55.

Zhong, F.N. (1997), 'An analysis of the level of artificial inflation in China's meat output statistics and the causes of inflation', *Chinese Rural Economy*, No. 10, pp. 63-66.

Zhou, J.L. (2001), 'Study on the dairy market in China', Ph.D. dissertation, China Agricultural University, Beijing.

Zhou, L. (1993), 'Continual increase in China's livestock production: the reasons explained', *Chinese Rural Economy*, No. 5, pp. 27-29.

Zhou, Z.Y., Tian, W.M. and Liu, X.A. (2003), 'Developments and trends in household animal raising practice in China: a survey report', in Zhou, Z.Y. and Tian, W.M., *China's Regional Feedgrain Markets: Developments and Prospects*, Grains Research and Development Corporation, Canberra.

Zhu, X.G. (2000), 'An analysis of China's grain demand and supply', in Zhu, X.G. (ed.), *China's Grain Production and Agricultural Extension*, China Agricultural Science and Technology Press, Beijing, pp. 3-17.

Notes

[1] The State Statistical Bureau (SSB) data are based on household surveys. However, it is believed that subjects in SSB household surveys tend to under-report their consumption. In addition, the SSB household survey does not include the amount of animal products consumed away from home. Hence, the SSB per capita consumption estimates are most likely lower than the actual consumption level (Wang and Fan 1999).

[2] Despite the fact that Huang and Rozelle used higher income elasticities, the per capita consumption of animal products they used was low, which is probably the major reason for their low demand projection for animal products.

PART II
GRAIN TRADE

Chapter 9

China's Grain Trade: Recent Developments

Wei-Ming Tian, Zhen-Hai Yang, Xian Xin and Zhang-Yue Zhou

Having examined China's grain production and consumption in earlier chapters, we turn our attention in this part to trade aspects of China's grain. We first highlight in this chapter some recent developments in China's grain trade, both domestically and internationally. Later chapters will address China's grain trade prospects and how China's grain trade will be affected by market reforms.

In this chapter, we discuss grain trade in general. It would be ideal if we could address foodgrain and feedgrain trade separately. Unfortunately, data currently available do not allow meaningful separation of foodgrain and feedgrain trade. However, wherever possible, we will point out what kinds of grains are imported and exported and for what purposes.

9.1 Patterns of Domestic Grain Trade

9.1.1 Regional Deficit and Surplus

Some provinces in China have a grain surplus but others are in deficit. Factors contributing to this include variations in natural resources, population size, and other social and economic conditions. Regional surplus or deficit occurs not only at the overall grain demand-supply level but also at the crop level, i.e., being surplus in some crops but deficit in others (for details, see Chapter 3).

In the past, when transportation was very limited, regional grain production patterns largely affected regional grain consumption patterns. Thus, in most regions, the staple food continues to be the one that the region is good at producing. In central China, wheat is the major food item. In northern China, particularly in upland areas, corn, millet and sorghum used to be staple foodgrains. But in the southern part of China, rice is the staple food. This pattern has existed in China for thousands of years.

Such a production-consumption pattern has also influenced the patterns of grain trade. Notably, grains were largely traded in the regions where they were produced. Only a limited amount of wheat was moved to southern China although a limited amount of rice used to be transported to the north. During the decades of rationing (1950s to 1980s), the composition of the ration was based mainly on local consumption habits.

Since the early 1980s, there have been some changes to the composition of grain varieties consumed at the regional level. Contributing factors include changing dietary culture (northern people eating more rice, and southern people eating more wheat products), migration of population (northern Chinese who work in southern China demand wheat, southern Chinese working in the north demand rice), and increased demand for feedgrain in southern provinces (to meet increased demand for animal products). There have also been changes in the supply side due to changed regional comparative advantages in grain production. Improvement in transportation facilities and gradual deregulation of marketing arrangements are also important. Combined, these two factors have led to changes in grain deficit and surplus patterns and hence the resulting changes in the patterns of regional grain trade. One major phenomenon that has emerged in the past two decades is the change from *nan liang bei diao* (transporting grains from the south to the north, chiefly rice) to *bei liang nan yun* (moving grains from the north to the south, chiefly corn). Further changes in regional grain consumption and trade patterns are expected in the future though they will be gradual.

To display patterns of regional grain trade, it is essential to have data on regional grain deficit and surplus as well as the direction and volume of trade flows among regions. However, reliable data are not available. One way to obtain grain deficit and surplus estimates is to construct a grain demand-supply balance sheet. Although there have been efforts to estimate grain deficit and surplus status at the national level using a demand-supply balance sheet approach (e.g., by the Ministry of Agriculture), similar efforts for regional estimates have been scarce. Recently, China's State Statistical Bureau assigned each provincial statistical bureau to study development of their regional grain market. As a result, some bureaus are able to provide estimated demand-supply balance sheets for their provinces (Xian 2003). However, the approaches used in different provinces are not consistent and the methods used in some provinces are problematic; accuracy and reliability, therefore, remain questionable. Nonetheless, given that there are no better alternatives, we based our judgement on Xian (2003) and compiled a table (Table 9.1) to indicate (1) whether a province is currently grain deficit, surplus or in balance and which crop is in deficit or surplus; and (2) the trend in deficit or surplus in a province and its likely impact on the national grain market.[1]

As Table 9.1 shows, grain demand and supply in major agricultural provinces in central China are basically in balance or in surplus. Changes in their demand and supply situation generally tend to have greater impact on the national grain market compared with other provinces. The three municipal cities (Beijing, Tianjin and Shanghai) are all in grain deficit, which is expected to grow. Changes in their grain demand and supply situations tend to have a small impact on the national market due to their relatively smaller share of grain demand and supply and population among the national total. The demand and supply situations in those poorer south-west or north-west provinces are mixed, some being largely in balance or with a small surplus, and others with a deficit. However, changes in their surplus or deficit situations would have a smaller impact on the national market. Except for

Liaoning, all the north-east provinces (Heilongjiang, Jilin and Inner Mongolia) will remain in grain surplus, though the level of surplus may decline in the years to come. Provinces in the south-east coastal regions (i.e., Zhejiang, Fujian, Guangdong and Hainan) all have a grain deficit which will be increasing. With the exception of Hainan, a smaller province, changes in the deficit situation of these provinces will also have a large impact on the national market.

Table 9.1 Grain deficit or surplus at the regional level: a subjective judgement

CN = corn, RI = rice, WH = wheat

Province	Current (2000)			Trend	
	Surplus or deficit?	*What is in surplus?*	*What is in shortage?*	*Changes in surplus or deficit*	*Impact on the national grain market*
Beijing	Deficit		WH, CN, RI	Growing deficit	Small
Tianjin	Deficit		WH, CN, RI	Growing deficit	Small
Hebei	Largely in balance	CN	WH, RI	Becoming deficit	Large
Shanxi	Largely in balance	CN	WH, RI	Remaining in balance	Small
Inner Mongolia	Surplus	CN		Reducing surplus	Small
Liaoning	Deficit			Growing deficit	Medium
Jilin	Surplus	CN		Remaining in surplus	Large
Heilongjiang	Surplus	RI		Reducing surplus	Large
Shanghai	Deficit		RI, WH, CN	Growing deficit	Small
Jiangsu	Largely in balance		CN	Remaining in balance	Large
Zhejiang	Deficit		CN, WH	Growing deficit	Large
Anhui	Largely in balance	WH, RI	CN	Remaining in balance	Large
Fujian	Deficit		CN, WH	Growing deficit	Large
Jiangxi	Surplus	RI	CN, WH	Reducing surplus	Large
Shandong	Largely in balance	WH	CN	Turning to deficit	Large
Henan	Surplus	WH	RI	Reducing surplus	Large
Hubei	Surplus	RI	CN	Reducing surplus	Large
Hunan	Surplus	RI	CN, WH	Reducing surplus	Large
Guangdong	Deficit		CN, WH	Growing deficit	Large
Guangxi	Largely in balance		WH	Remaining in balance	Large
Hainan	Deficit		WH	Growing deficit	Small
Chongqing	Largely in balance		CN, WH	Turning to deficit	Medium

Province	Current (2000)			Trend	
	Surplus or deficit?	*What is in surplus?*	*What is in shortage?*	*Changes in surplus or deficit*	*Impact on the national grain market*
Sichuan	Largely in balance		CN, WH	Remaining in balance	Large
Guizhou	Deficit		RI, WH	Remaining in deficit	Small
Yunnan	Largely in balance		RI	Turning to deficit	Medium
Tibet	Largely in balance			Remaining in balance	Small
Shaanxi	Deficit		WH, RI	In balance	Medium
Gansu	Largely in balance			Remaining in balance	Medium
Qinghai	Deficit		WH, RI, CN	Growing deficit	Small
Ningxia	Surplus	RI, CN	WH	Remaining in surplus	Small
Xinjiang	Surplus	CN	RI	Largely in balance	Small

Source: Authors' own judgements.

The geographic location of provinces with deficit, surplus or balance in grain supply is shown in Map 9.1.

9.1.2 Regional Trade Flows

In recent years, significant amounts of surplus corn from north-east provinces have been transported to other parts of the country, mainly for feed purposes. Corn is shipped by sea to the south coastal provinces, chiefly Guangdong. It is also transported by rail to other provinces; major receiving regions include Hebei, Beijing, Tianjin, Shandong, Hunan, Jiangxi, and also sometimes to Sichuan. Rice used to be shipped from southern provinces to northern ones. While some better quality indica rice is still transported to the north, good quality japonica rice is now shipped to southern provinces, as a result of changed tastes for japonica rice by residents in southern China. Wheat used to be largely consumed in the production region due to the very small amount of surplus (except in Henan, which is a major provider of surplus wheat to other provinces). The shortage in wheat in other provinces is usually met through imports. Since the mid-1990s, the wheat trade pattern within China has tended to be less stable because of changing import situations. With reduced wheat imports in the past few years, there have been increased wheat trade flows within China, chiefly from Henan province.

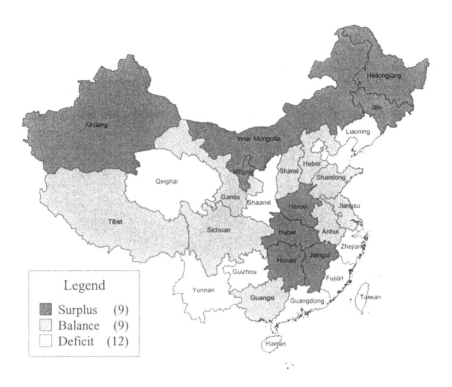

Map 9.1 Regional grain deficit or surplus, China

Source: Based on Table 9.1

The lack of reliable regional grain trade data makes it difficult to present accurate trade flows between regions. Nonetheless, based on Table 9.1, we devised the following map (Map 9.2) to show likely changes in grain surplus and deficit situations at the regional level, which may be used as a surrogate to roughly indicate the likely movements of grains within China. This, however, is a rather static presentation because import and export cannot be brought into consideration.

Our discussion in this section on China's regional grain surplus and deficit and regional trade flows is based on our many years of research work on China's grain economy; it is, however, rather subjective, and, due to the lack of appropriate data and information, it cannot be backed up. Research into China's regional grain trade patterns is called for and should be rewarding.[2] Later in this book, we will construct a regional feedgrain demand and supply balance sheet for China and show feedgrain trade flows at the regional level. The findings are presented in Chapter 10.

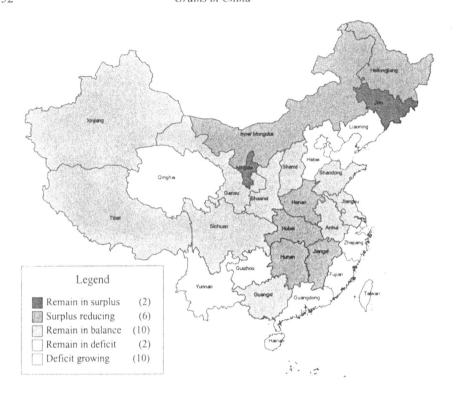

Map 9.2 Changing grain surplus or deficit at the regional level, China

Source: Based on Table 9.1.

9.2 Grains Import and Export

9.2.1 Composition and Level of Grain Import and Export

Since 1990, the patterns of China's grain import and export have changed drastically. Data in Table 9.2 bear out the following observations: (1) China's grain trade followed no regular pattern – large net import and large net export coexisted (and sometimes changed drastically); (2) China has both imported and exported rice but has been a net exporter except for 1995 and 1996; (3) China was a major corn exporter during 1990-2003 except for 1995 and 1996; and (4) China has even become a small net wheat exporter in the recent years (2002 and 2003).

The Chinese government gives a high priority to national food security. Changes in the trade balance of major cereals as shown in Table 9.2 are largely in accordance with domestic supply situations. In the early 1990s, China imported wheat in large volumes but exported corn and rice. This was regarded as a rational approach to increase both economic returns and availability of grains in the domestic market. China was able to produce corn and rice at relatively low costs. In addition, the ratio of rice price to wheat price during that time period was higher in the international market than in China.

Table 9.2 China's grain trade since 1990 ('000 tonnes)

Year	Import				Export			
	Total	Rice	Wheat	Corn	Total	Rice	Wheat	Corn
1990	13610	49	12530	369	4890	330	...	3404
1991	13450	140	12370	1	9760	690	...	7782
1992	11750	104	10580	...	12681	950	...	10340
1993	7520	96	6420	...	14773	1430	291	11097
1994	9200	514	7300	...	10840	1520	268	8740
1995	20810	1596	11590	5180	899	50	225	110
1996	10830	761	8250	440	1240	264	565	160
1997	4170	330	1861	...	8340	938	458	6607
1998	3880	240	1489	251	8890	3745	275	4686
1999	3390	170	450	70	7380	2700	164	4300
2000	3150	240	880	3	13780	2948	188	10466
2001	3440	290	740	39	8760	1870	713	6000
2002	2850	238	632	8	14820	1990	977	11675
2003	2087	259	447	1	22004	2612	2514	16391

Sources: China Customs Administration 2002; Ministry of Agriculture 2004.

In the mid-1990s, China's grain supply was believed to be in shortage. However, whether there was a shortage and to what extent cannot be ascertained due to a lack of data and information, particularly on the grain stock level. It could be that some irregular reactions in the market (e.g., panic buying by urban consumers and hoarding by farmers and state grain marketing enterprises, and increasing grain prices), made it difficult for the government to secure grains for its own distribution to urban residents. On the other hand, we believe that the grain shortage, if any, was not serious, but the panic by the public and the government was caused by speculations in the market, especially by government-run enterprises. The higher grain prices in the market were also associated with the higher inflation at that time. Nonetheless, the government decided to import grains in large volumes and also took measures to promote grain production.

As a result of policy measures that stimulated grain production, by the late 1990s and early 2000s, China had accumulated large volumes of grains. In response to declining domestic prices, the government encouraged farmers to adjust their production structure in order to reduce grain production, and also encouraged grain export (chiefly corn, see Chapter 2). During this time period, China's net grain export increased. China even became a small net wheat exporter in 2002 and 2003 (see Table 9.2).

However, China cannot continue with its currently large amount of grain export. This is because: (1) China's grain output has been low in the past few years, (2) its grain consumption has been increasing (see Table 9.3), (3) given that China net exports, its grain reserve stock must be declining, depleted for domestic consumption and for exporting, and (4) if grain output is not increased dramatically, the export will decline or China may have to import grains. Following grain price increases in late 2003 and early 2004, the government, already alarmed about China's overall grain demand and supply situation, has taken measures to boost grain production. China's domestic production is likely to increase in 2004, and its grain import may also increase while exports will decline.

Table 9.3 Production and estimated total consumption of grains, 1995-2003
        (mt)

Year	Production	Consumption			
		Total	*Foodgrains*	*Feedgrains*	*Other usages*
1995	466.62	456.26	274.64	130.02	51.60
1996	504.54	460.50	273.25	135.73	51.52
1997	494.17	465.31	271.86	141.44	52.01
1998	512.30	469.83	274.43	143.06	52.34
1999	508.39	474.06	275.95	145.53	52.58
2000	462.18	477.05	277.80	146.70	52.55
2001	452.64	482.42	280.30	148.90	53.22
2002	457.06	488.21	282.82	151.13	54.26
2003	430.70	494.37	285.37	153.40	55.60

Sources: SSBa (2004, p. 117) for production data; Xian (2003, p. 8) for consumption data (including beans and tubers).

9.2.2 Sources and Destinations of Grain Import and Export

China's grain import and export can change to a great extent between years as shown in Table 9.1. Such drastic changes often have an impact on the pattern of grains trade, sometimes leading to changes in the import source countries and export destination countries. Table 9.4 presents import sources and export destinations of China's grains in 2003.

Historical grain trade data show that China's import source countries have been relatively stable. In the case of wheat, the three major suppliers have been the United States, Canada and Australia. Imported wheat is distributed to many diverse provinces and is chiefly used for producing certain products that require higher quality wheat flour. China's negligible wheat net export of 2002 and 2003 is likely a short-lived phenomenon and does not warrant further discussion. (However, the improved supply of better quality wheat could result in a substitution for imported wheat in the longer term.)

Table 9.4 China's import and export of major grains, in sources and destinations, 2003

Wheat

Source	Import kt	$US mill.	Destination	Export kt	$US mill.
United States	213	39.2	South Korea	871	96.8
Canada	204	36.1	Philippines	651	75.7
Australia	7	1.3	Vietnam	296	36.1
			Indonesia	121	16.2
			North Korea	95	13.4
Others	neg.	neg.	Others	204	26.9
Total	424	76.6	Total	2237	265.0

Rice

Source	Import kt	$US mill.	Destination	Export kt	$US mill.
Thailand	257	96.4	Côte d'Ivoire	1016	146.5
Vietnam	neg.	neg.	Russia	266	63.1
Uruguay	neg.	neg.	PN Guinea	139	29.9
Italy	neg.	neg.	Indonesia	126	22.7
South Korea	neg.	neg.	Japan	122	37.2
Others	neg.	neg.	Others	920	183.4
Total	257	96.5	Total	2589	483.0

Corn

Source	Import kt	$US mill.	Destination	Export kt	$US mill.
Peru	0	0.1	South Korea	8037	868.4
United States	neg.	neg.	Malaysia	2464	261.5
Burma	neg.	neg.	Indonesia	1605	174.2
United Kingdom	neg.	neg.	Iran	1601	170.7
Taiwan	neg.	neg.	Japan	1310	145.2
Others	neg.	neg.	Others	1372	146.5
Total	0	0.1	Total	16389	1766.5

neg. = negligible

Source: MOA web 2004.

Thailand has been the major exporter of rice to the Chinese market. China is a net rice exporter. The relatively small rice import is mainly distributed through supermarkets to cater for diverse tastes. During the past decade, destination countries for China's rice exports have changed dramatically between years. For example, rice exports to Indonesia and the Philippines depend heavily on shortage of rice in those countries. In 1998, Indonesia imported 1.36 million tonnes of rice from China but in 1997 it only imported 9506 tonnes. The Philippines imported 1.37 million tonnes in 1998 but only imported 0.18 million tonnes in 1997. In the early 1990s, Cuba was a large importer of Chinese rice, importing annually around

0.2 million tonnes. Major provinces that provide rice for exports are Jiangxi and Hunan in central China and Heilongjiang in north-east China.

In recent years, China's corn import has been small except in 1995. Its corn export, however, has been at a relatively large volume. Given that China was a major corn exporter in the past few years, we will look further into China's corn export destinations and how these destinations have changed over time (Table 9.5).

Table 9.5 clearly shows that China's major corn export destinations have shifted in the past two decades. In the mid-1980s, Hong Kong, Japan and Russia were the major receivers of China's corn export. In recent years, the export to these three markets has been very small. On the other hand, South Korea has become China's major corn importer, accounting for about 50% of China's total corn export. Malaysia has also become another major destination for China's corn export.

Table 9.5 China's corn export by destinations

| Year | Import (mt) | Export (mt) | Export by destination (%) | | | | | | | |
			South Korea	North Korea	Malaysia	Indonesia	Hong Kong	Japan	Russia	Other
1984	0.06	0.95					39.13	31.73	0.00	29.14
1985	0.09	6.34					17.56	41.31	26.94	14.19
1986	0.59	5.64					17.86	45.86	28.01	8.27
1987	1.54	3.92	-	1.85	0.00	0.00	8.40	42.58	42.59	4.58
1988	0.11	3.91	-	3.51	0.53	0.10	6.25	42.03	44.76	2.82
1989	0.07	3.50	-	3.53	2.45	-	16.37	36.93	33.31	7.41
1990	0.37	3.40	0.00	5.21	0.48	0.00	23.12	28.68	33.44	9.07
1991	0.00	7.78	25.70	2.21	1.78	0.47	29.16	23.13	12.36	5.19
1992	-	10.34	29.19	4.95	5.25	0.14	25.00	20.02	7.41	8.04
1993	-	11.10	0.19	8.96	8.76	2.38	5.61	19.82	12.35	41.93
1994	-	8.74	0.08	6.93	13.06	7.23	5.08	18.67	7.23	41.72
1995	5.18	0.11	21.41	9.92	30.33	22.41	0.96	8.40	6.57	0.00
1996	0.44	0.16	34.98	51.37	3.89	0.00	0.01	9.73	0.00	0.02
1997	-	6.61	53.58	9.69	18.93	10.28	0.00	2.20	0.63	4.69
1998	0.25	4.69	54.53	4.17	25.47	0.89	0.00	4.67	0.05	10.22
1999	0.07	4.30	29.09	3.77	33.55	13.39	0.00	2.47	0.00	17.73
2000	0.00	10.47	57.30	n.a.	20.10	n.a.	n.a.	n.a.	n.a.	n.a.
2001	0.04	5.99	51.42	6.19	22.53	6.68	0.78	6.85	0.14	5.14
2002	0.01	11.67	52.58	1.20	21.30	11.50	0.63	2.71	0.06	10.03
2003	0.00	16.40	49.04	0.83	15.04	9.80	0.51	7.99	0.03	16.76

Source: China Customs Administration, various issues.

Major provinces that provide corn for exports are the three north-east provinces, namely, Jilin, Heilongjiang and Inner Mongolia (Table 9.6). These three provinces alone provided about 90% and 87% of China's corn export in 2001 and 2002, respectively. Jilin has been the most important supplier. Although China's corn import is small, over 90% of the imported corn is used in Guangdong province (see Table 9.6).

Table 9.6 China's major corn export providers, and major corn import users, 2001 and 2002

Province	Export (t)		Share (%)	
	2001	*2002*	*2001*	*2002*
Jilin	4473892	7926011	74.61	68.83
Liaoning	384416	987700	6.41	8.58
Inner Mongolia	199006	1398376	3.32	12.14
Heilongjiang	724553	742526	12.08	6.45
Shanxi	1100	-	0.02	-
Beijing	300	32	0.01	0.00
Hebei	213297	460695	3.56	4.00
Yunnan	50	150	0.00	0.00
Guangdong	10	31	0.00	0.00
Total	5996624	11515521	100	100
	Import (t)		**Share (%)**	
	2001	*2002*	*2001*	*2002*
Anhui	-	1	-	0.015
Henan	-	-	-	-
Guangdong	35867	6175	99.41	93.05
Liaoning	137	158	0.38	2.38
Shanghai	11	295	0.03	4.45
Yunnan	64	7	0.18	0.105
Total	36079	6636	100	100

Sources: China Customs Administration, various issues.

In addition to rice, wheat and corn, the other cereal China imports is barley. In the past decade, China has been regularly importing barley, in the range of 1.4 to 2.7 million tonnes per annum. The major source countries of the barley imports are France, Canada and Australia, with Australia taking a major share. Imported barley is chiefly for brewery purposes, for which domestically produced barley is not of adequate quality. China has in recent years made limited progress in improving barley varieties. How China's barley import needs will evolve depends on barley variety improvements in China and on demand for brewery products made out of barley.

9.3 Concluding Comments

Restrained by transportation facilities, China's grain consumption had a strong regional characteristic. The crop that a region was good at producing became the staple food in that region. This consumption pattern has largely determined regional grain trade patterns, which in turn reinforce the local consumption pattern. While China's grain consumption patterns have remained largely intact for thousands of years, some changes have become observable since the early 1980s when China's economic reform started. The most notable changes are (1) increased consumption of wheat products in southern China and rice in northern China, and

(2) reduced grain transport from the south to the north and increased transport from the north to the south.

As far as the international grain trade is concerned, there has been no clear pattern in recent years. Volumes of net import or net export and composition of grains imported and exported have tended to change rather dramatically between years. Import source countries for rice and wheat have been relatively stable. But destinations for China's grain exports have tended to change frequently. Though China has been a net grain exporter in the past few years, it is likely to become a net importer in the near future.

Many factors that affect China's grain production, consumption and domestic market reforms and that affect world agricultural market reforms will affect China's future grain trade. In previous chapters, we have examined various factors that may influence China's grain production and consumption. In the following chapters, by considering production and consumption, we examine how market reforms, both domestic and international, will affect China's grain trade. Given that feedgrain will become increasingly important in China's overall grain economy, in Chapter 10 we will focus on China's regional feedgrain demand and supply and trade flows, assuming China will fulfil its WTO accession commitment by liberalising domestic grain trade. In Chapter 11, we simulate how China's overall grain trade may be affected by international agricultural market reforms. Chapter 12 will bring feedgrain consumption and foodgrain consumption together and draw implications of increased feedgrain demand on foodgrain consumption and on grain trade.

References

China Customs Administration, *China Customs Statistical Yearbook*, various issues, China Customs Administration, Beijing.
MOA (Ministry of Agriculture) (2004), China Agricultural Information Net, at http://www.agri.gov.cn/analysis/, accessed on 28 May 2004.
Mullen, J. (2004), 'The contribution of ACIAR to domestic grain market reform in China', paper presented at the 48th Annual Conference of the Australian Agricultural and Resource Economics Society, 11-13 February 2004, Melbourne.
SSBa (State Statistical Bureau) (2004), *China Statistical Abstract 2004*, China Statistical Press, Beijing.
SSBb, *China Statistical Yearbook*, various issues, China Statistical Press, Beijing.
Xian, Z.D. (ed.) (2003), *A Study on China's Grain*, China Statistical Press, Beijing.

Notes

[1] We made the judgment on the likely trend in deficit or surplus in a province by combining our knowledge of a province's resource endowments and its grain production level and per capita grain output level. Provincial population, grain production and per capita grain output are presented in Table A9.1 in the Appendix. When we predict the likely impact of a change in a province's grain surplus or deficit on the national market, we state the impact mainly from the demand point of view, i.e., the size of the population in a province in relation to the national total. Potential

impacts of the likely structural adjustment of production in the future are also taken into account.

2   In two ACIAR-funded projects, attempts were made to study China's regional grain trade flows but "the projects failed to meet their objective of measuring inter-regional grain flows within China" (Mullen 2004).

Appendix Table A9.1 Population and grain production by province in China, 1998 and 2002

Province	Population (million)		Grain production (mt)		Per capita output (kg)	
	1998	*2002*	*1998*	*2002*	*1998*	*2002*
National	1247.61	1284.53	512.3	457.1	410	356
Beijing	12.46	14.23	2.4	0.8	192	58
Tianjin	9.57	10.07	2.1	1.4	220	137
Hebei	65.69	67.35	29.2	24.4	444	362
Shanxi	31.72	32.94	10.8	9.3	341	281
Inner Mongolia	23.45	23.79	15.8	14.1	672	591
Liaoning	41.57	42.03	18.3	15.1	440	359
Jilin	26.44	26.99	25.1	22.1	948	821
Heilongjiang	37.73	38.13	30.1	29.4	797	771
Shanghai	14.64	16.25	2.1	1.3	145	80
Jiangsu	71.82	73.81	34.2	29.1	476	394
Zhejiang	44.56	46.47	14.4	9.4	322	203
Anhui	61.84	63.38	25.9	27.7	419	436
Fujian	32.99	34.66	9.6	7.6	290	220
Jiangxi	41.91	42.22	15.6	15.5	371	367
Shandong	88.38	90.82	42.6	32.9	483	363
Henan	93.15	96.13	40.1	42.1	430	438
Hubei	59.07	59.88	24.8	20.5	419	342
Hunan	65.02	66.29	26.5	25.0	407	377
Guangdong	71.43	78.59	19.5	14.8	273	188
Guangxi	46.75	48.22	15.6	14.9	333	308
Hainan	7.53	8.03	2.1	1.9	280	235
Chongqing	30.6	31.07	11.2	10.8	367	348
Sichuan	84.93	86.73	35.2	31.3	414	361
Guizhou	36.58	38.37	11.0	10.3	301	270
Yunnan	41.44	43.33	13.2	14.2	318	329
Tibet	2.52	2.67	0.9	1.0	337	368
Shaanxi	35.96	36.74	13.0	10.1	362	274
Gansu	25.19	25.93	8.7	7.8	346	302
Qinghai	5.03	5.29	1.3	0.9	255	173
Ningxia	5.38	5.72	2.9	3.0	548	528
Xinjiang	17.47	19.05	8.4	8.4	479	439

Source: SSBb (1999, pp. 113, 395; 2003, pp. 98, 430).

Chapter 10

Regional Feedgrain Demand, Supply and Trade Flows after the WTO Accession

Xian Xin, Guang-Hua Wan and Xiao-Yun Liu

As has been shown in earlier chapters, demand for animal products and thus the derived demand for feedgrains is growing quickly in China. Many believe that feedgrain demand will become an increasingly important component of China's future grain demand. Many also expect that China's feedgrain market will undergo some changes given that China is now a member of the WTO. Some of the major expected changes include replacing non-tariff barriers by tariff-rate quotas, allowing non-state enterprises to engage in grain trade, stopping export subsidies to agricultural products, and relaxing restrictions on inter-regional feedgrain movement. These changes are expected to have tremendous effects on China's feedgrain market. Further, it is noted that a significant regional imbalance exists between feedgrain demand and supply in China (see Chapter 7). With increasing external factors coming into play under the WTO framework, the regional distribution of feedgrain demand, supply and trade patterns will change.

So, how will the regional feedgrain demand, supply and trade flows change in response to the changing trade environment? An answer to such an important question is invaluable to policy makers and trade practitioners. Unfortunately, little effort has been made to examine China's feedgrain market at the regional level. Earlier studies have primarily focused on the feedgrain market at the more aggregated national level. This is partly attributable to the fact that neither government organisations nor other institutions can provide a regional feedgrain balance sheet and inter-regional feedgrain trade flows.

To fill this gap, this chapter examines changes in regional feedgrain demand, supply and regional trade flows in response to market changes. More specifically, it examines how the regional feedgrain markets react to technological improvements in feedgrain production and animal production, income growth, livestock export growth, and trade liberalisation. To address these issues, we will use a non-linear spatial equilibrium model including a trade sector. Feedgrain demand, supply, price and trade flow variables are endogenised in the model.

In the next section, a feedgrain balance sheet is constructed, covering regional feedgrain demand and supply, import and export. In Section 10.2, a spatial equilibrium model for simulating China's feedgrain economy is developed. Data issues and base scenarios of China's regional feedgrain market are presented in

Section 10.3. Findings on how regional feedgrain demand, supply and trade flows react to shocks are reported in Section 10.4. Section 10.5 concludes the chapter.

10.1 Feedgrain Demand-Supply Balance Sheet

Feedgrain mainly refers to coarse grain, including corn, sorghum, millet, barley, oats and other minor cereals. In this chapter, feedgrain refers to all grains used to feed livestock.[1] In China, there is no comprehensive information available on regional feedgrain supply, demand and trade flows. In this section, we first estimate regional feedgrain demand and production and the results are given in Table 10.1.

Feedgrain consumption patterns vary among regions, due to regional differences in resource endowment, animal types and breeds and feeding style. Regional feedgrain demand is obtained by multiplying the outputs of livestock with the corresponding region-specific conversion ratios. The total regional demand for feedgrain is the sum of feedgrain demand by all types of livestock.

Table 10.1 shows feedgrain consumption is concentrated in a few provinces. Sichuan, Shandong, Henan and Hebei together account for 40% of the national total. Hunan, Jiangsu, Anhui, Jilin, Liaoning, Guangdong and Hubei account for 33%. The remaining 27% is consumed in the other 19 provinces.

Regional production data are obtained by multiplying regional grain output with estimated percentage for region-specific feedgrain use. Although feedgrain production takes place in almost all regions in China, major producing areas are located geographically from the northeast to the southwest. Table 10.1 shows ten provinces produced 66% of China's total feedgrains in 1999. The other 20 provinces produced only 34%.

Feedgrain export and import data are also given in Table 10.1. In 1999, China exported a total of 4.3 million tonnes of corn and only imported 0.07 million tonnes of corn. To ensure grain security, including feedgrain security, import and export of feedgrains were managed under the state trading system in the past. However, the trading volume has varied significantly in the last two decades (see Chapter 9 for more details). Three north-east provinces (Jilin, Liaoning, Heilongjiang) and the east of Inner Mongolia are the main feedgrain producers and exporters. In 1999, these four regions accounted for more than 98% of China's total corn export.

Regional feedgrain balance was obtained by negative demand and net export from feedgrain production. From the last column of Table 10.1, it can be seen that northern China, except Hebei, are characterised by feedgrain surplus, while southern China is characterised by feedgrain deficit. It is noted that Shandong, Guangxi, Jiangxi, Hubei and Jiangsu are more or less self-sufficient in feedgrain. Other provinces have demand-supply gaps of more than 20%. Hence, inter-regional flows of feedgrains are substantial in China. The feedgrain deficit-surplus status is depicted in Map 10.1.

Table 10.1 Regional feedgrain demand and production, China, 1999
      ('000 tonnes)

Region	Demand [a]	Production [a]	Export [b]	Import [b]	Surplus [c]
Beijing	1382	776	26	0	-632
Tianjin	903	593	0	0	-310
Hebei	14212	9641	20	0	-4591
Shanxi	2108	3206	37	0	1060
Inner Mongolia	3354	6610	741	0	2516
Liaoning	6520	9078	834	0	1724
Jilin	6993	14688	2229	0	5645
Heilongjiang	5011	12713	418	0	7284
Shanghai	1764	446	0	0	-1318
Jiangsu	7742	7564	0	0	-179
Zhejiang	2428	3029	0	0	601
Anhui	7219	5467	0	50	-1702
Fujian	3656	1897	0	0	-1759
Jiangxi	4262	4137	0	0	-125
Shandong	15252	13882	0	0	-1370
Henan	14642	11326	0	20	-3296
Hubei	6212	6051	0	0	-161
Hunan	10404	6972	0	0	-3432
Guangdong	6304	4639	0	0	-1665
Guangxi	4930	4617	0	0	-312
Hainan	764	464	0	0	-301
Sichuan	16726	12619	0	0	-4107
Guizhou	1588	3907	0	0	2320
Yunnan	4211	5188	0	0	977
Tibet	313	31	0	0	-283
Shaanxi	2292	3977	0	0	1684
Gansu	1395	2243	0	0	849
Qinghai	460	69	0	0	-391
Ningxia	485	1071	0	0	586
Xinjiang	1945	2632	0	0	687
National	155476	159532	4305	70	0

Chongqing is included in Sichuan. Taiwan, Hong Kong and Macao are not included.
[a] Feedgrain demand and production data are from the authors' own estimation based on sample survey data.
[b] Export and import data are from SSB (2000).
[c] Negative values mean deficits.

10.2 Simulating Feedgrain Demand and Supply: Theoretical Framework

Having constructed the feedgrain demand-supply balance sheet for China, we now turn to developing the spatial equilibrium model that can be used to simulate China's feedgrain economy. Stephen Enke was recognised to be among the first to address spatial equilibrium models (SEM) in 1951 although Cournot described the spatial equilibrium problem as early as in 1838 (MacAulay 2001). SEM was later developed by Samuelson (1952) and Takayama and Judge (1964, 1971).

Samuelson (1952) used net social welfare (hereafter NSW) as the objective function. Martin (1981) gave mathematical details of the price form of the net social revenue (hereafter NSR) model. The advantages of the NSR model over the NSW model is the generality in the former, which allows for asymmetric sets of supply and demand coefficients.[2]

Map 10.1 Feedgrain deficit/surplus, 1999

The spatial equilibrium model has been used widely to solve agricultural distribution problems at regional and international levels. MacAulay (1976) used a recursive spatial equilibrium model to analyse cattle trade between Canada and the US. Koo (1986) conducted a spatial equilibrium analysis of wheat trade between the US, Canada and Europe. Applications of SEM to China include Halbrendt et al. (1989), Hearn et al. (1990) and Webb et al. (1992).

More recently, Rutherford (1996) used a linear transportation/processing cost minimising approach to model live cattle exports in Australia. Minot and Goletti (2000) developed a complicated agricultural spatial equilibrium model to examine the impacts of further trade liberalisation of rice markets of Vietnam. Dominic (2001) used a SEM to analyse China's live cattle and beef sector.

In this chapter, based on the work of Takayama and Judge (1964, 1971) and others, a non-linear Feedgrain Spatial Equilibrium Model (FSEM) is proposed for simulating inter-regional feedgrain production, demand and trade flows for China. The model is a quadratic programming problem, with a quadratic objective function measuring the NSR. The constraints include supply and demand equations, outflow and inflow equations, and arbitrage equations. Normally, the supply of transport services is assumed to be perfectly elastic and the demand for transport services is assumed to be a downward line.

As pointed out by MacAulay (2001), the NSR formulation of the spatial equilibrium model is essentially a primal-dual formulation in which the primal model is subtracted from its dual model and the constraints from both models are included. The competitive market will be cleared at a zero NSR because arbitrage conditions bid any excess profits away by trading in the commodity concerned.[3] Under the zero conditions, transport service suppliers earn the social average profit.

Usually, the supply and demand functions are specified to take linear forms as follows:

$$y = \alpha - Bp_y \tag{1.1}$$

$$x = \theta + \Gamma p_x \tag{1.2}$$

where:

p_y and p_x are $n \times 1$ vectors of unrestricted demand and supply prices in n regions;

y and x are $n \times 1$ vectors of demand and supply quantities;

α and θ are $n \times 1$ vectors of the intercepts of the demand and supply equations, respectively;

B and Γ are $n \times n$ matrices of slope coefficients for the demand and supply functions, respectively.

The primal-dual form of the standard spatial equilibrium model can be defined as follows:

Objective function:

$$G(y, x, X, \rho_y, \rho_x) = p_y{'}y - p_x{'}x - T{'}X \tag{2.1}$$

Subject to:

$$-G_y X + \alpha - B(\rho_y - w) \leq 0 \tag{2.2}$$

$$-G_x X - \theta - \Gamma(\rho_x + v) \leq 0 \qquad (2.3)$$

$$-\alpha + B(\rho_y - w) \leq 0 \qquad (2.4)$$

$$-\theta + \Gamma(\rho_x + v) \leq 0 \qquad (2.5)$$

$$-T + G_y{'}\rho_y + G_x{'}\rho_x \leq 0 \qquad (2.6)$$

$$w, v, X, \rho_y, \rho_x \geq 0 \qquad (2.7)$$

where:

X is an $n^2 \times 1$ vector of quantities shipped between each of the n regions;

T is an $n^2 \times 1$ vector of transport costs for those shipments;

ρ_y is an $n \times 1$ vector of non-negative demand prices, which is equal to p_y-w, and w is an $n \times 1$ vector of slack values;

ρ_x is an $n \times 1$ vector of non-negative supply prices, which is equal to p_x+v, and v is an $n \times 1$ vector of slack values to ensure that ρ_x is non-negative;[4]

G_y is an $n \times n^2$ matrix ensuring inflows must equal or exceed the given demand quantity;

G_x is an $n \times n^2$ matrix ensuring outflows cannot exceed the supply.

$$G_y = \begin{bmatrix} 1 & & & 1 & & & 1 & & \\ & 1 & & & 1 & & & 1 & \\ & & .. & & & .. & & & .. \\ & & 1 & & & 1 & & & 1 \end{bmatrix}_{n \times n^2}$$

$$G_x = \begin{bmatrix} -1-1...-1 & & \\ & -1-1...-1 & \\ & .. & & .. & \\ & & & -1-1...-1 \end{bmatrix}_{n \times n^2}$$

The FSEM has 6 block constraints besides the objective function. Block (2.2) is to maintain demand quantity balances, dictating that inflows cannot be less than demand. Block (2.3) is imposed to keep supply quantity balances, namely, the outflows cannot be greater than supply.

Blocks (2.4) and (2.5) are demand and supply equations. Feedgrain markets in this model are assumed to follow the rules of spatial arbitrage, which means that trade flows between two regions occur when the price difference reaches the transfer costs. Block (2.6) ensures that price differentials do not exceed transportation costs between regions. Block (2.7) is the usual non-negativity condition.

The above model can be used to examine the roles of technological progress, income growth and other feedgrain production and demand shifters, including policy intervention. The shifter variables can be easily incorporated into the model by simply adding them to the right-hand side of supply and demand equations.

It is also possible to incorporate a number of policy intervention mechanisms by simply modifying equation (2.6). These mechanisms include shipment rate adjustment or setting barriers to internal trade, export subsidy and import constraint. The model can also be used to examine short-run or long-run effects of shipment rate adjustment on feedgrain economy by altering the corresponding parameters. These features of the above theoretical framework make it possible to make simulations and carry out sensitive analysis.

10.3 Data and Base Scenarios

Regional price elasticities for feedgrain demand and production are estimated based on survey data and data from *Costs and Benefits of Agricultural Products* published by China's State Development and Planning Commission and other organisations.

Microeconomic theory dictates that feedgrain demand is a derived demand and thus should be expressed as a function of feedgrain and livestock prices. However, the regression results indicate low R-squares. More importantly, the coefficients of the price variable make no economic sense in many cases. Consequently, livestock output is used as a proxy for the price variable in the final regressions. To obtain regional feedgrain price elasticity, lagged feedgrain output is introduced into the models, which reflects the long-run effect of feedgrain price changes on feedgrain production.

The distances between regions are measured along railway lines between provincial capitals, and are available from the Ministry of Transportation. There are altogether 30 provinces in China for our research. The rest of the world (ROW) is regarded as the 31st region. China's feedgrain import and export is embodied in the shipments of 30 provinces with ROW. The quality of feedgrain is assumed to be homogenous across regions.

The data on transportation fee and other cost incurred during feedgrain transportation by railway are taken from the State Development and Planning Commission. The price elasticity of feedgrain supply and demand for ROW are estimated to be 0.55 and -0.81, respectively, using IFPRI time series data.

In the FSEM, both quantities and prices of feedgrain demand and supply are specified to be endogenous. Imports, exports and world prices of feedgrain enter the model as endogenous variables as well.

Based on the feedgrain demand-supply balance sheet (as in Table 10.1), the FSEM is used to derive the base scenario for further simulations. Feedgrain demand, supply and prices are obtained by using non-linear programming solver (GAMS) to maximise the net social revenue. The optimal value for NSR is zero. The FSEM can be used to simulate the short-run impact (one year after free trade) or the long-run impact (after full adjustment), depending on the parameters.

Simulations on the impact both in the short-run and long-run are carried out. The short-run results are given in Table 10.2. The long-run results are presented in Table A10.1. Both the short-run and long-run results are compared with those given in the 1999 balance sheet and the comparison indicates that internal trade liberalisation has significant effects on provincial feedgrain demand, supply and prices. The results tend to suggest that the short-run effect is slightly greater than the long-run effect. The difference between the long-run and short-run effects is given in Table A10.2.

The base scenario indicates that, in the short-run (Table 10.2), the internal trade liberalisation would drive the price down by 4.3% from the 1999 level. Feedgrain demand will increase by 2.2%, while the supply will fall by 0.4%. The price decline despite an increase in demand and a decrease in supply may be explained by rationalisation of transportation routes or reduction of rent. However, the effects are not evenly distributed among provinces. For most feedgrain surplus regions, the price will rise, especially in the three north-east provinces. For most deficit provinces, the prices tend to decrease when internal trade is liberalised. The findings strongly suggest that barriers exist in internal feedgrain trade. The demand for feedgrain tends to rise in almost all provinces except the north-east provinces, where supply decreases.

The base scenario of regional trade flows between supplier and destination regions is reported in Table A10.3. Table A10.3 shows trade flows from column regions to row regions. For example, the value of 634 in the cell at the intersection of the 'Inner Mongolia' column and the 'Beijing' row represents a net outflow of 634,000 tonnes of feedgrain from Inner Mongolia to Beijing.

In the long run (that is, after full adjustment), feedgrain demand, production, price, deficit/surplus values differ from those in the short run. At the national level, China will see a 1% decline in both demand and domestic production, and a 3.5% rise in price (Table A10.2). After full adjustment, regional trade flows differ from those in the short run (see Table A10.4).

10.4 Simulation Results

We will first report how feedgrain demand and supply will change after the introduction of several shocks, namely, technological improvements in feedgrain production and animal raising; income increase; increase in animal product export; and imposition/relaxation of regional trade restrictions. Then we report how regional trade flows will be affected by these shocks. Finally, we present the 2010 scenarios of China's feedgrain demand, supply, trade flows and imports.

Table 10.2 Feedgrain demand, supply and price, base scenario, short-run model

Region	Supply NLP ('000 t)	Supply 1999 ('000 t)	Supply Change (%)	Demand NLP ('000 t)	Demand 1999 ('000 t)	Demand Change (%)	Price NLP (¥/t)	Price 1999 (¥/t)	Price Change (%)	Deficit/surplus NLP ('000 t)	Deficit/surplus 1999 ('000 t)	Deficit/surplus Change (%)
Beijing	773	776	-0.4	1406	1382	1.8	1077	1110	-3.0	-634	-606	4.6
Tianjin	592	593	-0.2	912	903	1.0	1072	1090	-1.6	-320	-310	3.2
Hebei	9802	9641	1.7	13212	14212	-7.0	1086	970	11.9	-3410	-4571	-25.4
Shanxi	3215	3206	0.3	2084	2108	-1.2	1009	990	2.0	1131	1098	3.0
Inner Mongolia	6569	6610	-0.6	3442	3354	2.6	984	1030	-4.4	3127	3256	-3.9
Liaoning	9202	9078	1.4	6303	6520	-3.3	979	910	7.6	2899	2558	13.3
Jilin	14956	14688	1.8	6681	6993	-4.5	969	880	10.1	8275	7695	7.5
Heilongjiang	13108	12713	3.1	4631	5011	-7.6	961	820	17.2	8477	7702	10.1
Shanghai	438	446	-1.7	1882	1764	6.7	1115	1240	-10.1	-1443	-1318	9.5
Jiangsu	7482	7564	-1.1	8067	7742	4.2	1105	1180	-6.4	-585	-178	228.7
Zhejiang	2950	3029	-2.6	2674	2428	10.1	1050	1240	-15.4	276	601	-54.1
Anhui	5347	5467	-2.2	7834	7219	8.5	1097	1260	-12.9	-2486	-1752	41.9
Fujian	1860	1897	-1.9	3931	3656	7.5	1152	1300	-11.4	-2071	-1759	17.7
Jiangxi	3999	4137	-3.3	4815	4262	13.0	1141	1420	-19.7	-817	-125	553.3
Shandong	13958	13882	0.5	14928	15252	-2.1	1084	1050	3.2	-971	-1370	-29.1
Henan	11545	11326	1.9	13928	14642	-4.9	1099	1020	7.7	-2383	-3316	-28.1
Hubei	5878	6051	-2.9	6659	6212	7.2	1116	1260	-11.4	-781	-161	385.4
Hunan	6801	6972	-2.5	11047	10404	6.2	1127	1250	-9.8	-4246	-3432	23.7
Guangdong	4468	4639	-3.7	6891	6304	9.3	1151	1350	-14.8	-2423	-1665	45.5
Guangxi	4427	4617	-4.1	5441	4930	10.4	1128	1350	-16.5	-1014	-313	224.1
Hainan	431	464	-7.1	900	764	17.9	1182	1650	-28.3	-469	-300	56.4
Sichuan	12493	12619	-1.0	17527	16726	4.8	1123	1210	-7.1	-5035	-4107	22.6
Guizhou	3803	3907	-2.7	1790	1588	12.7	1029	1270	-19.0	2014	2319	-13.2
Yunnan	5048	5188	-2.7	4754	4211	12.9	1017	1260	-19.3	294	977	-69.9
Tibet	31	31	-1.3	332	313	6.1	1182	1300	-9.1	-301	-282	6.9
Shaanxi	3990	3977	0.3	2282	2292	-0.4	1026	1020	0.6	1708	1685	1.4
Gansu	2278	2243	1.5	1368	1395	-1.9	1015	990	2.5	910	848	7.3
Qinghai	68	69	-2.0	471	460	2.5	1093	1130	-3.3	-404	-391	3.3
Ningxia	1071	1071	0.0	485	485	0.0	1000	1000	0.0	586	586	0.0
Xinjiang	2326	2632	-11.6	2227	1945	14.5	955	1180	-19.1	98	586	-85.7
National	158907	159533	-0.4	158907	155476	2.2	1081	1129	-4.3			

Each of the shocks is introduced into the model at varying degrees, e.g., different elasticities of production (from 0.1 to 1) or different R&D growth rates (from 1% to 10%). Table 10.3 provides an overview of the simulation results of selected scenarios at the national level. Details of the simulation results with varying degrees of shocks at the provincial level are given in the appendix to this chapter (in Tables A10.1-19). In the sections that follow, we highlight the major findings from each of the simulation scenarios at both the provincial and national levels.

Table 10.3 Simulation, China's feedgrain supply and demand under a free trade regime ('000 tonnes)

Scenarios	Supply		Demand		Price		Deficit (demand -supply)	Domestic trade volume
	+/-%	Total	+/-%	Total	+/-%	Total		
Base		158907		158907		1081	0	29789
Scen. 1	1.46	161227	1.46	161227	-2.54	1054	0	30345
Scen. 2	-2.86	154362	-2.86	154362	-13.80	932	0	28546
Scen. 3	0.41	159559	2.03	162133	1.98	1102	2574	31902
Scen. 4	0.86	160274	2.51	162896	4.12	1126	2622	44403
Scen. 5	-2.12	155538	-2.12	155538	-4.87	1028	0	16342
Scen. 6	27.90	203242	30.25	206976	13.76	1230	3734	41566
Scen. 7	25.22	198983	27.26	202225	3.42	1118	3242	35239

Base Scenario: Derived by using a non-linear programming solver (GAMS) based on the 1999 estimated feedgrain demand and supply balance sheet.
Scenario 1: Technological improvements in feedgrain production, elasticity of production=0.8, R&D growth rate=0.4.
Scenario 2: Technological improvements in animal raising, leading to a 10% decrease in derived demand for feedgrain.
Scenario 3: Income growth, per capita income growth=4%, income elasticity of demand for feedgrain=0.8.
Scenario 4: Growth in export of livestock products, increases in export by 5%.
Scenario 5: Imposition of restrictions on regional trade flows (very heavy restrictions).
Scenario 6: Demand and supply in 2010, elasticity of production=0.5, R&D growth=4%, income growth=4%, income elasticity of demand for feedgrain=0.8.
Scenario 7: Demand and supply in 2010, elasticity of production=0.5, R&D growth=4%, income growth=4%, income elasticity of demand for feedgrain=0.6.

10.4.1 Changes in Feedgrain Demand and Production

Technological improvements in feedgrain production In Chapter 8 we pointed out that technological improvement may play an important role in China's grain output growth. It is argued that grain yields can be raised with technological improvements (Lin et al. 1996, pp. 136-43). Tian and Wan (2000) used a frontier production function to measure regional technical efficiency based on the production cost data during 1983-96. Their results also suggest that there is potential to increase corn yield in China if effort is devoted to eliminating inefficiency.

We assume a different technological progress rate and different elasticities of production with respect to technological progress. The simulations show that regional supply, demand and price of the feedgrain market is sensitive to technological improvement in feedgrain production (see Tables A5 and A6). Here R&D investment was used to capture technological improvement in feedgrain production. When production elasticity becomes larger, *ceteris paribus*, China's feedgrain production and demand increase (Table A10.5). Feedgrain production and demand in China also increase with increases in investment of agricultural R&D (Table A10.6). Feedgrain price will decline in both cases. With the same technological improvements, outputs of feedgrain in north-west China increase more slowly than in other parts of China.

At the national level, assuming that elasticity of production=0.8 and R&D growth rate=0.4, there will be a 1.46% increase in both feedgrain demand and supply. The price will be reduced by 2.54% (see Table 10.3, Scenario 1).

Technological improvements in animal raising   The derived demand for feedgrain will decrease if there are technological improvements in animal raising. Feed-meat conversion ratio and animal raising period, two correlated indicators, can be used to indicate technological improvements. Using time series data, Xin (1997) showed that technological improvements in the hog industry accounted for more than 50% of output growth.

Assume that technological improvements in animal raising lead to a 10% decrease in derived demand for feedgrain. Holding other shifters constant, the simulations show that, at the national level, feedgrain production and demand will decline by nearly 3%, while feedgrain price will fall by 14% (Table 10.3, Scenario 2; Table A10.7).

Changes in real per capita income   Per capita consumption of all animal products is sensitive to income growth (Xin 2001). Effects of income growth on feedgrain demand also depend on income elasticities. Assuming different income growth rates, the simulations show that 1% growth in real per capita income will lead to 0.7% increase in national demand for feedgrains (see Table A10.8). When the growth rate of real per capita income is 10%, national demand for feedgrain will increase by 3.3%. In this case, the national feedgrain price will rise by 7.5%, while there will only be a less than 2% increase in domestic production. Net import will be 2.6 million tonnes. In the most likely case, with the income growth rate at 4%, China's feedgrain demand and price will rise by 2%, while domestic production will rise by only 0.4%, resulting in a net import of about 2.6 million tonnes (Table 10.3, Scenario 3).

The sensitivity analysis shows that the growth of China's demand for feedgrain ranges from 0.7% to 2.3% when the income elasticity assumes a value between 0.2 and 1 (see Table A10.9).

Growth in export of livestock products China's export of livestock products has been small and its export markets are limited, with most shipments going to Hong Kong, Macao, Russia, North Korea and Japan. It is expected that the quality of livestock product could be improved as China reinforces, after entering the WTO, the development of the livestock sector. This suggests that export of animal products may be increased.

Assume that China's export of livestock products increases by 5%. China's total demand for feedgrain will increase by 2.5% and feedgrain price will increase by 4%, while domestic production will increase by less than 1%. In this case, China will import 2.6 million tonnes of feedgrain (Table 10.3, Scenario 4; Table A10.10).

Restriction of regional trade flows Theoretically, the price gap between different regions should reflect transport costs. When the gap is larger than transport costs, restrictions are in place. Given that the base scenario is a free trade arrangement, an increase in transportation cost is equivalent to an imposition of trade restrictions. In our simulation, it is assumed that the level of restriction is proportional to the distances of shipment.

The simulations suggest that when restrictions on inter-regional movement of feedgrain are imposed, China experiences a decline in feedgrain production, demand and price (Table 10.3, Scenario 5; Table A10.11). The imposition of restrictions on inter-regional movement of feedgrain would increase animal production costs and thus reduce livestock production. When the restrictions increase, feedgrain production, demand and price will decline further. When the restriction is only 10% of transport costs, feedgrain production will decline by 0.07 million tonnes. When the restriction on inter-regional movement of feedgrain are imposed heavily, say, 5 times the transport costs, China's domestic feedgrain production will fall by more than 2%, or 3.7 million tonnes.

Hence, restrictions on inter-regional movement of feedgrain lead to a decline in both domestic feedgrain demand and production. There will also be a fall in the average national feedgrain price. Producers in the major feedgrain surplus regions suffer most and the price level in their regions will decline by about 50% if heavy restrictions are imposed.

10.4.2 Changes in Regional Trade Flows

Technological improvements in feedgrain production Since no demand shocks are assumed, the technological improvements in feedgrain production will result in a decline of feedgrain price, which in turn will drive up demand for feedgrain. The national trade volume will be almost the same as in the base scenario, which is around 30 million tonnes (see Table A10.12). The direction of regional trades will change, but not significantly. The outflow from four northern regions (three north-east provinces plus eastern Inner Mongolia) amounts to 23 million tonnes. The inflows of seven major deficit regions amount to 22 million tonnes.

Technological improvements in animal raising Since the derived demand for feedgrain declines with technological improvements in animal raising, the inter-regional trade volume tends to decrease. Total domestic trade volume is likely to be 28.5 million tonnes. The outflow from the four northern provinces is 22 million tonnes. The inflows of seven major deficit regions amount to 21.2 million tonnes (see Table A10.13).

Changes in real per capita income The demand for feedgrain and feedgrain price tend to increase with rising real per capita income and supply shifters. The national trade volume will be around 32 million tonnes, slightly higher than the base scenario. The growth in trade volume comes from feedgrain imports, which is 2.6 million tonnes (see Table A10.14). The outflow from the four northern provinces is 22.5 million tonnes. The inflows of the seven major deficit regions amount to 23.4 million tonnes.

Growth in export of livestock products The growth in export of livestock products leads to an increase in inter-regional trade volume to 44.4 million tonnes if China can export 5% of its livestock products (see Table A10.15). The outflow from the four northern provinces is 34.7 million tonnes. The inflows of the seven major deficit regions amount to 34.6 million tonnes.

Restriction of regional trade flows If restrictions on inter-regional flows are imposed heavily, the trade volume will decrease by 50%. The outflow from the four northern provinces will be only 12.7 million tonnes, which is about equal to the inflows of the seven major deficit regions (see Table A10.16).

10.4.3 Scenario for 2010

If technological improvement (with elasticity of production 0.5 and annual growth rate of R&D investment 4%) and income growth (annual growth rate 4%) maintain their current rates to 2010, China's demand for feedgrain and domestic production of feedgrain will increase by 30% and 28%, respectively. Domestic production may not meet increasing demand, and thus the price will rise by almost 14% by 2010 (Table 10.3, Scenario 6; Table A10.17). Feedgrain import will be 3.7 million tonnes in 2010. Internal trade volume will be 41.6 million tonnes in 2010. The four north provinces will ship around 28.7 million tonnes surplus feedgrain to the deficit regions and the seven major feedgrain deficit regions will outsource 30 million tonnes in 2010. If the income elasticity of demand for feedgrain drops to 0.6 in 2010, China's demand for feedgrain and domestic production will be slightly smaller (Table 10.3, Scenario 7; Table A10.17). For internal trade volume and directions of the flows, see Tables A10.18 and A10.19, and Map 10.2.

Map 10.2 Feedgrain deficit/surplus, 2010

10.5 Summary and Concluding Comments

Although there has been increased research into China's feedgrain demand and supply, very little effort has been made to examine the issues at a regional level. This study presents an early attempt to fill this gap. Using a non-linear spatial equilibrium model, this study examines possible changes in regional feedgrain demand, supply, price and regional trade flows in response to trade liberalisation, technological improvement in feedgrain production and animal production, income growth, and livestock export growth.

This study finds that China would gain if the government took measures to eliminate restrictions on inter-regional movement of feedgrain. Major feedgrain producers and users would benefit more from such internal trade liberalisation: the former will gain through increased feedgrain prices, and the latter will be able to obtain their feedgrains at a lower price. While technological improvements in feedgrain production will increase both feedgrain supply and demand and reduce feedgrain price, technological improvements in animal raising will reduce feedgrain supply, demand and price.

Given that China is now a member of the WTO, it is reasonable to anticipate that China will gradually relax domestic restrictions on internal feedgrain trade flows. When this takes place, there will be changes in patterns of feedgrain demand and supply and domestic feedgrain trade flows. According to our simulation results, if China's current income growth is maintained at its current rate, and China can successfully increase its export of animal products to the world market, China's demand for feedgrain will increase.

Despite the fact that technological improvements may increase China's domestic supply (increased feedgrain productivity) or reduce its demand for feedgrains (improved feeding efficiency), in balance, China will not be able to meet the increased demand with domestic resources, and imports will be needed. It is noted that, based on our simulation scenarios, the demand for feedgrain import is relatively small compared with that suggested by some other studies (see Chapter 8). This may be due partially to data deficiencies in our simulations, and partially to the fact that our predictions are based on more recent data and information than those used by previous studies. Nonetheless, we believe that the size of this projected import demand is acceptable, given the realities of China's current feedgrain import and export regime. Admittedly, many unexpected circumstances may affect China's feedgrain demand and supply, and hence import needs. However, our study tends to suggest that in the near future China's import of feedgrain is unlikely to be very large unless extraordinary circumstances occur.

Like many other studies that try to research China's feedgrain demand and supply issues, our study also suffers from some limitations. A major limitation is data deficiency. Despite our best efforts, some data cannot be obtained because they simply do not exist. Related to lack of data, some regional differences could not be built into the model, and, instead, parameters for larger regions (embracing several provinces) were used as surrogates. In addition, only one port is used in the simulation to cater for imports, which is hardly a reflection of reality: the inclusion of multi-ports is technically executable, but would significantly complicate the simulation process. Despite these limitations, this study represents a useful exercise in examining China's feedgrain issues at the regional level, and also offers some valuable findings. When better data become available, further studies should be undertaken.

References

Dominic, S. (2001), 'China's live cattle and beef marketing and distribution', Ph.D. thesis, University of Queensland, Australia.

Halbrendt, C.K., Gempesaw II, C.M. and Chen, C.S. (1989), 'A spatial equilibrium model of inter-provincial rice trade in China', *Sri Lankan Journal of Agricultural Economics*, Vol. 21, pp. 124-41.

Hearn, D., Halbrendt, C.K., Gempesaw II, C.M. and Webb, S.E. (1990), 'An analysis of transport improvements in China's corn sector: a hybrid spatial equilibrium approach', *Journal of Transportation Research Forum*, Vol. 31, pp. 154-66.

Koo, W.W. (1986), 'A spatial equilibrium analysis of the U.S. wheat industry', North Dakota Research Report No. 99, Agricultural Experiment Station, North Dakota State University, Fargo.

Koo, W.W. and Uhm, I.H. (1990), 'A spatial equilibrium analysis of US wheat exports under alternative transport costs and trade restrictions', *Logistics and Transportation Review*, Vol. 22, pp. 27-41.

Lin, Y.F., Shen, M.G., and Zhou, H. (eds) (1996), *Priorities of China's Agricultural Research*, China Agricultural Press, Beijing.

MacAulay, T.G. (1976), 'A recursive spatial equilibrium model of the North American beef industry for policy analysis', Ph.D. thesis, University of Guelph, Canada.

MacAulay, T.G. (2001), 'Spatial equilibrium modelling', materials distributed at the workshop on Spatial Equilibrium Modelling, 4-5 August 2001, Asian Agribusiness Research Centre, University of Sydney.

Martin, L.J. (1981), 'Quadratic single and multi-commodity models of spatial equilibrium: a simplified exposition', *Canadian Journal of Agricultural Economics*, Vol. 29, pp. 21-48.

Minot, N. and Goletti, F. (2000), *Rice Market Liberalization and Poverty in Viet Nam*, International Food Policy Research Institute Research Report 114, IFPRI, Washington D.C.

Rutherford, A. (1996), 'Locating value adding activities in northern Australia's beef industry: an interregional trade modelling approach', Ph.D. thesis, University of Queensland, Brisbane.

Samuelson, P.A. (1952), 'Spatial price equilibrium and linear programming', *The American Economic Review*, Vol. 42, pp. 283-303.

SSB (State Statistical Bureau) (2000), *Rural Statistical Yearbook of China*, China Statistical Press, Beijing.

Takayama, T. and Judge, G.G. (1964), 'An interregional activity analysis model for the agricultural sector', *Journal of Farm Economics*, Vol. 46, pp. 349-65.

Takayama, T. and Judge, G.G. (1971), *Spatial and Temporal Price and Allocation Models*, North-Holland Publishing Company, Amsterdam.

Tian, W.M. and Wan, G.H. (2000), 'Technical efficiency and its determinants in China's grain production', *Journal of Productivity Analysis*. Vol. 3, pp. 159-174.

Webb, S.E., Halbrendt, H., Gana, C.K. and Tuan, F. (1992), 'An application of a spatial equilibrium model to analyse the impact on China's trade of a policy change', in Larson, D.W. (ed.), *Transportation Research: Needs and Issues for Chinese Agriculture*, Proceedings of a Special Session on Transportation at a Conference in Prospects for Chinese Agricultural Development in the 1990s, 20-25 August 1992.

Xin, X. (1997), 'Enhancing pork output', *Journal of Rural Sociology and Economics*, Vol. 46, pp. 83-88.

Xin, X. (2001), 'Production, consumption and trade of food in China', paper presented at the *Workshop on Factors which Affect Supply and Demand of Food, and APEC Economies Response to Them*, Tokyo, Japan, 7-9 March 2001.

Notes

[1] It should be noted that aquaculture/fishery production also affects feedgrain demand and supply. However, due to lack of data, this part is not included in this study.

[2] For more detail, refer to MacAulay (2001) and Dominic (2001).

[3] This can also be explained because the value of the objective function of the primal part of the problem must equal the value of the dual part at the optimum.

4   w and v are ignored in the above formulation and for most practical purposes can be ignored provided that any calculated solutions are not likely to include negative prices or quantities (MacAulay 2001, p. 16).

Table A10.1 Feedgrain demand, supply and price, base scenario, long-run model

(1kt=1000 tonnes)

Region	Supply			Demand			Price			Deficit/surplus		
	NLP (kt)	1999 (kt)	Change (%)	NLP (kt)	1999 (kt)	Change (%)	NLP (¥/t)	1999 (¥/t)	Change (%)	NLP (kt)	1999 (kt)	Change (%)
Beijing	771	776	-0.6	1394	1382	0.9	1094	1110	-1.5	-623	-606	2.7
Tianjin	593	593	0.0	903	903	0.0	1089	1090	-0.1	-310	-310	0.1
Hebei	10182	9641	5.6	13065	14212	-8.1	1103	970	13.7	-2883	-4571	-36.9
Shanxi	3255	3206	1.5	2062	2108	-2.2	1027	990	3.7	1192	1098	8.6
Inner Mongolia	6535	6610	-1.1	3409	3354	1.6	1001	1030	-2.8	3126	3256	-4.0
Liaoning	9249	9078	1.9	6249	6520	-4.2	996	910	9.4	3000	2558	17.3
Jilin	15043	14688	2.4	6622	6993	-5.3	986	880	12.1	8421	7695	9.4
Heilongjiang	13204	12713	3.9	4585	5011	-8.5	978	820	19.3	8620	7702	11.9
Shanghai	434	446	-2.8	1866	1764	5.8	1132	1240	-8.7	-1432	-1318	8.7
Jiangsu	7445	7564	-1.6	7993	7742	3.2	1122	1180	-4.9	-549	-178	208.2
Zhejiang	2894	3029	-4.5	2652	2428	9.2	1067	1240	-14.0	242	601	-59.8
Anhui	5265	5467	-3.7	7769	7219	7.6	1115	1260	-11.5	-2504	-1752	42.9
Fujian	1836	1897	-3.2	3900	3656	6.7	1169	1300	-10.1	-2064	-1759	17.3
Jiangxi	3892	4137	-5.9	4782	4262	12.2	1158	1420	-18.5	-889	-125	611.2
Shandong	14097	13882	1.5	14765	15252	-3.2	1101	1050	4.8	-668	-1370	-51.2
Henan	12349	11326	9.0	13774	14642	-5.9	1116	1020	9.4	-1426	-3316	-57.0
Hubei	5465	6051	-9.7	6607	6212	6.4	1133	1260	-10.1	-1141	-161	608.8
Hunan	6407	6972	-8.1	10958	10404	5.3	1144	1250	-8.4	-4551	-3432	32.6
Guangdong	4037	4639	-13.0	6841	6304	8.5	1168	1350	-13.5	-2804	-1665	68.4
Guangxi	3943	4617	-14.6	5402	4930	9.6	1145	1350	-15.2	-1459	-313	366.2
Hainan	342	464	-26.2	895	764	17.2	1199	1650	-27.3	-553	-300	84.4
Sichuan	12177	12619	-3.5	17369	16726	3.8	1141	1210	-5.7	-5192	-4107	26.4
Guizhou	3487	3907	-10.7	1775	1588	11.8	1046	1270	-17.6	1712	2319	-26.2
Yunnan	4671	5188	-10.0	4671	4211	10.9	1054	1260	-16.3	0	977	-100.0
Tibet	30	31	-4.7	329	313	5.2	1199	1300	-7.8	-300	-282	6.3
Shaanxi	4045	3977	1.7	2253	2292	-1.7	1043	1020	2.2	1792	1685	6.3
Gansu	2317	2243	3.3	1350	1395	-3.2	1032	990	4.3	967	848	14.0
Qinghai	68	69	-1.4	466	460	1.3	1110	1130	-1.8	-398	-391	1.8
Ningxia	1085	1071	1.3	479	485	-1.3	1017	1000	1.7	607	586	3.5
Xinjiang	2274	2632	-13.6	2206	1945	13.4	972	1180	-17.6	69	687	-90.0
National	157392	159532	-1.3	157392	155476	1.2	1100	1129	-2.6			

Table A10.2 Feedgrain demand, supply and price, base scenario, long-run versus short-run model

Region	Supply Long (kt)	Supply Short (kt)	Supply Change (%)	Demand Long (kt)	Demand Short (kt)	Demand Change (%)	Price Long (¥/t)	Price Short (¥/t)	Price Change (%)	Deficit/surplus Long (kt)	Deficit/surplus Short (kt)	Deficit/surplus Change (%)
Beijing	771	773	-0.2	1394	1406	-0.9	1094	1077	1.6	-623	-634	-1.8
Tianjin	593	592	0.2	903	912	-0.9	1089	1072	1.6	-310	-320	-3.0
Hebei	10182	9802	3.9	13065	13212	-1.1	1103	1086	1.6	-2883	-3410	-15.5
Shanxi	3255	3215	1.2	2062	2084	-1.0	1027	1009	1.7	1192	1131	5.4
Inner Mongolia	6535	6569	-0.5	3409	3442	-1.0	1001	984	1.7	3126	3127	0.0
Liaoning	9249	9202	0.5	6249	6303	-0.9	996	979	1.7	3000	2899	3.5
Jilin	15043	14956	0.6	6622	6681	-0.9	986	969	1.8	8421	8275	1.8
Heilongjiang	13204	13108	0.7	4585	4631	-1.0	978	961	1.8	8620	8477	1.7
Shanghai	434	438	-1.1	1866	1882	-0.9	1132	1115	1.5	-1432	-1443	-0.8
Jiangsu	7445	7482	-0.5	7993	8067	-0.9	1122	1105	1.5	-549	-585	-6.2
Zhejiang	2894	2950	-1.9	2652	2674	-0.8	1067	1050	1.6	242	276	-12.5
Anhui	5265	5347	-1.5	7769	7834	-0.8	1115	1097	1.6	-2504	-2486	0.7
Fujian	1836	1860	-1.3	3900	3931	-0.8	1169	1152	1.5	-2064	-2071	-0.3
Jiangxi	3892	3999	-2.7	4782	4815	-0.7	1158	1141	1.5	-889	-817	8.9
Shandong	14097	13958	1.0	14765	14928	-1.1	1101	1084	1.6	-668	-971	-31.2
Henan	12349	11545	7.0	13774	13928	-1.1	1116	1099	1.6	-1426	-2383	-40.2
Hubei	5465	5878	-7.0	6607	6659	-0.8	1133	1116	1.5	-1141	-781	46.0
Hunan	6407	6801	-5.8	10958	11047	-0.8	1144	1127	1.5	-4551	-4246	7.2
Guangdong	4037	4468	-9.6	6841	6891	-0.7	1168	1151	1.5	-2804	-2423	15.7
Guangxi	3943	4427	-10.9	5402	5441	-0.7	1145	1128	1.5	-1459	-1014	43.8
Hainan	342	431	-20.6	895	900	-0.6	1199	1182	1.4	-553	-469	17.9
Sichuan	12177	12493	-2.5	17369	17527	-0.9	1141	1123	1.5	-5192	-5035	3.1
Guizhou	3487	3803	-8.3	1775	1790	-0.8	1046	1029	1.7	1712	2014	-15.0
Yunnan	4671	5048	-7.5	4671	4754	-1.7	1054	1017	3.6	0	294	-100.0
Tibet	30	31	-3.5	329	332	-0.8	1199	1182	1.4	-300	-301	-0.6
Shaanxi	4045	3990	1.4	2253	2282	-1.3	1043	1026	1.7	1792	1708	4.9
Gansu	2317	2278	1.7	1350	1368	-1.3	1032	1015	1.7	967	910	6.3
Qinghai	68	68	0.6	466	471	-1.1	1110	1093	1.6	-398	-404	-1.4
Ningxia	1085	1071	1.3	479	485	-1.3	1017	1000	1.7	607	586	3.5
Xinjiang	2274	2326	-2.2	2206	2227	-1.0	972	955	1.8	69	98	-30.3
National	157392	158907	-1.0	158907	158907	-1.0	1100	1063	3.5	0	0	

Table A10.3 Internal shipment of feedgrain, base scenario, short-run model (kt)

Region	Shanxi	Inner Mongolia	Liaoning	Jilin	Heilongjiang	Zhejiang	Guizhou	Yunnan	Shaanxi	Gansu	Ningxia	Xinjiang	Inflow
Beijing		634											634
Tianjin				320									320
Hebei				1019	2391								3410
Shanghai					1443								1443
Jiangsu					585								585
Anhui				2486									2486
Fujian				1795		276							2071
Jiangxi					817								817
Shandong				971									971
Henan	1131			1252									2383
Hubei		350		431									781
Hunan			2899		1347								4246
Guangdong					1893		530						2423
Guangxi							1014						1014
Hainan							469						469
Sichuan		2143						293	1708	604	284		5032
Tibet											301		301
Qinghai										305		98	403
Outflow	1131	3127	2899	8274	8476	276	2013	293	1708	909	585	98	29789

Table A10.4 Internal shipment of feedgrain, base scenario, long-run model (kt)

Region	Shanxi	Inner Mongolia	Liaoning	Jilin	Heilongjiang	Zhejiang	Guizhou	Shaanxi	Gansu	Ningxia	Xinjiang	Inflow
Beijing				622								622
Tianjin			310									310
Hebei		669			2213							2882
Shanghai				1432								1432
Jiangsu				548								548
Anhui				2504								2504
Fujian					1822	241						2063
Jiangxi				889								889
Shandong				668								668
Henan	1192			233								1425
Hubei				1141								1141
Hunan			2689		1861							4550
Guangdong				381	2169		252					2802
Guangxi							1459					1459
Hainan					553							553
Sichuan		2456						1791	568	306	68	5189
Tibet										299		299
Qinghai									398			398
Outflow	1192	3125	2999	8418	8618	241	1711	1791	966	605	68	29734

Table A10.5 Simulation, regional feedgrain market, varying technological progress (R&D growth rate=4%)

Region	Elasticity of production=0.1			Elasticity of production=0.5			Elasticity of production=0.8			Elasticity of production=1.0		
	Supply	Demand	Price	Supply	Demand	Price	Supply	Demand	Price	Supply	Demand	Price
Beijing	0.31	0.36	-0.64	0.99	0.84	-1.50	1.65	1.40	-2.50	2.64	2.24	-3.98
Tianjin	0.31	0.37	-0.64	0.99	0.87	-1.51	1.65	1.44	-2.51	2.63	2.30	-4.00
Hebei	0.30	0.45	-0.63	0.97	1.06	-1.49	1.61	1.76	-2.48	2.57	2.81	-3.95
Shanxi	0.30	0.42	-0.68	0.97	0.98	-1.60	1.61	1.62	-2.66	2.58	2.59	-4.25
Inner Mongolia	0.31	0.38	-0.70	0.98	0.90	-1.64	1.62	1.50	-2.73	2.59	2.39	-4.36
Liaoning	0.26	0.34	-0.70	0.88	0.81	-1.65	1.46	1.35	-2.75	2.34	2.15	-4.38
Jilin	0.26	0.36	-0.71	0.87	0.85	-1.67	1.45	1.41	-2.78	2.31	2.25	-4.43
Heilongjiang	0.25	0.40	-0.72	0.85	0.94	-1.68	1.42	1.56	-2.80	2.26	2.49	-4.46
Shanghai	0.30	0.34	-0.62	0.97	0.81	-1.45	1.62	1.34	-2.41	2.58	2.14	-3.85
Jiangsu	0.30	0.37	-0.62	0.96	0.87	-1.46	1.60	1.44	-2.43	2.56	2.30	-3.88
Zhejiang	0.30	0.33	-0.66	0.97	0.78	-1.54	1.61	1.30	-2.56	2.58	2.07	-4.09
Anhui	0.30	0.33	-0.63	0.97	0.78	-1.47	1.62	1.30	-2.45	2.59	2.07	-3.91
Fujian	0.31	0.33	-0.60	0.98	0.76	-1.40	1.63	1.27	-2.34	2.61	2.03	-3.73
Jiangxi	0.31	0.28	-0.60	1.00	0.67	-1.42	1.66	1.11	-2.36	2.65	1.76	-3.76
Shandong	0.29	0.44	-0.64	0.94	1.04	-1.49	1.56	1.73	-2.48	2.49	2.76	-3.96
Henan	0.23	0.45	-0.63	0.81	1.05	-1.47	1.34	1.75	-2.45	2.14	2.79	-3.90
Hubei	0.26	0.32	-0.62	0.87	0.75	-1.45	1.44	1.25	-2.41	2.30	2.00	-3.84
Hunan	0.26	0.33	-0.61	0.86	0.77	-1.43	1.44	1.28	-2.39	2.29	2.04	-3.81
Guangdong	0.27	0.29	-0.60	0.89	0.69	-1.41	1.47	1.15	-2.34	2.35	1.83	-3.73
Guangxi	0.27	0.29	-0.61	0.88	0.68	-1.43	1.47	1.14	-2.39	2.34	1.81	-3.80
Hainan	0.29	0.22	-0.58	0.93	0.52	-1.37	1.55	0.87	-2.27	2.48	1.39	-3.63
Sichuan	0.32	0.36	-0.61	1.01	0.85	-1.44	1.68	1.42	-2.39	2.68	2.27	-3.82
Guizhou	0.32	0.32	-0.67	1.01	0.76	-1.57	1.69	1.26	-2.61	2.70	2.01	-4.17
Yunnan	0.32	0.32	-0.68	1.01	0.76	-1.59	1.69	1.27	-2.64	2.69	2.02	-4.22
Tibet	0.32	0.33	-0.58	1.02	0.79	-1.37	1.70	1.31	-2.28	2.72	2.08	-3.63
Shaanxi	-0.01	0.52	-0.67	0.22	1.21	-1.58	0.36	2.01	-2.62	0.56	3.21	-4.18
Gansu	-0.02	0.54	-0.68	0.21	1.27	-1.59	0.34	2.11	-2.65	0.51	3.36	-4.23
Qinghai	0.02	0.45	-0.63	0.30	1.06	-1.48	0.49	1.77	-2.46	0.76	2.82	-3.93
Ningxia	-0.02	0.52	-0.69	0.20	1.23	-1.62	0.33	2.04	-2.69	0.50	3.26	-4.29
Xinjiang	-0.00	0.39	-0.72	0.24	0.91	-1.69	0.39	1.51	-2.82	0.61	2.41	-4.49
National	0.26	0.37	-0.65	0.88	0.88	-1.53	1.46	1.46	-2.54	2.33	2.33	-4.05

Note: Figures in the table are the percentage changes compared with the short-run base scenario (Table 10.2, NLP result).

Table A10.6 Simulation, regional feedgrain market, varying technological progress (Elasticity of production=0.5)

Region	R&D growth rate=1%			R&D growth rate=5%			R&D growth rate=10%		
	Supply	Demand	Price	Supply	Demand	Price	Supply	Demand	Price
Beijing	0.40	0.40	-0.71	2.06	1.75	-3.12	4.11	3.48	-6.20
Tianjin	0.40	0.41	-0.71	2.06	1.80	-3.13	4.10	3.58	-6.22
Hebei	0.39	0.50	-0.71	2.01	2.20	-3.09	4.01	4.37	-6.14
Shanxi	0.39	0.46	-0.76	2.01	2.02	-3.33	4.01	4.02	-6.61
Inner Mongolia	0.39	0.43	-0.78	2.03	1.87	-3.41	4.04	3.72	-6.78
Liaoning	0.35	0.38	-0.78	1.83	1.68	-3.43	3.63	3.34	-6.82
Jilin	0.35	0.40	-0.79	1.81	1.76	-3.46	3.59	3.49	-6.88
Heilongjiang	0.34	0.44	-0.80	1.77	1.95	-3.49	3.51	3.87	-6.94
Shanghai	0.39	0.38	-0.69	2.02	1.68	-3.01	4.02	3.33	-5.99
Jiangsu	0.39	0.41	-0.69	2.00	1.80	-3.04	3.98	3.58	-6.04
Zhejiang	0.39	0.37	-0.73	2.02	1.62	-3.20	4.01	3.22	-6.36
Anhui	0.39	0.37	-0.70	2.03	1.62	-3.06	4.03	3.22	-6.08
Fujian	0.40	0.36	-0.66	2.04	1.59	-2.92	4.07	3.15	-5.79
Jiangxi	0.40	0.31	-0.67	2.07	1.38	-2.94	4.13	2.74	-5.85
Shandong	0.38	0.49	-0.71	1.95	2.16	-3.10	3.87	4.28	-6.16
Henan	0.31	0.50	-0.70	1.67	2.18	-3.06	3.32	4.33	-6.07
Hubei	0.34	0.36	-0.69	1.80	1.57	-3.01	3.57	3.11	-5.98
Hunan	0.34	0.36	-0.68	1.79	1.59	-2.98	3.56	3.17	-5.92
Guangdong	0.35	0.33	-0.67	1.84	1.43	-2.92	3.65	2.85	-5.80
Guangxi	0.35	0.32	-0.68	1.84	1.42	-2.98	3.65	2.82	-5.92
Hainan	0.37	0.25	-0.65	1.94	1.09	-2.84	3.86	2.16	-5.64
Sichuan	0.41	0.40	-0.68	2.10	1.77	-2.99	4.18	3.53	-5.94
Guizhou	0.41	0.36	-0.74	2.11	1.57	-3.26	4.21	3.12	-6.48
Yunnan	0.41	0.36	-0.75	2.11	1.58	-3.30	4.20	3.14	-6.56
Tibet	0.41	0.37	-0.65	2.12	1.63	-2.84	4.23	3.24	-5.65
Shaanxi	0.04	0.57	-0.75	0.45	2.51	-3.27	0.82	4.99	-6.50
Gansu	0.03	0.60	-0.75	0.41	2.63	-3.31	0.75	5.22	-6.57
Qinghai	0.08	0.50	-0.70	0.60	2.20	-3.07	1.14	4.38	-6.10
Ningxia	0.03	0.58	-0.77	0.40	2.55	-3.36	0.73	5.07	-6.67
Xinjiang	0.05	0.43	-0.80	0.49	1.89	-3.52	0.90	3.75	-6.99
National	0.35	0.42	-0.72	1.82	1.82	-3.17	3.62	3.62	-6.30

Note: Figures in the table are the percentage changes compared with the short-run base scenario (Table 10.2, NLP result).

Table A10.7 Simulation, improvements in animal raising technology

Region	Supply	Demand	Price	Region	Supply	Demand	Price
Beijing	-1.85	-3.12	-13.59	Henan	-3.52	-1.45	-13.31
Tianjin	-1.88	-2.94	-13.64	Hubei	-2.99	-3.86	-13.11
Hebei	-2.08	-1.38	-13.48	Hunan	-3.00	-3.75	-12.98
Shanxi	-2.06	-2.06	-14.49	Guangdong	-2.81	-4.38	-12.72
Inner Mongolia	-2.00	-2.65	-14.86	Guangxi	-2.83	-4.43	-12.97
Liaoning	-2.86	-3.41	-14.95	Hainan	-2.39	-5.73	-12.37
Jilin	-2.94	-3.11	-15.10	Sichuan	-1.71	-3.04	-13.02
Heilongjiang	-3.12	-2.35	-15.22	Guizhou	-1.66	-3.84	-14.22
Shanghai	-2.04	-3.43	-13.13	Yunnan	-1.67	-3.80	-14.38
Jiangsu	-2.13	-2.93	-13.24	Tibet	-1.60	-3.60	-12.38
Zhejiang	-2.06	-3.64	-13.94	Shannxi	-8.72	-0.15	-14.27
Anhui	-2.02	-3.64	-13.33	Gansu	-8.88	0.31	-14.41
Fujian	-1.95	-3.78	-12.70	Qinghai	-8.06	-1.36	-13.39
Jiangxi	-1.81	-4.58	-12.83	Ningxia	-8.92	0.01	-14.63
Shandong	-2.36	-1.54	-13.50	Xinjiang	-7.55	-3.47	-13.52
National	-2.86	-2.86	-13.80				

Note: Figures in the table are the percentage changes compared with the short-run base scenario (Table 10.2, NLP result).

Table A10.8 Simulation, regional feedgrain market, different income growth rates (Elasticity of demand for feedgrain=0.8)

Region	Income growth rate=1%			Income growth rate=4%			Income growth rate=8%			Income growth rate=10%		
	Supply	Demand	Price	Supply	Demand	Price	Supply	Demand	Price	Supply	Demand	Price
Beijing	0.03	0.68	0.21	0.27	2.07	1.95	0.78	2.99	5.70	1.02	3.44	7.51
Tianjin	0.03	0.68	0.21	0.27	2.04	1.96	0.79	2.90	5.72	1.04	3.32	7.54
Hebei	0.03	0.65	0.21	0.30	1.78	1.93	0.87	2.13	5.65	1.15	2.28	7.45
Shanxi	0.03	0.66	0.22	0.30	1.89	2.08	0.87	2.46	6.08	1.14	2.73	8.01
Inner Mongolia	0.03	0.67	0.23	0.29	1.99	2.13	0.84	2.76	6.23	1.11	3.12	8.22
Liaoning	0.04	0.69	0.23	0.41	2.12	2.14	1.20	3.13	6.27	1.58	3.63	8.26
Jilin	0.05	0.68	0.23	0.42	2.07	2.16	1.23	2.98	6.33	1.62	3.43	8.35
Heilongjiang	0.05	0.67	0.24	0.45	1.94	2.18	1.31	2.61	6.38	1.72	2.93	8.41
Shanghai	0.03	0.69	0.20	0.29	2.12	1.88	0.86	3.14	5.51	1.13	3.64	7.26
Jiangsu	0.03	0.68	0.20	0.31	2.04	1.90	0.89	2.90	5.55	1.18	3.31	7.32
Zhejiang	0.03	0.69	0.22	0.30	2.15	2.00	0.86	3.24	5.85	1.14	3.78	7.71
Anhui	0.03	0.69	0.21	0.29	2.16	1.91	0.85	3.25	5.59	1.12	3.78	7.37
Fujian	0.03	0.69	0.20	0.28	2.18	1.82	0.82	3.32	5.33	1.08	3.88	7.02
Jiangxi	0.03	0.71	0.20	0.26	2.31	1.84	0.76	3.71	5.38	1.00	4.41	7.09
Shandong	0.04	0.65	0.21	0.34	1.81	1.94	0.99	2.21	5.66	1.30	2.39	7.46
Henan	0.05	0.69	0.21	0.50	1.79	1.91	1.48	2.16	5.58	1.94	2.33	7.36
Hubei	0.05	0.69	0.20	0.43	2.19	1.88	1.25	3.35	5.50	1.65	3.93	7.25
Hunan	0.05	0.69	0.20	0.43	2.17	1.86	1.26	3.30	5.44	1.66	3.85	7.17
Guangdong	0.04	0.70	0.20	0.39	2.32	1.74	0.77	4.57	3.50	0.96	5.69	4.35
Guangxi	0.04	0.70	0.20	0.41	2.28	1.86	1.19	3.64	5.44	1.56	4.31	7.17
Hainan	0.04	0.73	0.19	0.34	2.50	1.77	1.00	4.28	5.19	1.32	5.17	6.84
Sichuan	0.03	0.68	0.20	0.25	2.06	1.87	0.72	2.95	5.46	0.95	3.38	7.20
Guizhou	0.03	0.69	0.22	0.24	2.19	2.04	0.69	3.34	5.96	0.92	3.91	7.86
Yunnan	0.03	0.69	0.22	0.24	2.18	2.06	0.70	3.32	6.03	0.92	3.89	7.95
Tibet	0.02	0.69	0.19	0.23	2.15	1.77	0.67	3.23	5.19	0.88	3.76	6.84
Shaanxi	0.13	0.63	0.22	1.25	1.58	2.05	3.66	1.51	5.98	4.82	1.46	7.89
Gansu	0.14	0.62	0.22	1.27	1.51	2.07	3.72	1.29	6.04	4.91	1.16	7.97
Qinghai	0.12	0.65	0.21	1.15	1.78	1.92	3.38	2.12	5.61	4.45	2.27	7.40
Ningxia	0.14	0.63	0.23	1.28	1.55	2.10	3.74	1.44	6.13	4.93	1.36	8.09
Xinjiang	0.13	0.67	0.24	1.23	1.98	2.20	3.59	2.73	6.43	4.73	3.09	8.47
National	0.04	0.68	0.21	0.41	2.03	1.98	1.19	2.90	5.74	1.57	3.32	7.56

Note: Figures in the table are the percentage changes compared with the short-run base scenario (Table 10.2, NLP result).

Table A10.9 Simulation, regional feedgrain market, different income elasticities of demand (Income growth rate=4%)

Region	Elast. of demand for feedgrain=0.2			Elast. of demand for feedgrain=0.6			Elast. of demand for feedgrain=0.8			Elast. of demand for feedgrain=1		
	Supply	Demand	Price	Supply	Demand	Price	Supply	Demand	Price	Supply	Demand	Price
Beijing	0.03	0.68	0.21	0.18	1.64	1.33	0.27	2.07	1.95	0.40	2.30	2.90
Tianjin	0.03	0.68	0.21	0.18	1.62	1.33	0.27	2.04	1.96	0.40	2.26	2.91
Hebei	0.03	0.65	0.21	0.20	1.44	1.31	0.30	1.78	1.93	0.44	1.87	2.88
Shanxi	0.03	0.66	0.22	0.20	1.52	1.41	0.30	1.89	2.08	0.44	2.04	3.10
Inner Mongolia	0.03	0.67	0.23	0.20	1.58	1.45	0.29	1.99	2.13	0.43	2.19	3.17
Liaoning	0.04	0.69	0.23	0.28	1.67	1.46	0.41	2.12	2.14	0.61	2.37	3.19
Jilin	0.05	0.68	0.23	0.29	1.63	1.47	0.42	2.07	2.16	0.63	2.30	3.22
Heilongjiang	0.05	0.67	0.24	0.30	1.55	1.48	0.45	1.94	2.18	0.67	2.11	3.25
Shanghai	0.03	0.69	0.20	0.20	1.67	1.28	0.29	2.12	1.88	0.44	2.38	2.80
Jiangsu	0.03	0.68	0.20	0.21	1.62	1.29	0.31	2.04	1.90	0.46	2.26	2.83
Zhejiang	0.03	0.69	0.22	0.20	1.69	1.36	0.30	2.15	2.00	0.44	2.43	2.98
Anhui	0.03	0.69	0.21	0.20	1.69	1.30	0.29	2.16	1.91	0.43	2.43	2.85
Fujian	0.03	0.69	0.20	0.19	1.71	1.24	0.28	2.18	1.82	0.42	2.47	2.71
Jiangxi	0.03	0.71	0.20	0.18	1.80	1.25	0.26	2.31	1.84	0.39	2.66	2.74
Shandong	0.04	0.65	0.21	0.23	1.46	1.32	0.34	1.81	1.94	0.50	1.91	2.88
Henan	0.05	0.65	0.21	0.34	1.45	1.30	0.50	1.79	1.91	0.75	1.89	2.84
Hubei	0.05	0.69	0.20	0.29	1.72	1.28	0.43	2.19	1.88	0.64	2.48	2.80
Hunan	0.05	0.69	0.20	0.29	1.71	1.27	0.43	2.17	1.86	0.64	2.46	2.77
Guangdong	0.04	0.70	0.20	0.27	1.78	1.24	0.39	2.32	1.74	0.48	2.88	2.19
Guangxi	0.04	0.70	0.20	0.28	1.78	1.27	0.41	2.28	1.86	0.60	2.63	2.77
Hainan	0.04	0.73	0.19	0.23	1.93	1.21	0.34	2.50	1.77	0.51	2.95	2.64
Sichuan	0.03	0.68	0.20	0.17	1.63	1.27	0.25	2.06	1.87	0.37	2.28	2.78
Guizhou	0.03	0.69	0.22	0.16	1.72	1.39	0.24	2.19	2.04	0.35	2.48	3.04
Yunnan	0.03	0.69	0.22	0.16	1.71	1.40	0.24	2.18	2.06	0.36	2.47	3.07
Tibet	0.02	0.69	0.19	0.15	1.69	1.21	0.23	2.15	1.77	0.34	2.42	2.64
Shaanxi	0.13	0.63	0.22	0.85	1.31	1.39	1.25	1.58	2.05	1.86	1.57	3.05
Gansu	0.14	0.62	0.22	0.87	1.26	1.41	1.27	1.51	2.07	1.90	1.46	3.08
Qinghai	0.12	0.65	0.21	0.79	1.44	1.31	1.15	1.78	1.92	1.72	1.87	2.86
Ningxia	0.14	0.63	0.23	0.87	1.29	1.43	1.28	1.55	2.10	1.91	1.53	3.12
Xinjiang	0.13	0.67	0.24	0.84	1.58	1.50	1.23	1.98	2.20	1.83	2.17	3.27
National	0.04	0.68	0.21	0.28	1.61	1.35	0.41	2.03	1.98	0.61	2.25	2.93

Note: Figures in the table are the percentage changes compared with the short-run base scenario (Table 10.2, NLP result).

Table A10.10 Simulation, growth in livestock product exports

Region	Supply	Demand	Price	Region	Supply	Demand	Price
Beijing	0.56	2.59	4.08	Henan	1.06	2.01	4.00
Tianjin	0.57	2.53	4.10	Hubei	0.90	2.85	3.94
Hebei	0.62	1.98	4.04	Hunan	0.90	2.81	3.90
Shanxi	0.62	2.22	4.35	Guangdong	0.66	3.45	3.00
Inner Mongolia	0.60	2.43	4.46	Guangxi	0.85	3.05	3.89
Liaoning	0.86	2.69	4.49	Hainan	0.72	3.51	3.71
Jilin	0.88	2.59	4.53	Sichuan	0.51	2.56	3.91
Heilongjiang	0.93	2.32	4.57	Guizhou	0.50	2.84	4.27
Shanghai	0.61	2.70	3.94	Yunnan	0.50	2.83	4.32
Jiangsu	0.64	2.52	3.97	Tibet	0.48	2.76	3.72
Zhejiang	0.62	2.77	4.18	Shannxi	2.62	1.55	4.28
Anhui	0.61	2.77	4.00	Gansu	2.66	1.39	4.33
Fujian	0.59	2.82	3.81	Qinghai	2.42	1.97	4.02
Jiangxi	0.54	3.10	3.85	Ningxia	2.68	1.49	4.39
Shandong	0.71	2.04	4.05	Xinjiang	2.57	2.41	4.60
National	0.86	2.51	4.12				

Note: Figures in the table are the percentage changes compared with the short-run base scenario (Table 10.2, NLP result).

Table A10.11 Simulation, regional feedgrain market, imposed restrictions on feedgrain movements

Region	Restriction=0.1			Restriction=0.5			Restriction=1			Restriction=5		
	Supply	Demand	Price	Supply	Demand	Price	Supply	Demand	Price	Supply	Demand	Price
Beijing	0.01	-0.03	0.05	0.03	-0.13	0.22	0.05	-0.21	0.37	0.21	-0.86	1.52
Tianjin	0.00	-0.01	0.01	0.00	-0.01	0.02	-0.00	0.02	-0.04	-0.07	0.29	-0.51
Hebei	0.02	-0.10	0.14	0.10	-0.45	0.64	0.18	-0.85	1.20	0.87	-4.03	5.67
Shanxi	-0.09	0.37	-0.61	-0.44	1.88	-3.09	-0.89	3.81	-6.27	-4.51	19.28	-31.68
Inner Mongolia	-0.12	0.48	-0.88	-0.60	2.44	-4.44	-1.21	4.93	-8.97	-6.09	24.85	-45.22
Liaoning	-0.18	0.46	-0.94	-0.91	2.33	-4.75	-1.83	4.69	-9.59	-9.22	23.64	-48.29
Jilin	-0.20	0.53	-1.05	-1.03	2.69	-5.30	-2.08	5.42	-10.69	-10.47	27.29	-53.80
Heilongjiang	-0.23	0.64	-1.14	-1.18	3.21	-5.74	-2.37	6.46	-11.58	-11.92	32.52	-58.24
Shanghai	0.06	-0.22	0.39	0.30	-1.07	1.92	0.58	-2.09	3.76	2.87	-10.27	18.47
Jiangsu	0.05	-0.18	0.31	0.24	-0.89	1.49	0.47	-1.73	2.91	1.57	-5.79	9.77
Zhejiang	-0.03	0.10	-0.20	-0.16	0.54	-1.06	-0.33	1.12	-2.20	-1.67	5.75	-11.33
Anhui	0.04	-0.13	0.24	0.18	-0.62	1.17	0.34	-1.19	2.26	1.66	-5.80	10.96
Fujian	0.11	-0.38	0.70	0.53	-1.88	3.46	1.05	-3.73	6.85	5.22	-18.46	33.96
Jiangxi	0.09	-0.29	0.61	0.43	-1.42	3.02	0.84	-2.80	5.96	3.92	-13.03	27.76
Shandong	0.02	-0.08	0.12	0.10	-0.38	0.55	0.18	-0.71	1.02	0.83	-3.31	4.75
Henan	0.07	-0.18	0.25	0.32	-0.88	1.23	0.63	-1.70	2.38	3.06	-8.26	11.58
Hubei	0.09	-0.21	0.40	0.45	-1.03	1.97	0.88	-2.01	3.87	3.71	-8.46	16.26
Hunan	0.12	-0.27	0.50	0.57	-1.32	2.46	1.12	-2.59	4.84	5.53	-12.79	23.91
Guangdong	0.15	-0.34	0.69	0.76	-1.68	3.42	1.50	-3.32	6.76	7.03	-15.62	31.80
Guangxi	0.11	-0.24	0.50	0.54	-1.18	2.47	1.06	-2.32	4.87	4.86	-10.65	22.33
Hainan	0.18	-0.36	0.94	0.90	-1.79	4.67	1.79	-3.55	9.27	8.57	-17.02	44.43
Sichuan	0.06	-0.28	0.47	0.30	-1.36	2.30	0.59	-2.68	4.52	2.92	-13.22	22.27
Guizhou	-0.05	0.20	-0.41	-0.24	1.00	-2.07	-0.49	2.04	-4.23	-2.73	11.27	-23.39
Yunnan	-0.06	0.25	-0.53	-0.31	1.28	-2.68	-0.63	2.61	-5.44	-1.19	4.92	-10.26
Tibet	0.12	-0.54	0.94	0.60	-2.67	4.65	1.19	-5.30	9.23	6.27	-27.92	48.63
Shaanxi	-0.27	0.34	-0.44	-1.38	1.73	-2.25	-2.81	3.53	-4.59	-14.25	17.89	-23.31
Gansu	-0.34	0.44	-0.55	-1.72	2.22	-2.80	-3.50	4.51	-5.68	-15.71	20.27	-25.51
Qinghai	0.12	-0.14	0.20	0.58	-0.69	0.97	1.12	-1.33	1.85	7.19	-8.56	11.94
Ningxia	-0.43	0.54	-0.71	-2.19	2.72	-3.58	-4.42	5.51	-7.25	-20.34	25.35	-33.34
Xinjiang	-0.68	0.65	-1.22	-2.20	2.12	-3.94	-2.20	2.12	-3.94	-2.20	2.12	-3.94
National	-0.05	-0.05	-0.13	-0.23	-0.23	-0.63	-0.44	-0.44	-1.25	-2.12	-2.12	-4.87

Note: Figures in the table are the percentage changes compared with the short-run base scenario (Table 10.2, NLP result).

Table A10.12 Simulation, trade flows, progress in feedgrain production technology (kt)
(Elasticity of production=0.8; R&D growth rate=0.4)

Region	Shanxi	Inner Mongolia	Liaoning	Jilin	Heilongjiang	Zhejiang	Guizhou	Yunnan	Shaanxi	Gansu	Ningxia	Xinjiang	ROW	Inflow
Beijing					644									644
Tianjin			325											325
Hebei				3529										3529
Shanghai					1472									1472
Jiangsu			579											579
Anhui				2510										2510
Fujian			831		974	296								2101
Jiangxi			795											795
Shandong				1034										1034
Henan	1160	895	446	22										2523
Hubei					779									779
Hunan					4315									4315
Guangdong				1373			1070							2443
Guangxi							1009							1009
Hainan					471									471
Sichuan		2319						333	1657	517	268			5094
Tibet											307			307
Qinghai										357		58		415
Outflow	1160	3214	2976	8468	8655	296	2079	333	1657	874	575	58	0	30345

Table A10.13 Simulation, trade flows, improvements in animal raising technology (kt)

Region	Shanxi	Inner Mongolia	Liaoning	Jilin	Heilongjiang	Zhejiang	Guizhou	Yunnan	Shaanxi	Gansu	Ningxia	Xinjiang	ROW	Inflow
Beijing					604									604
Tianjin			304											304
Hebei		627		2804										3431
Shanghai					1388									1388
Jiangsu				508										508
Anhui				2309										2309
Fujian			1646			312								1959
Jiangxi			668											668
Shandong			232	167	670									1069
Henan	1108				1480									2588
Hubei				700										700
Hunan					4036									4036
Guangdong				1554			693							2247
Guangxi							898							898
Hainan							428							428
Sichuan		2461						390	1363	300	201			4715
Tibet											290			290
Qinghai										403				403
Outflow	1108	3087	2851	8043	8178	312	2019	390	1363	703	491	0	0	28546

Table A10.14 Simulation, trade flows (kt) (Real per capita income growth rate is 4%; elasticity of feedgrain demand=0.8)

Region	Shanxi	Inner Mongolia	Liaoning	Jilin	Heilongjiang	Zhejiang	Guizhou	Yunnan	Shaanxi	Gansu	Ningxia	Xinjiang	ROW	Inflow
Beijing			660											660
Tianjin					336									336
Hebei				3616										3616
Shanghai					1481									1481
Jiangsu			726											726
Anhui				2639										2639
Fujian				1718	205	227								2150
Jiangxi			54				862							916
Shandong			969	224										1193
Henan	1101				1473									2574
Hubei		510	391											901
Hunan					4456									4456
Guangdong													2565	2565
Guangxi							1120							1120
Hainan					490									490
Sichuan		2566						202	1721	790		82		5361
Tibet											308			308
Qinghai										127	283			410
Outflow	1101	3076	2800	8197	8441	227	1982	202	1721	917	591	82	2565	31902

Table A10.15 Simulation, trade flows, growth in livestock product exports (kt)

Region	Shanxi	Inner Mongolia	Liaoning	Jilin	Heilongjiang	Zhejiang	Guizhou	Yunnan	Shaanxi	Gansu	Ningxia	Xinjiang	ROW	Inflow
Beijing					604									604
Tianjin			304		340									644
Hebei		627	2808	2804	803									7042
Shanghai					1388									1388
Jiangsu				508										508
Anhui				2309										2309
Fujian			1646		1951	312								3910
Jiangxi			668		603		341							1613
Shandong			232	167	670									1069
Henan	1105	567			1480									3152
Hubei				700	918									1619
Hunan				4495	4036									8531
Guangdong				1554			693						2632	4879
Guangxi							898							898
Hainan							428							428
Sichuan		2461						390	1363	300	201	105		4820
Tibet											290			290
Qinghai										403	297			700
Outflow	1105	3654	5659	12538	12793	312	2360	390	1363	703	788	105	2632	44403

Table A10.16 Simulation, inter-regional movements, imposed restrictions (kt)
(Restrictions are assumed to be five times transport costs)

Region	Shanxi	Inner Mongolia	Liaoning	Jilin	Heilongjiang	Zhejiang	Guizhou	Shaanxi	Gansu	Ningxia	Inflow
Beijing					620						620
Tianjin			323								323
Hebei		206	237	2349							2792
Shanghai				593	644						1237
Anhui				1943							1943
Fujian					1175	73					1248
Jiangxi							32				32
Shandong					361						361
Henan	585				295						880
Hunan					2313		144				2457
Guangdong							1033				1033
Guangxi							220				220
Hainan							279				279
Sichuan		1666						686			2352
Tibet								46		161	207
Qinghai									274	84	358
Outflow	585	1872	560	4885	5408	73	1708	732	274	245	16342

Table A10.17 Simulation, regional feedgrain market, 2010

Region	2010 (income elasticity=0.8)			2010 (income elasticity=0.6)		
	Supply	Demand	Price	Supply	Demand	Price
Beijing	26.66	30.52	13.69	24.91	27.34	3.37
Tianjin	26.70	30.23	13.74	24.92	27.28	3.39
Hebei	26.94	27.77	13.57	24.98	26.72	3.35
Shanxi	26.92	28.84	14.60	24.97	26.96	3.60
Inner Mongolia	26.84	29.77	14.97	24.96	27.18	3.69
Liaoning	27.91	30.98	15.06	25.22	27.45	3.71
Jilin	28.02	30.50	15.21	25.24	27.34	3.75
Heilongjiang	28.24	29.31	15.33	25.30	27.07	3.78
Shanghai	26.89	31.01	13.22	24.97	27.45	3.26
Jiangsu	27.01	30.22	13.34	25.00	27.28	3.29
Zhejiang	26.92	31.34	14.04	24.97	27.53	3.46
Anhui	26.87	31.35	13.43	24.96	27.53	3.31
Fujian	26.78	31.57	12.80	24.94	27.58	3.15
Jiangxi	26.61	32.83	12.92	24.90	27.87	3.18
Shandong	27.29	28.02	13.60	25.06	26.78	3.35
Henan	28.74	27.88	13.41	25.42	26.75	3.31
Hubei	28.08	31.69	13.21	25.26	27.61	3.26
Hunan	28.09	31.52	13.07	25.26	27.57	3.22
Guangdong	26.41	36.17	7.54	25.07	28.11	2.67
Guangxi	27.88	32.60	13.07	25.21	27.81	3.22
Hainan	27.33	34.66	12.46	25.07	28.28	3.07
Sichuan	26.48	30.40	13.12	24.87	27.32	3.23
Guizhou	26.41	31.65	14.32	24.85	27.60	3.53
Yunnan	26.43	31.59	14.49	24.85	27.59	3.57
Tibet	26.33	31.28	12.47	24.83	27.52	3.07
Shaanxi	35.26	25.81	14.37	27.03	26.28	3.54
Gansu	35.46	25.09	14.52	27.08	26.12	3.58
Qinghai	34.43	27.73	13.48	26.82	26.71	3.32
Ningxia	35.51	25.57	14.74	27.09	26.22	3.63
Xinjiang	35.06	29.69	15.44	26.98	27.16	3.80
National	27.90	30.25	13.76	25.22	27.26	3.42

Note:
Elasticity of feedgrain production=0.5

Annual growth rate of R&D investment =4%

Income growth rate=4%

Figures in the table are the percentage changes compared with the short-run base scenario (Table 10.2, NLP result).

Table A10.18 Simulation, trade flows, 2010 (kt)

(Elasticity of feedgrain production=0.5; annual growth rate of R&D investment=4%; elasticity of feedgrain demand=0.8; income growth rate=4%)

Region	Shanxi	Inner Mongolia	Liaoning	Jilin	Heilongjiang	Zhejiang	Guizhou	Yunnan	Shaanxi	Gansu	Ningxia	Xinjiang	ROW	Inflow
Beijing			857											857
Tianjin			317	121										438
Hebei		1025		3414										4439
Shanghai				489	1420									1909
Jiangsu					1002									1002
Anhui				3505										3505
Fujian					2582	232								2814
Jiangxi			1100				234							1334
Shandong				1345										1345
Henan	1396			1552										2948
Hubei			1241											1241
Hunan					5817									5817
Guangdong													3736	3736
Guangxi							1554							1554
Hainan							664							664
Sichuan		2842						126	2526	1374		187		7054
Tibet											397			397
Qinghai											445	66		511
Outflow	1396	3866	3515	10427	10821	232	2452	126	2526	1374	843	253	3736	41566

Table A10.19 Simulation, trade flows, 2010 (kt)

(Elasticity of feedgrain production=0.5; annual growth rate of R&D investment=4%; elasticity of feedgrain demand=0.6; income growth rate=4%)

Region	Shanxi	Inner Mongolia	Liaoning	Jilin	Heilongjiang	Zhejiang	Guizhou	Yunnan	Shaanxi	Gansu	Ningxia	Xinjiang	ROW	Inflow
Beijing				735										735
Tianjin					374									374
Hebei		743	1610	1649										4002
Shanghai					1657									1657
Jiangsu				771										771
Anhui				2923										2923
Fujian				1207	919	272								2397
Jiangxi				1001										1001
Shandong					1266									1266
Henan	1251		1580											2831
Hubei				976										976
Hunan					4951									4951
Guangdong							831						2010	2841
Guangxi							1228							1228
Hainan					360		185							546
Sichuan		2741						258	1940	573	321	101		5934
Tibet											345			345
Qinghai										461				461
Outflow	1251	3484	3190	9263	9527	272	2244	258	1940	1034	667	101	2010	35239

Chapter 11

China's Future Grain Demand and International Trade Reforms

Wei-Ming Tian and Zhang-Yue Zhou

11.1 China's Grain Demand and the World Market

As has been pointed out in earlier chapters, direct human consumption of grains in China has declined. On the other hand, consumption of animal products in China has increased rapidly, which has led to the increased derived demand for feedgrains. It is commonly held that China's ability to increase grain production is limited and that large imports of feedgrain are required in the long term. Hence, it is useful to examine China's future foodgrain and feedgrain demand in a broader context and in conjunction with the developments in the international grain market. This has become even more important given that China is now a member of the WTO, which leads the domestic market to being more closely linked with the international market, and thus more affected by the reforms in international trade arrangements.

Although the Uruguay Round (UR) of multilateral trade negotiations have achieved some success in pushing forward trade policy reforms worldwide, agricultural trade at present is still heavily distorted by a wide range of intervention measures, such as high tariff protection the world around, huge government support to producers in major developed countries, and wide use (and abuse) of SPS (sanitary and phytosanitary) measures, TBT (technical barriers of trade) and various safe-guard measures (WTO 2001b; USDA 2001a and 2001b). Further reforms are included in the "built-in agenda" in Article 20 of the Agreement of Agriculture and the new round of negotiations is now underway (WTO 2003a and 2003b).

As a WTO member, in the years to come China will need to implement all its commitments that are included into the Protocols for China's Accession. In the meantime, China is also able to participate in the new round of trade negotiations. While the outcomes are still uncertain, it is expected that the direction towards a freer trade system will be maintained. To what extent further liberalisation of agricultural trade may affect the development of the world grain market and what opportunities may be brought about to both China and other players are of great importance.

In this chapter, simulations with the GTAP model are carried out to evaluate quantitatively how the world grain market will change under different scenarios of trade policy reforms in general and how China's grain trade may be affected by such reforms. Policy implications are then derived for China and for other major grain-exporting countries.

After this introduction, progress in agricultural trade reforms after the Uruguay Round is briefly described and the major issues related to trade of grains and livestock (due to its impact on the demand for feedgrains) are highlighted. The third section describes the methodologies used for policy simulations and presents the designs of the scenarios. The results of the simulation are reported in the fourth section. The last section summarises the chapter with concluding remarks.

11.2 Evolving Agricultural Trade Environment

11.2.1 Changes in International Agricultural Trade Arrangements

It is believed that the significant accomplishment of the Uruguay Round of trade negotiations is to establish a "rule-based multilateral trade system". With respect to agricultural trade, the Uruguay Round is the first time in history that all agricultural products have been brought together under effective multilateral rules and disciplines. The Agreement of Agriculture sets requirements for members to reduce their import tariffs, export subsidies and trade-distorting domestic support in line with specified targets. The Uruguay Round also establishes disciplines on the use of SPS measures, TBT and agreement on a new process for settling trade disputes.

However, while the Uruguay Round has resulted in reforms of trade policies throughout the world, agricultural tariffs remain very high for some products in some countries, limiting the trade benefits to be derived from the new rules. Developed countries continue to provide substantial support to agricultural producers, as revealed by high Producer Support Estimates in OECD countries (OECD 2003). Although many countries turned their support into categories of "green-box" or "blue-box" measures, the huge amounts of support cause concerns as to whether such supports are actually non- or less- trade-distorting.

While a target for concluding the new round of trade negotiations by 1 January 2005 was agreed at the WTO ministerial meeting in Doha, it has been demonstrated at the Cancun meeting that there is a lack of common grounds among the members to advance the Doha development agenda (Hoekman and Newfarmer 2003). Major disputes are concentrated on issues related to agricultural trade. Whether and when the Doha Round can resume its vigour is yet to be seen.

11.2.2 Changes in China's Agricultural Trade Arrangements

The Chinese government has traditionally placed a top priority on national food security and grain policies have greatly affected China's agricultural policies. Since the early 1990s, there have been some important developments in China's grain polices. Subsequently, overall agricultural policies experienced some changes that were closely related to grain demand and supply situations. Recent developments in China's grain policies have been reviewed in Chapter 2. Here we focus on China's commitments to agricultural reforms that affect its agricultural trade arrangements.

China became a WTO member in late 2001. However, well before China's acceptance to the WTO, the government started to carry out market-oriented reforms but in a gradual way to prepare China for entering the WTO. China initiated a number of steps to reduce trade barriers. For example, China's average tariff was reduced from over 40% in the early 1990s to 15.3% by January 2001, which includes many lines of agricultural commodities. The extent of reduction was much greater than what was required by the Uruguay Round (UR) agreements for both developing and developed countries. As with tariff cuts, China has autonomously implemented a wide range of reform measures in removing non-tariff barriers (NTBs). China has reduced coverage of licence controls substantially since 1992. Trading rights have been granted to foreign and joint venture firms first and then to domestic non-state firms. These measures have made China's trade regime much more liberal than that which prevailed in the 1980s. In the meantime, the Chinese government has also taken steps to improve its domestic regulatory framework covering the legal system, firm system, and government institutions.

China's commitments to reform its agricultural sector and trade arrangements under the WTO accession are substantial and comprehensive. Table 11.1 summarises China's major commitments to reform its agricultural trade in its bid for WTO accession.

While the Chinese leaders perceive that accession to the WTO will bring about economic benefits (e.g., improved access to foreign markets, increased foreign investments and associated technology transfers into China which may help China to accelerate economic growth), as well as political benefits (e.g., improving China's reputation and exerting influence on world affairs, pressure on Taiwan to establish a closer link with mainland China), they also recognise the likely threats and costs, such as expected hardship in structural adjustment, constraints on policy options, and influence on the Chinese society by western cultures. Nonetheless, it seems that the Chinese government intends to adhere to some essential principles. Since China's acceptance to the WTO in late 2001, it has begun to honour its commitments. Deregulation of grain marketing was on the agenda in 2002 in selected provinces (mainly grain-deficit regions). Further reforms of the grain marketing systems are now underway (see Chapter 2).

Table 11.1 Major commitments in agricultural trade reforms made by China in its bid for WTO accession

Commodities	Commitments
Cereals	A tariff-rate-quota system is applied to wheat, rice and corn. The quotas are to be increased annually at different rates until 2004. The final quotas are 9.636 million tonnes for wheat, 7.2 million tonnes for corn and 5.32 million tonnes for rice. Part of the quotas is retained for non-state trading enterprises according to pre-specified proportions. With respect to corn, this share will increase from 25% in 2002 to 40% in 2004. The in-quota tariff rate remains at 1% while out-quota rate declines from 71% in 2002 to 65% in 2004. A "tariff-only" system will be applied to other minor cereals, including barley (3%). Ban on TCK wheat from the US is lifted.
Cotton, wool and wool top	A tariff-rate-quota system is applied. The quotas are to be increased to 894000 tonnes for cotton, 287000 tonnes for wool and 80000 tonnes of wool top by 2004. The in-quota tariffs are 1% for cotton, 1% for wool and 3% for wool top while the out-quota tariffs are reduced to 40% for cotton and 38% for wool and wool top by 2004. Two-thirds of cotton import quota is retained to non-state trading enterprises.
Vegetable oils	A tariff-rate-quota system is applied to soybean oil, rapeseed oil and palm oil. The quotas are to increase significantly. By 2005, the import quotas will rise to 3.5871 million tonnes for soybean oil, 1.243 million tonnes for rapeseed oil and 3.168 million tonnes for palm oil. The in-quota tariff rates are uniformly 9% during the implementing period. The out-quota tariff rates will be reduced from 52.4% in 2002 to 9% in 2005. Two-thirds of the import quota is retained to non-state trading enterprises. China commits to adopt the "tariff-only" system starting from 2006.
Oilseeds and meals	A tariff-only system is applied to soybean with a tariff rate of 3%. The tariff of soybean meal remains at 5%.
Animal products	A tariff-only system is applied. Import tariffs are to be reduced gradually by varying extents. A sharp reduction of tariff is committed for frozen beef, frozen pork, edible offal of bovine animals, frozen cuts and offal of poultry, and dairy products. China commits to remove scientifically unjustified restrictions on importation of meat products.
Fishery products [*]	A tariff-only system is applied. Import tariffs are to be reduced gradually by varying extents. A sharp reduction of tariff is committed for many frozen products of sea fish species and lobster.
Horticultural products	A tariff-only system is applied. Import tariffs are to be reduced gradually by varying extents. A sharp reduction of tariff is committed for a range of fruits and nuts produced in temperate zone. China commits to remove scientifically unjustified restrictions on importation of horticultural products.
Processed food and beverages	A tariff-only system is applied. Import tariffs are to be reduced gradually by varying extents. A sharp reduction of tariff is committed for malt, wines, beer, tobacco, and so on.

Services	Commitments
General	China permits all approved enterprises, including non-state domestic enterprises and foreign enterprises, to engage in a full range of trading and distribution services in a progressive way.
Specific to agriculture	China permits all approved enterprises to engage in all services affiliated to agriculture, forestry and livestock, including wholesale, retail and warehousing.

[*] Fishery products are not classified as agricultural commodities in the Uruguay Round.

Source: Compiled from WTO (2001a).

11.2.3 Major Issues Affecting Trade of Grains and Other Agricultural Products

China's future grain import needs are to a great extent affected by China's demand for feedgrains, which in turn is determined by the speed of expansion of China's livestock industries. However, China's animal product output is currently limited by a number of factors. (1) The frequent incidence of food safety hazards in China has caused great concerns to Chinese consumers, and has had a negative influence on domestic demand for animal products. (2) China's ability to produce quality animal products is still limited and this reduces China's chance to expand its livestock production for export. (3) China's effort to expand export of animal products is also hindered by the increased use of SPS and TBT measures in the EU and in some Asian importing countries.

Table 11.2 shows that China's trade in animal product is very small. It also shows trade balances for a few other major agricultural products. In the past, Hong Kong and Macao were China's traditional export markets of animal products. While China is able to maintain its dominant position in supplying live animals to these markets, it faces acute competition for exporting other animal products to these markets. China's access to other remunerative markets, such as Japan, Korea and the EU, is seriously limited by problems such as an inability to control animal diseases and inappropriate management of the use of antibiotics, growth stimulants and other additives. Poultry products are exceptional among the animal products, in that China exports them in large volumes. Taking advantage of cheap labour, China is able to produce processed poultry meat products at low costs and exports them to Japan (and also EU before the mid-1990s).

Table 11.2 China's net exports, selected animal and agricultural products

Products	1999	2000	2001	2002	2003p
	Value (million US$)				
Meats and edible offal (HS02)	192	116	243	38	n.a.
Fishery products (HS03)	1064	1058	1260	1308	n.a.
Cereals (HS10)	638	1069	427	1168	n.a.
Oilseeds and kernels (HS12)	-833	-2195	-2433	-1837	n.a.
	Quantity ('000 t)				
Wheat	-341	-731	-26	345	1445
Corn	4254	10476	5961	11667	12609
Rice	2526	713	1577	1752	2091
Other cereals	-2457	191	-2187	-1778	n.a.
Soybean	-4113	-10204	-13678	-11010	-21170

p: preliminary; n.a.: not available.

Source: China Administration of Customs, various issues.

Changes in the world trade environment may bring opportunities for the development of China's livestock sector. The Uruguay Round multilateral trade negotiations pushed forward trade liberalisation in agricultural commodities, including animal products. This may improve China's chance to access overseas markets. China is in an advantageous position by being located very close to Japan, Korea and other Asian importing markets, which consist of the largest net import market of food products in the world now and the volumes of import are expected to rise in the future.

Implementation of the WTO accession commitments means that domestic grain prices will be more aligned with world prices. Given that China's domestic prices were notably higher than world prices in the late 1990s, a decline in the domestic grain prices was expected. This would further lead to lower feedgrain prices and thus lower production costs of animal products. This would increase the competitiveness of China's animal products in the world market.

The livestock sector is expected to play a key role in reshaping China's agriculture in the coming years. The likely decline of feedgrain prices will favour the development of intensive animal-raising practices. The expanding scale of the sector and the shift from backyard feeding to modern feeding operations will increase China's demand for feed ingredients, including grains and protein meals (Zhou et al. 2003).

China's trade position in feedgrains is partially dependent on its trade patterns in animal products, and the export competitiveness is, in turn, related to feed costs. Thus, major elements that need to be assessed are China's border intervention on feedgrains, border protection of major importers of animal products, and export subsidies and domestic support to feedgrain and animal producers of major competitors.

Rapid growth in the non-agricultural economy will affect both the demand for and the supply of food in China. Rising incomes are clearly changing food consumption patterns. Demand for meat, fruits, vegetables, and other high-value commodities is rising continuously. The per capita demand for staple foodgrains, such as wheat and rice, is likely to fall further as consumers substitute higher value foods for staple foodgrains. Greater exposure of urban people to exotic cultures may affect lifestyles as well, especially of youth. As these changes in food consumption patterns are transmitted back to farmers in the form of price changes, agricultural production patterns are shifting to cater to the rising demand for meat, fruits, vegetables, and other high-value crops.

Having provided some background on the progress in agricultural trade reforms and some major issues related to the trade of grains and animal products, we now turn our attention in the next section to methodological issues related to our policy simulation exercises.

11.3 Simulating China's Grain Demand: Methodology

11.3.1 The GTAP Model

The GTAP model is used to evaluate the impacts of different policy environments on China's grain trade. GTAP is a CGE model specially designed for trade policy analysis and is widely used around the world to address various issues in world trade. More detailed description of the GTAP model can be found in Hertel (1997).

Recently, the GTAP model has also been frequently used in studies on impacts of China's WTO accession (e.g., Arndt et al. 1996; Wang 1997; College of Economics and Management 1999; Martin 1999; Hertel et al. 1999; Walmsley and Hertel 2000; Anderson et al. 2002). These studies use different assumptions of policy environments in China as well as in other countries and vary in country and commodity aggregations. It is commonly found by such studies that China's trade policy reforms would benefit not only China itself, but also the whole world.

The GTAP version 5, formally released in late 2001, includes 57 countries (or country groups) and 66 sectors. The base year of the dataset is 1997. A twenty-two sector by thirteen-region version of the GTAP model is employed for this study in order to simplify the work. The detailed categorisation of sectors and regions is reported in Tables 11.3 and 11.4. It can be seen from Table 11.3 that the simulation work gives a high emphasis to those regions that are China's actual or potential trade partners in agricultural commodities. Similarly, agriculture and related sectors remain less aggregated while manufacturing and service sectors are highly aggregated. This treatment is based on considerations of operational simplicity and usefulness of the results for the intended purposes.

Table 11.3 Regional grouping in the policy simulations

Region code	Members included
China	Mainland China
HKG	Hong Kong Special Administration of China
TWN	Taiwan Province of China
JPN	Japan
KOR	Republic of Korea
ASEAN	Thailand, Malaysia, Indonesia, Philippines, Singapore, Vietnam
SA	India, Bangladesh, Sri Lanka, rest of South Asia
LA	All countries in Latin America except Mexico
AUNZ	Australia, New Zealand
WEUR	EU, Switzerland, rest of EFTA
EEUR	Hungary, Poland, rest of Central European Association, former Soviet Union
NAFTA	USA, Canada, Mexico
ROW	All countries and regions not included above

Table 11.4 Sector grouping in the policy simulations

Code	Sectors covered	Code	Sectors covered
RICE	Paddy rice, processed rice	WHT	Wheat, wheat flour
GRO	Cereal grains nec	V_F	Vegetables, fruits, nuts
OSD	Oil seeds	SUGAR	Sugar cane, sugar beet, sugar
FIBER	Plant-based fibres	OFOOD	Crops nec, food products nec, beverages and tobacco products
CTL	Cattle, sheep, goats, horses	OAP	Animal products nec
DAIRY	Raw milk, dairy products	WOOL	Wool, silk-worm cocoons
FISH	Fishing	CMT	Meat: cattle, sheep, goats, horse
OMT	Meat products nec	VOIL	Vegetable oils and fats
FOR	Forestry	OthPrimary	Coal, oil, gas, minerals nec
Leather	Leather products	Textile	Textiles, wearing apparel
Mnfcs	All other manufactures	Svces	All services

11.3.2 Scenarios

We project the global economy for the year of 2010 (when commitments under the new round of negotiations may be implemented) by exogenously changing factor endowments and population for all economies and by imposing growth forecasts for regional GDPs and rates of technical progress in different sectors. An economy-wide technological change variable is endogenised to take up any slack in GDP forecasts. Comparative static simulations for different scenarios of worldwide trade policy reforms are undertaken for 2010.

The WTO accession of mainland China and Taiwan entails extensive reforms of their trade policies as well as domestic policies. However, it is assumed that there are no trade barriers by the existing members that are applied bilaterally with respect to China or Taiwan and thus what they need to do is to complete their policy reforms as committed under the UR. Many policy reforms under the context of WTO cannot be easily quantified due to lack of appropriate data and framework for aggregated regions and sectors. These include the induction of tariff-rate-quota systems (TRQ) by some countries, implementation of SPS and TBT measures, intellectual property protection, phase-out of MFA quotas, impacts on FDI of implementing TRIMs, and related institutional reforms. To reduce this complexity, we assume that mainland China and Taiwan will reduce their import tariff equivalents as they committed in their WTO accession protocols while all other countries are assumed to have uniform reforms as required under the UR by their development status. It is assumed that the required cuts of import tariffs on agricultural commodities and non-agricultural goods are 24% and 26% for developed countries, and 19% and 24% for developing countries, respectively. With respect to export subsidies, the reductions are assumed to be 14% for the developed and 11% for the developing countries, respectively.

Since we are unable to include TRQ committed by mainland China and Taiwan formally, a question arises on whether in-quota or above-quota tariff rates should be used in the simulations.[1] We adopted a simple but pragmatic approach to look at this issue. We use the in-quota rates to design shocks for the projection and then check whether the derived imports for relevant commodities are larger than committed quotas. If this is the case, we shift to use above-quota tariffs and obtain new results. Otherwise, we proceed to the next phase of the exercise, namely the policy simulations.

Based on discussions in the previous section, here we consider three sets of policies that may affect China's trade position in grains significantly, namely import tariffs, export subsidies and domestic support. It is expected that the future reforms under the WTO context are likely to be in certain uniformity for all members, although special and different treatments to developing countries are likely to remain. Considering this possibility, the simulated scenarios assess the policy reforms by different aspects, rather than by measures undertaken by specific region or regions. The simulation work covers these scenarios:

- Scenario 1: All regions cut their import tariff rates (tariff equivalents) with an approach by a variant of Swiss formulae proposed in the Tokyo Round. Thus, trade barriers as envisaged by tariff peaks and tariff escalation can be effectively removed.

- Scenario 2: All economies remove their export subsidies on agricultural products completely.

- Scenario 3: All developed economies remove their domestic support to agricultural products completely.

- Scenario 4: All regions carry out a comprehensive reform package consisting of all three aspects shown in the above three scenarios.

In essence, the above designs imply that the prospects of China's grain market will be evaluated within a framework of worldwide trade policy reforms. Further information for designs of various scenarios and the key assumptions are given in Table 11.5.

11.3.3 Data and Parameters

In designing the scenarios, changes in population, factor endowments and policies are either derived on the basis of available data from various international organisations, or derived with reference to other second-hand information.

Since the results obtained from simulations with GTAP are mainly in the forms of proportional changes over the base-year data, it is useful to know the trade pattern. China's import and export values of all traded goods and services as reflected in the GTAP base-data (for 1997) are reported in Table 11.6. It can be seen that, for the commodities in which this study is largely interested, China maintained a trade surplus in rice, coarse grains, live animals, fishery products, and meats of non-ruminant animals, but had deficits in wheat, dairy products, wool and meats of ruminant animals. However, regardless of surplus or deficit, the size of trade was not large as indicated by the shares in world total, except for wool on the import side and non-ruminant animals on the export side.

Table 11.5 Characteristics and key assumptions of the scenarios

Scenario	Key assumptions
Projection scenario of 2010	China and Taiwan implement their commitments made in accession to the WTO; all other countries continue their unfinished reforms as committed under the Uruguay Round. No further reforms are entailed from the new round of multilateral trade negotiations.
Tariff cut	All economies cut their tariffs in line with the Swiss formulae for all traded goods and services; the parameter **a** is set at 60% for developing economies and 40% for developed economies.*
Removal of export subsidies	All economies remove export subsidies to agricultural products completely on the base of 2010 reference scenario.
Removal of domestic support	All developed economies remove domestic support to agricultural products completely on the base of 2010 reference scenario.
Comprehensive reforms	All economies cut their tariff rates with the formulae approach abovementioned and remove all export subsidies; developed economies remove domestic support to agricultural products.

* The tariff cut formulae suggested by Switzerland can be written as $t_1=(a\times t_0)/(a+t_0)$, where t_1 is the tariff rate at the end of reform and t_0 is the initial tariff. It can be seen from the formulae that the parameter **a** determines not only the bound rate at the end, but also the speed for tariff cut. Suppose parameter **a** equals 45%. If the initial tariff is 10%, the tariff will be reduced to 8.18% at the end, reducing about 12%; If the initial tariff is 300%, the tariff will be reduced to 39.13%, declining by 87%. It can be observed from this example that the tariff cut with such a formula is conducive to eliminating tariff peaks and tariff escalation. Here, we give a higher parameter **a** to developing economies to reflect the special and differential treatments given to the developing economies.

After checking the original data of GTAP it was found that China's income elasticities of demand for agricultural products seem to be too high in comparison with findings from recent empirical studies (for instance, Yuan 2001). If such high income elasticities were used, the assumed strong economic growth could result in substantial expansions of domestic consumption, which in turn would lead to substantial increase in imports. To reflect the situation more realistically, we revised income elasticities of demand for China based on information available from the literature as well as on our own research work.[2] Table 11.7 compares the original and the revised income elasticities of household demand.

Another important revision is related to the tariff rates reflected in the base year. In the original GTAP dataset, China's tariff rates for cereals are those above-quota tariff rates. However, these rates were not effective as evidenced by comparing domestic market prices and the world prices. To deal with this problem, we used GTAP's tariff revision facility to shock the tariff rates to levels consistent with the situation in 1997.

Table 11.6 China's trade pattern, base year, 1997

Code	Import		Export		Balance of trade
	Value (m US$)	*Share in world trade (%)*	*Value (m US$)*	*Share in world trade (%)*	**(m US$)**
RICE	379	5.4	403	6.1	24
WHT	524	2.9	18	0.1	-506
GRO	594	3.6	932	6.5	338
V_F	602	1.2	1282	3.0	680
OSD	1410	8.0	294	1.8	-1117
SUGAR	258	2.1	144	1.3	-114
FIBER	1386	13.3	4	0.0	-1382
OFOOD	3753	1.7	6649	3.2	2896
CTL	7	0.1	53	0.8	46
OAP	746	4.8	1437	9.6	691
DAIRY	262	0.9	52	0.2	-210
WOOL	410	16.2	57	2.4	-352
FISH	103	1.0	597	6.2	494
CMT	315	1.5	75	0.4	-239
OMT	897	3.0	1207	4.2	310
VOIL	2838	8.2	537	1.7	-2301
FOR	930	7.7	134	1.3	-796
OthPrimary	7313	2.0	4646	1.4	-2668
LEATHER	2730	3.3	21231	27.7	18501
TEXTILE	20844	6.0	47286	14.2	26442
Mnfcs	146724	3.7	131619	3.4	-15105
Svces	22056	2.0	20506	1.8	-1550
Total	215082	3.4	239165	3.9	24083

Source: GTAP data for 1997.

Table 11.7 Comparing partial equilibrium elasticities of household demand to income before and after adjustments

Code	Original	Revised	Change
RICE	0.41	0.12	-0.29
WHT	0.41	0.22	-0.19
GRO	0.41	0.16	-0.25
CTL	1.12	0.63	-0.49
OAP	1.12	0.58	-0.54
DAIRY	0.77	0.77	0.00
WOOL	0.92	1.01	0.09
FISH	0.87	0.67	-0.20
CMT	1.12	0.63	-0.49
OMT	1.12	0.47	-0.65

Although we have devoted much effort to improving the data and parameters, not all the shortcomings in the current versions of the GTAP model can be identified or corrected. At the present level of aggregation, it is also difficult to reflect detailed commitments on different commodities. Furthermore, some policy measures cannot be quantified under the GTAP model. As a result, the simulation results derived in this study should be treated as indicative prospects under various policy changes, rather than as strict forecasts of the future.

11.4 Findings

11.4.1 Projection of 2010

Using the procedure described above, a decision was made to shock upward the import tariffs of rice and shock downward the import tariffs of wheat and corn to their in-quota rates of 1% because none were found to be bound by the market access quota in the initial trial simulation. The tariff of wool was shocked to the out-quota rate after observing the volume of import. The tariffs of all other listed commodities were reduced with varied percentages except for ruminant animals, whose tariff was raised. Figure 11.1 shows average tariffs in the base data and in the simulation results obtained. It can be seen that China's tariff rates will be reduced substantially for wheat and corn, indicating improved access to China's market. The tariff rates for animals and animal products also decline notably and this may result in a substitution between imports of feedgrains and livestock products after WTO accession.

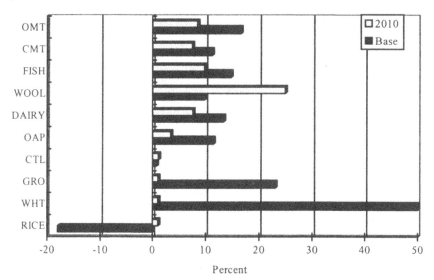

Figure 11.1 Average tariffs, base data and simulation results

Table 11.8 presents the major results obtained from simulating the 2010 projection. According to Table 11.8, with assumed strong growth of the Chinese economy and changes in endowment, a substantial structural adjustment will take place after WTO accession. The agricultural sector will decline in importance, although outputs of all agricultural commodities continue to grow at varying rates. Among the agricultural products, cereals, especially wheat, have slower growth rates. For the commodities listed in Table 11.8, there is a uniform pattern of increased imports and decreased exports except for rice, for which China's product is relatively competitive in the eastern Asian market. It is noted that, although there will be sharp rises in imports for most of the commodities in proportional terms, the real increases in volume are small due to the small numbers in the base year. The minimal market access quotas for cereals are unlikely to be fully utilised even at the in-quota low tariff rates.

Table 11.8 Simulation, 2010 projection*

Code	Production (%)	Import (%)	Export (%)	Trade balance (m US$)
RICE	24.5	-68.2	245.3	1167
WHT	8.8	180.3	7.2	-1324
GRO	19.8	103.9	19.1	-181
CTL	66.9	956.9	-95.6	-126
OAP	30.5	290.8	-62.7	-3019
DAIRY	69.1	199.5	-25.2	-504
WOOL	88.4	178.3	-94.6	-1054
FISH	33.0	426.9	-76.8	-821
CMT	116.1	122.4	-3.2	-424
OMT	30.6	156.2	-30.5	-1583

* The figures are proportional changes over base-year for production, import and export, and absolute changes in values of trade balance.

In terms of trade values, wheat, non-ruminant animals and their meats, and wool are the commodities that contribute most to the increased agricultural trade deficit (see Table 11.8). While China has been a net importer of wheat and wool for a long time, it was a net exporter of live animals and animal meats. Several studies by Chinese researchers have predicted that China has comparative advantages in livestock products and as a result China could increase its export of such products on the assumption that the WTO accession will lead to improved access to overseas markets and that the likely increase in feedgrain imports may reduce feed costs of animal products (see, for example, Huang 2000; Sun 2001).[3] However, the results obtained in this study clearly disagree with these speculations. The results from this study are also in conflict with the findings from a previous simulation using GTAP version 4, which suggested increased export of animal products by China, although only at a small volume (College of Economics and Management 1999). Such conflicts in modelling outcomes could be attributed to modifications in GTAP model itself, such as revisions on the parameters, changed market conditions as reflected by the base-year data set, and more importantly, assumption of reduction of bilateral tariff equivalents with regard to agricultural imports from China. Apart from these model-related factors, China's inability to improve the quality of its animal products to the standards required by major importers such as Japan is a real constraint to increase export. This situation is likely to persist for a while.

The findings above tend to suggest that China may increase imports of agricultural products significantly. However, it is pointed out that China is unlikely to become either a major exporter or a major importer in the world markets of grains and livestock products in the near future. China's accession to the WTO may not be immediately translated to opportunity for grain exporters. As for feedgrains, substantial export to China in the near future is unlikely if China is unable to expand its export of animal products. On the other hand, the opportunity for exporting animal products to China seems to be promising, although penetration into the Chinese market will be a huge challenge.

Sensitivity analyses are carried out to check robustness of the results. For simplicity, we consider only the rate of China's GDP growth. A 10% variation is assumed in this case. The results suggest that changes in China's GDP growth rate have limited impact on performance of the world economy. This can be expected for although the Chinese economy has been growing rapidly, China is still a small player in the world market at present. However, the results suggest that China itself will be affected significantly. The sensitivity analysis shows that, in general, production is not very sensitive to changes in China's GDP growth, though wheat is an exception. Among animal products, wool and beef belong to the commodities that are relatively sensitive to GDP changes. A similar situation applies to exports, where only non-ruminant animals (OAP) and fishery products are relatively sensitive. In contrast, China's imports are very sensitive to changes in GDP. The high sensitivity of wheat import to GDP growth is due to its small size of trade in the base year. Imports of other grains (GRO) and ruminant meats are also relatively sensitive due to a similar reason.

11.4.2 Policy Reform Scenarios

Three sets of international trade reforms are first evaluated individually and then in a comprehensive policy package. These scenarios are not designed specifically to address the bilateral trade issues between China and its trade partners, such as agreed FTA with ASEAN, rather they assess the impacts of worldwide reforms such as those under the mandate of WTO. However, by nature of the design of these scenarios, the three major distorting factors to trade of grains and livestock products, namely tariff protection, export subsides and domestic support, are fully taken into account. For instance, with the modality of cutting import tariffs with Swiss formulae, the high levels of trade protection in Western Europe, Japan and Korea can be weakened substantially. Since cereals and livestock products are among the commodities receiving the highest tariff protection in those countries, reduction of tariffs in such a manner can help greatly to remove trade barriers that prevent China from entering those markets. Similarly, complete removal of export subsidies and domestic support, which are almost exclusively used by developed countries, reduce the competition pressure on the Chinese grain producers.

The policy reform scenarios are benchmarked against the 2010 projection. Table 11.9 summarises the simulation results of the four scenarios. The results reveal that if distortions in agricultural trade can be removed, China's agricultural sector will benefit not only for animal products, but also for major cereals. Although changes in China's production of the selected commodities are not particularly large, the changes in trade are noticeable. Under all four scenarios, China's trade balances of the three cereals improve significantly, especially for rice. Among the three core tasks of trade policy reforms, tariff cuts have the most important impacts, which is followed by removal of domestic support. In fact, if these scenarios could turn into reality, China would become not only a net exporter of rice, for which China has comparative advantage, but also a net exporter of coarse grains, although China's ability to export coarse grains is very limited.

Table 11.9 Simulation, policy reform scenarios*

Code	Production (%)	Import (%)	Export (%)	Trade balance (m US$)	Production (%)	Import (%)	Export (%)	Trade balance (m US$)
	Tariff cuts				*Removal of export subsidies*			
RICE	1.0	2.3	43.8	611	0.0	-0.2	1.5	22
WHT	0.9	-4.7	81.7	40	0.1	-1.0	-1.6	4
GRO	0.5	-1.1	7.1	118	0.3	-1.2	2.6	46
CTL	-0.1	-0.5	15.5	1	0.0	1.3	-5.2	-1
OAP	0.0	2.8	-2.4	-85	0.0	2.3	-2.8	-68
DAIRY	-0.4	2.2	22.4	-11	2.1	-12.8	20.4	43
WOOL	-0.4	9.6	17.9	-185	-0.3	3.7	-11.3	-4
FISH	-0.1	2.9	7.8	-2	0.0	1.6	-0.1	-5
CMT	-0.5	-0.2	6.9	-4	0.2	-1.9	22.5	23
OMT	0.5	2.3	15.8	100	0.3	-1.2	3.1	44
	Removal of domestic support				*Comprehensive reforms*			
RICE	-0.2	0.0	0.8	7	0.9	2.2	48.8	675
WHT	0.1	-5.5	12.4	65	1.0	-11.0	96.8	114
GRO	0.7	-1.3	8.1	134	1.5	-3.6	19.4	328
CTL	0.0	-2.4	4.9	2	-0.1	-0.9	14.5	1
OAP	0.0	1.1	-0.2	-13	-0.1	6.5	-5.5	-173
DAIRY	0.1	-0.7	1.7	4	1.9	-11.5	46.3	38
WOOL	0.4	-1.2	4.9	2	-0.3	12.3	10.0	-189
FISH	0.1	-9.6	27.4	93	0.0	-6.2	40.6	100
CMT	0.4	-0.5	1.3	3	0.2	-2.6	32.3	24
OMT	0.1	-0.7	0.7	19	0.9	0.4	20.0	166

* The figures are proportional changes over 2010 reference scenario for production, import and export, and absolute change in values of trade balance.

The situation for animal products differs from that of cereals. With the reforms, China's import of wool and non-ruminant animals will increase, while trade balances for other animals and animal products (ruminant animals, dairy, fishery products and meats) will improve to various degrees. Overall, China's trade position in the world agricultural market is strengthened. Although China's access to overseas markets of animal products is improved under these scenarios, the impacts are quite limited. This is partially due to the fact that China is a big producer of animal products but a small player in the world market of animal products. Thus, a large proportional change in trade cannot be translated into a large volume of trade. Besides, when the world market prices of feedgrain begin to rise as a consequence of removing trade distorting policies by major exporters, the production costs of livestock products will inevitably increase, which in turn erodes China's competitiveness in such products.

There are weaknesses in this simulation analysis. We were unable to include the measure of tariff-rate quotas into policy simulation due to its complexity in treatment as well as lack of information, although this is an important aspect in China's WTO accession protocols. However, we did discuss whether such quotas are likely to be fulfilled. Besides, it is uncertain if the TRQ system can be maintained upon completion of the new round of negotiations. The other major weakness is that the GTAP model by design is unable to take into account the structural changes in China's livestock industry from backyard animal-raising to specialised households or to feedlot operations. Different practices use different composition of feed materials (see Zhou et al. 2003), which in turn affects the amount of feedgrains demanded.

11.4.3 Discussion

The results from the policy simulations with GTAP highlight some interesting phenomena, which have important implications for both China and its major agricultural trade partners.

Firstly, although China is the largest producer in a wide range of agricultural products, it has not been a major player in the world agricultural market. It is unlikely to become a major player in the near future. While WTO accession may enhance China's trade relationships with other major players in agricultural products, the potential for China to increase both exports and imports seem to be limited. Such a prospect can be attributed to both internal and external factors. Internally, with an assumed strong growth of the Chinese economy, domestic demand for agricultural products tends to increase. However, demand surge will be mainly in those high valued food products, such as livestock and horticultural products, while demand for cereals and other ordinary food products may even decline as substitution takes place. Thus, although China is thought to have comparative advantages in livestock and horticultural products and have the potential to export (mainly to eastern Asian markets), such increases in outputs may be largely absorbed by the increased domestic demand. In the meantime, expansion of import of cereals and other bulk commodities into China is bound by the already weakening demand and also by supply responses of the producers to price rises. Externally, China faces some legal trade barriers under WTO's SPS and TBT framework for it to export food products to the high-income markets, such as Japan, Korea and EU, which cannot be easily overcome even with the new round of trade negotiations. However, reduction of export subsidies and domestic support used in developed countries will surely contribute to the improvement of China's competitiveness in a range of farm products, including cereals and livestock products. These factors in combination prevent the possibility of China becoming either a large importer or exporter in the world agricultural market.

Secondly, in the longer term, China is likely to turn from a net exporter into a net importer of agricultural products. Under the assumed changes in resource endowments, China's comparative advantages in agricultural products will decline in general, which in turn results in a shift of resources from agriculture towards non-agriculture. While the current level of support to agricultural commodities is still lower than the WTO commitments, the possibility for China to increase assistance to agricultural development is constrained mainly by its fiscal capacity at the national and regional levels and its willingness to do so. Given this reality, it is unlikely for China to grant substantial support to agriculture in the near future. In the meantime, although the new WTO negotiations may lead to a more liberal regime of agricultural trade, the phasing-out of various trade distorting measures in developed countries may take time to realise. With such a prospect, it is expected that China's agricultural import will increase at a rate that is higher than that of export. Although the total volume of net import may not be particularly large, it nevertheless offers opportunities for efficient producers to export certain products to the Chinese market.

Thirdly, the worldwide reforms of agricultural policies have important impacts on China's agricultural trade. As revealed by the simulation results of policy reform scenarios, with the reforms, the world market prices of cereals tend to increase in exporting regions and decrease in importing regions. This results in a worldwide adjustment of production locations and increase in trade volume. A similar situation also happens in the world livestock market. Our results suggest that, if the trade distorting measures in developed countries could be removed, China's competitiveness in the world agricultural market could be improved significantly. Thus, China will benefit from international trade reforms that remove trade-distorting measures.

Fourthly, the simulations reveal a complex relationship between China's trade in livestock products and in grains. In general, under the given situation of changing resource endowment in China as well as in other countries, China's overall comparative advantage in agriculture will decline and import of both livestock products and grains (except for rice) will tend to increase. However, in the case of worldwide reforms, China's trade position in both grains and animal products is in general improved. These results suggest that China is not very likely to become a large importer of either grains or animal products in the near future. China will need to import grains (chiefly, feedgrains) in large amounts only if it is able to export large amounts of livestock products to overseas markets. However, this prospect is not promising in the near future since it is difficult for China to overcome the trade barriers of the major importing countries.

Finally, our results reveal that worldwide reforms of agricultural policies benefit mainly major net exporters (such as Australia and Latin American countries) and net importers who have a high level of trade protection (such as

Western Europe, Japan, Korea). While the welfare improvements for China are small under these scenarios, such policy reforms do help to ease, to some extent, the pressure on China's agricultural sector for structural adjustment after WTO accession.

11.5 Conclusions and Implications

Entry to the WTO will improve China's access to overseas agricultural markets, particularly the eastern Asian region that is now, in aggregate, the world's largest net importing region of agri-food products. However, in the meantime, the Chinese farmers will inevitably face increased pressure of import competition, especially in those land-intensive commodities. Thus, substantial structural adjustment in China's national economy is likely to take place in the years to come, which in turn will generate notable impacts on China's trade pattern for agricultural products.

China's position in agricultural trade crucially depends on its rate of economic growth, changes in resource endowments, and the policy frameworks both in China and in other regions. To assess the likely impact on China's future grain demand as a result of its WTO accession and possible international agricultural trade reforms, in this chapter, we used the GTAP model to simulate several hypothetical scenarios of trade policy reforms worldwide. Given the fact that China's consumption of foodgrains has started to decline, China's future overall grain demand will be largely affected by its demand for feedgrain that in turn will be affected by the demand for animal products by both the domestic and overseas consumers. Hence, we focused our attention on examining how China's demand for feedgrain and the demand for China's animal products will evolve under various trade policy reform scenarios.

Our study revealed that some important changes in China's trade of grains and other important agricultural products are likely to take place. First of all, China is likely to turn from being a current net exporter into a net importer of grains (chiefly feedgrains) in the near future. The same applies to some other agricultural products. Second, the volume of China's imports and exports of grains and other agricultural products will remain relatively small in terms of their shares in domestic supply or demand, as well as in world trade. Third, removal of existing trade distortions by major developed countries will strengthen China's competitiveness not only in animal products but also in grains. Fourth, there is potential for further expansion of agricultural trade between China and the rest of the world but this prospect is dependent to some extent on policy reforms of other major players in the world market.

China's WTO accession is unlikely to affect the world agricultural market significantly: the opportunities for China to increase export of animal products and for other countries to export more cereals or even meat products to China are bound by a number of factors, which are unlikely to be overcome in the short run. While China's market access commitments open a better avenue for foreign livestock products to enter the Chinese market, it is unlikely for such products to take notable market shares due to both competition of domestic products and likely high marketing costs associated with distribution of imported products. On the other hand, China's ability to expand export of meat products is confined by high feed costs and inferior quality of products in the short term. It is expected that some niche Asian markets will continue to be the major destinations for China's exports of meat products. However, there is potential for China to expand market access to the EU and transitional economies in the longer term if China succeeds in improving the quality of its animal products. Nevertheless, China is unlikely to become a major competitor in the world meat market.

China's future demand for grains will be largely determined by the demand for its animal products, both domestically and internationally. Increased demand for its animal products will lead to higher derived demand for feedgrains and increased imports of feedgrains. It is pertinent for China to devote great effort to improving the quality of its animal products and other agricultural products in order to take the advantage rendered by WTO accession to access international markets. China also needs to actively participate in the new round of multilateral trade negotiations to work jointly with other players in the market to remove those trade-distorting measures.

References

Anderson, K., Huang, J.K. and Ianchovichina, E. (2002), 'Impact of China's WTO accession on rural-urban income inequality', paper presented to the Australian Agricultural and Resource Economics Society 2002 Annual Conference, Canberra, 13-15 February 2002.

Arndt, C., Hertel, T., Dimaranan, B., Huff, K. and McDougall, R. (1996), *China in 2005: Implications for the Rest of the World*, Centre for Global Trade Analysis, Purdue University.

China Administration of Customs, *China's Customs Yearbook*, various issues, Beijing.

College of Economics and Management (1999), *Reforms of the World Trade System and China's Options of Agricultural Trade*, Research Report, China Agricultural University.

Hertel, T. (ed.) (1997), *Global Trade Analysis: Modelling and Applications*, Cambridge University Press, London.

Hertel, T., Nin-Pratt, A., Rae, A. and Ehui, S. (1999), 'Productivity growth and "catching-up": implications for China's trade in livestock products', paper presented to the International Agricultural Trade Research Consortium Symposium on China's Agricultural Trade, San Francisco, June 25-26.

Hoekman, B. and Newfarmer, R. (2003), 'After Cancún: continuation or collapse?' *Trade Note*, December 17, 2003, The World Bank, Washington D.C.

Huang, J.K. (2000), 'WTO and China's agriculture', in the Institute of Agricultural Economics, *CAAS Annual Report on Economic and Technological Development in Agriculture 2000*, China Agricultural Press, Beijing, pp. 17-37.

Martin, W. (1999), 'WTO accession and China's agricultural trade policies', paper presented to the International Agricultural Trade Research Consortium Symposium on China's Agricultural Trade, San Francisco, June 25-26.

OECD (2003), *Agricultural Policies in OECD Countries: Monitoring and Evaluation 2003*, Paris.

Sun, D.S. (2001), *WTO and China's Agricultural Trade*, China Agricultural Press, Beijing.

USDA (2001a), 'Profiles of tariffs in global agricultural markets', Agricultural Economic Report No. 796, Washington D.C.

USDA (2001b), 'The road ahead: agricultural policy reform in the WTO', *Agricultural Economic Report No. 802*, Washington D.C.

Walmsley, T. and Hertel, T. (2000), 'China's accession to the WTO: timing is everything', Centre for Global Trade Analysis, Purdue University.

Wang, Z. (1997), 'The impact of China and Taiwan joining the World Trade Organization on U.S. and world agricultural trade: a computable general equilibrium analysis, Economic Research Service, U.S. Department of Agriculture, Technical Bulletin No. 1858, Washington D.C.

WTO (2001a), Schedule CLII - People's Republic of China, obtained from http://www.wto.org

WTO (2001b), Market Access: Unfinished Business Post-Uruguay Round Inventory and Issues, *Special Studies*, No. 6.

WTO (2003a), *Annual Report 2003*, Geneva.

WTO (2003b), *World Trade Report 2003*, Geneva.

Yuan, X.G. (2001), 'Study on the Consumption of Animal Products in China', Ph.D. dissertation, The Chinese Academy of Agricultural Sciences, Beijing.

Zhou, Z.Y., Tian, W.M. and Liu, X.A. (2003), 'Developments and trends in household animal raising practice in China: a survey report', in Zhou, Z.Y. and Tian, W.M. (eds), *China's Regional Feedgrain Markets: Developments and Prospects*, Grains Research and Development Corporation, Canberra.

Notes

[1]   In fact, TRQ is also employed by many other WTO members in a wide range of agricultural commodities. Thus, this issue can only be taken into account with a comprehensive treatment. However, this is beyond the scope of this study.

[2]   The behavioural elasticities used by GTAP are derived from the data and parameter files stored in each version. These elasticities are a function of the base flow data and of the currently selected parameters file.

[3]   Huang (2000, p. 22) predicts, using the China Agricultural Policy Simulation and Projection Model (CAPSim), that China would become an important exporter of pork, poultry meats and eggs but an importer of beef and mutton under the condition of a worldwide trade liberalisation (net exports in year 2010 reach 5.7 million tonnes for pork and 1.2 million tonnes for poultry meat, and net import of beef is 0.136 million tonnes). As a result, China needs to import feedgrains in large volume. Similarly, Sun's (2001) result, obtained with the China Agriculture and Trade Policy Model (CATP), is that by 2010 China's net exports of pork, poultry meat and beef will reach 1.25 million tonnes, 0.92 million tonnes and 0.23 million tonnes, respectively.

Chapter 12

Feedgrain Demand and Implications for Foodgrain Consumption and Trade

Yan-Rui Wu

As Chinese consumption of feed-related food increases, demand for feed and hence feedgrain has attracted much attention both inside and outside China, as revealed in earlier chapters. This is not only because of food security concerns but also because of the potential implication for international trade, given the sheer size of the Chinese market. This chapter, in relation to the findings in earlier chapters, looks at China's grain issues from various broad perspectives. In particular, it sheds light on the relationship between feedgrain requirement and foodgrain consumption in China. It especially focuses on examining the impact of economic growth and demographic changes on demand for feedgrain in the near future.

This chapter consists of four sections. Based on findings in earlier chapters of this book and some other studies, the next section examines the sources of growth in China's feedgrain demand in the past as well as in the future. This is followed by Section 12.2, which provides an assessment of feedgrain consumption. Subsequently, Section 12.3 addresses the likely implications of China's feedgrain demand on foodgrain consumption and international trade. The concluding remarks are given in Section 12.4.

12.1 Sources of Growth for Feedgrain Demand

In general, the use of feed determines the demand for feedgrain. Thus, production and consumption of meats, eggs, dairy and aquatic products are the driving forces of feedgrain demand. The demand for these feed-related products is in turn affected by several economic and social factors in China.

First, demand is income-driven. Feedgrain consumption as a part of China's grain requirement has become an issue as consumer income increases substantially. As China's current economic growth continues, the rising consumer affordability will lead to more consumption of feed-related products and hence more demand for feedgrain. Figure 12.1 clearly demonstrates the linear relationship between per capita expenditure on meat products and the level of disposable income among the Chinese regions.

Second, demand can also be generated from structural shifts in consumption patterns. Apart from an increase in the absolute amount of consumption, income growth can also result in structural shifts in food consumption patterns. As income increases, consumers' diets change to include more meat and less cereal products. This is confirmed by consumption patterns of rural and urban households in China, as shown in Figure 12.2. In the past two decades, per capita consumption of meat in both rural and urban households has increased. The increase in rural households was particularly dramatic in the early 1980s and late 1990s due to 1) an increase in rural incomes; and, more importantly, 2) the small quantity of consumption in the base period. Figure 12.2 also illustrates that per capita grain consumption has been declining dramatically in urban households in the past decade.

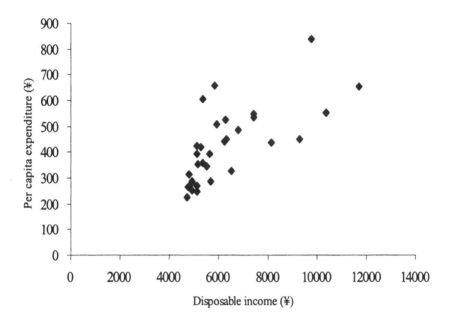

Figure 12.1 Expenditure on meat products and disposable income in Chinese regions, 2000

Source: SSBa (2001).

Third, demand for feed-related products and hence feedgrain is also affected by demographic changes in Chinese society. Urbanisation is one of the important demographic factors influencing demand for grain in general and feedgrain in particular. China has experienced rapid urbanisation in the past two decades (Figure 12.3). With the potential removal of the stringent household registration system, the process of urbanisation is likely to accelerate in the near future. Currently, there is a substantial gap in the consumption patterns of urban and rural consumers. For example, in 2001, per capita grain consumption by rural households (178 kg) was more than double that by urban households (80 kg). At the same time, urban per capita consumption of pork, red meat, poultry, eggs and aquatic products was much greater than rural consumption (see Figures 12.4 and 12.5). The gap for pork consumption is narrowing rapidly due to (1) the increase in rural income and (2) the saturation of pork consumption in urban China. However, in terms of the consumption of beef, mutton, poultry, eggs and aquatic products, rural China is about two decades behind its urban counterpart, according to Figures 12.4 and 12.5. As rural citizens move to the cities, they will adjust their dietary patterns accordingly. Urbanisation will thus directly contribute to the growth in demand for meat and other non-cereal foods, an observation supported by Wang et al. (2004).

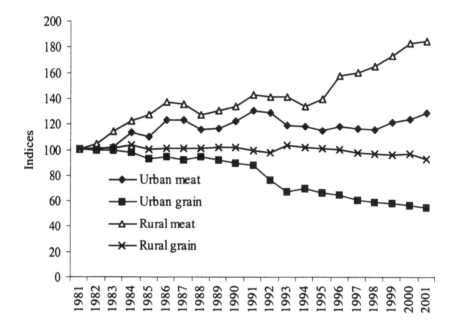

Figure 12.2 Meat and grain consumption indices, 1981-2001

Sources: Derived from SSBa (2001), SSBb (2001) and SSBc (2002).

In the 1980s and 1990s, demand for feedgrain in China increased due to the combined impact of the factors mentioned above. The following section attempts to quantify feedgrain demand and examines how the factors discussed above continue to affect China's demand for feedgrain.

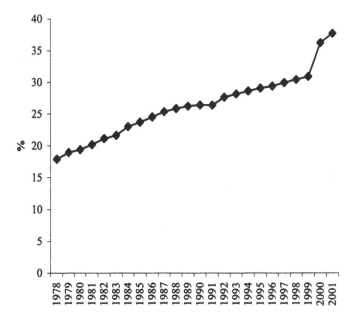

Figure 12.3 Urbanisation index, 1978-2001

Sources: SSBa, various issues.

12.2 Assessing Feedgrain Demand

Feedgrain demand in China has for a long time been a residual of overall grain consumption. One reason is that, for decades, feedgrain has not been the primary source of feed in China's animal feeding due to the dominance of backyard production (Tian and Chudleigh 1999). It is only recently that feedgrain may have become an important component of feed. However, the precise amount of feedgrain consumption is unknown. Several approaches have been used to derive estimates of feedgrain demand in China (see Section 8.2, Chapter 8, for details). As expected, previous estimates, shown in Table 12.1, vary considerably. However, the trend is clear: China's feedgrain demand has been increasing rapidly in the past two decades.

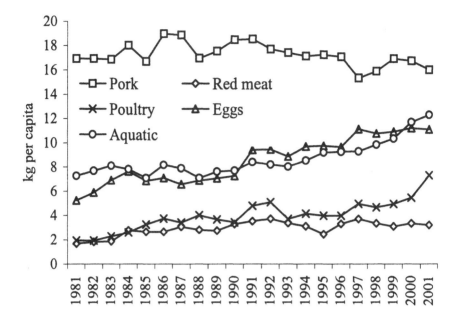

Figure 12.4 Urban consumption of feed-oriented products

Sources: SSBa, various issues.

Table 12.1 Estimated feedgrain consumption in China (mt)

Year	A	B	C	D	E	F	G
1985	48.7	84.6	72.7				
1990	125.6	108.9	86.7				
1995	143.6				117.7		
1999						155	162
2000				109	138.6		161
2001							163

Sources:

A and B: as cited in Chapter 8.
C: Wu and Wu (1997).
D: Huang and Rozelle (1998).
E: Wang and Davis (1998);
F: Chapter 10.
G: Yang (2003).

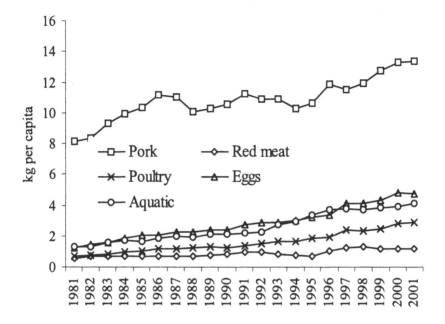

Figure 12.5 Rural consumption of feed-oriented products

Sources: SSBa, various issues.

Estimation of feedgrain demand is a very difficult task, as is the projection of future demand (see Chapter 8). Some existing literature follows the demand or supply approach to estimate and project China's feedgrain demand. Estimates and projections by these approaches, however, are significantly affected by the accuracy of livestock production data and survey data of household animal product consumption. Unfortunately, official data about livestock production and consumption do present some problems. Table 12.2 presents the production and consumption statistics of pork, red meat, poultry, eggs and aquatic products.

A striking feature in Table 12.2 is the huge gap between the production and consumption data. Output figures are more than double the household survey numbers in recent years. Where have the "surplus" products gone? One explanation is that the production statistics are over-reported and consumption data underestimated (Fuller et al. 2000).

It is not surprising that feedgrain demand estimates vary considerably due to the use of different data sources. Estimation is also complicated because of the choice of conversion ratios. No consensus has been reached on the conversion ratios. Among the studies cited in Chapter 8, the conversion ratios range from 3.1 to 8 for pork, 2.7 to 10 for beef, 1.9 to 5 for poultry, 2.5 to 5 for eggs and 1.5 to 2 for fish. While the technicalities in determining conversion ratios is beyond the scope of this chapter, our estimates here are derived from two sets of *ad hoc* ratios.

Table 12.2 Production and consumption of animal products
      (mt)

Year	Production					Consumption				
	Pork	Beef and mutton	Poultry meat	Eggs	Aquatic product	Pork	Beef and mutton	Poultry meat	Eggs	Aquatic product
1985	17.0	1.1	1.6	5.3	7.1	12.5	1.2	1.6	3.3	3.1
1990	23.0	2.4	3.2	7.9	12.4	14.4	1.7	2.1	4.2	4.1
1995	36.0	6.2	9.3	16.8	25.2	15.2	1.5	3.0	6.2	6.1
2000	40.3	8.1	12.8	22.4	42.8	18.4	2.4	4.8	9.0	7.7
2001	41.8	8.4	13.1	23.4	43.8	18.3	2.4	5.8	9.1	9.2

Sources: The production figures are drawn from SSBa (2001) and SSBc (2002). The consumption statistics are the author's own estimates using data from the same sources.

In general, growth in feedgrain demand can be decomposed into three main sources, i.e., an increase in the level of consumer income, population growth and urbanisation. For this purpose, certain assumptions have to be made:

- In the past five years (1997-2001), consumer disposable income in rural and urban China on average increased by 4.2% and 7.2%, respectively (SSBa 2001). It is assumed that this growth trend is sustainable in the coming decade.
- The estimates in this chapter are based on a set of assumed conversion ratios (i.e., 4.3 for pork, 2 for red meat, 2.7 for poultry and eggs and 0.5 for aquatic products). These conversion ratios were used by Li (1989) and Wu and Wu (1997).
- Income elasticities used in this chapter are drawn from Wang and Fan (1999). The income elasticities of demand for animal products by rural households are 0.25 (0.32) for pork, 0.57 (0.49) for red meats, 0.22 (0.48) for poultry, 0.36 (0.26) for eggs, 0.32 (0.49) for milk and 0.37 (0.51) for fish. (The numbers in parentheses refer to urban households.)
- Population growth is assumed to be 0.8% in the coming years. This is also the mean growth rate in the past five years (1997-2001).
- Urbanisation is assumed to take place at the pace of 2% per annum. This is slightly higher than the average rate in the last ten years.

Table 12.3 shows that the main source of growth in feedgrain demand will come from the increase in consumer income. This income effect tends to rise over time. The urbanisation effect will be the second largest source of growth in feedgrain demand. Population growth will still contribute to the increase in demand for feedgrain. It is, however, noted that apart from these three factors, other factors such as ageing also affect consumption patterns and hence demand for feedgrain. Furthermore, according to the forecast in Chapter 10, feedgrain demand in absolute terms will increase by more than 40 million tonnes in 2010 (from about 155 million tonnes in 1999).

Table 12.3 Decomposition of growth in feedgrain demand (%)

Sources	2005	2010
Income	48	50
Population	17	19
Urbanisation	35	31
Total	100	100

Source: Author's own estimates.

12.3 Implications for Foodgrain Consumption and Grain Trade

Consumption of foodgrain, as illustrated in Figure 12.6, has shown two different patterns in China. On the one hand, per capita consumption since 1981 has declined steadily in urban China, which indicates continuing income growth. On the other hand, there has been little change in the rural area. Thus, rural consumers have lagged behind their urban counterparts. However, the pattern in Figure 12.6 does show the tendency of decline in the demand for foodgrain in rural China since 1993. The overall trend for foodgrain consumption in China has been modestly downward in the past two decades. This trend is consistent with the declining share of foodgrain in total grain consumption (Figure 12.7).

The decline of foodgrain consumption share is projected to continue in the coming years. That is, foodgrain consumption is projected to account for 43% and 38% of China's total grain demand in 2005 and 2010. In the meantime, the share of feedgrain demand will rise from 38% in 2001 to about 40% and 49% in 2005 and 2010, respectively (see Table 12.4). Thus, by 2010, China's demand for feedgrain is expected to exceed that of foodgrain. Feedgrain will be the main source of growth in China's grain consumption.

From an international perspective, the pattern of grain consumption in China in 2010, according to Table 12.4, will be similar to that of Japan in 1980 and that of Korea in 1999; China's consumption pattern is expected to follow these currently developed Asian countries and to differ from the patterns of the US and Europe.

Chinese producers of feedgrains (e.g., corn and beans) are less competitive internationally due to land scarcity and low-yield crops (see Yang 2003). Corn prices are already much higher in Chinese markets than in international markets. As a result, developed regions in China are buying corn from international markets, though still on a small scale. China's imports of corn peaked together with the overall imports of grains in the mid-1990s (see Table 12.5). Due to good harvests in the late 1990s, China's grain imports have declined substantially in recent years. However, the trend of imports is expected to be upwards in the coming decade as predicted in Chapter 11. This growing tendency will be driven by the growth in demand for feedgrains as well as for beer. In addition, substantial domestic trade will also result from China's regional variation in grain production. China's vast landscape and different climates make inter-regional trade necessary for grains.

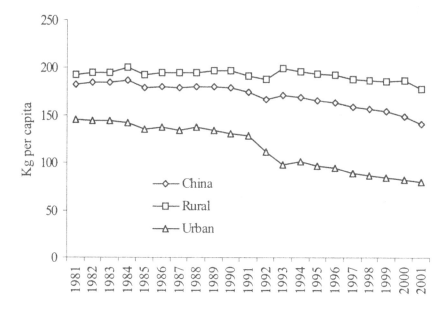

Figure 12.6 Per capita food grain consumption in China, 1981–2001

Source: Calculations from SSBa, various issues.

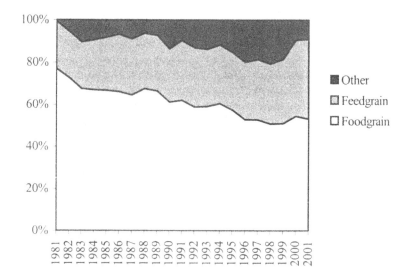

Figure 12.7 Composition of demand for grain, 1981–2001

Source: Calculations from SSBa, various issues.

Table 12.4 Pattern of feedgrain and foodgrain consumption, selected countries (%)

Countries	Year	Feed	Food	Other	Total
China	2001	37.8	53.1	9.0	100
	2005	39.9	43.4	16.7	100
	2010	48.8	38.3	13.0	100
Thailand	1999	37.1	50.0	13.0	100
Korea	1999	45.0	42.8	12.2	100
Japan	1980	48.4	41.1	10.5	100
	1999	46.1	41.1	12.8	100
Australia	1999	59.3	17.0	23.7	100
US	1999	65.9	12.8	21.3	100
Asia	1999	18.7	69.3	12.0	100
Europe	1980	63.3	23.2	13.5	100

Sources: The numbers for China are the author's own estimates. Non-Chinese statistics are based on the FAO online database (http://www.fao.org).

Table 12.5 Grain trade statistics (mt)

Year	Exports			Imports				Balance
	Rice	*Corn*	*All grain*	*Wheat*	*Rice*	*Corn*	*All grain*	
1990	0.33		5.83	12.53			13.72	-7.89
1991	0.69		10.86	12.37			13.45	-2.59
1992	0.95		13.64	10.58		0.13	11.75	1.89
1993	1.43		15.35	6.42		0.29	7.52	7.83
1994	1.52		13.46	7.18		6.18	9.20	4.26
1995	0.05		2.14	11.59		5.18	20.81	-18.27
1996	0.38		1.98	8.25	0.76	0.44	12.23	-10.25
1997	0.94		8.34	1.86	0.33		4.17	4.17
1998	3.75	4.69	8.89	1.49	0.24	0.25	3.88	5.01
1999	2.71	4.31	7.38	0.45	0.17	0.07	3.39	3.99
2000	2.95	10.47	13.78	0.88	0.24		3.15	10.63
2001	1.87	6.00	8.76	0.74	0.29		3.44	5.32
2002	1.99	11.67	14.82	0.63	0.24		2.85	11.97
2003	2.61	16.39	22.00	0.47	0.26		2.09	19.92

Sources: SSBa, various issues.

12.4 Concluding Remarks

To sum up, economic growth and subsequent structural changes have reshaped the Chinese grain market. In particular, feedgrain demand has emerged as the main source of growth in grain consumption. It is projected that, in the coming decade, feedgrain will overtake foodgrain to become the dominant source of grain demand growth in the Chinese market. The key driving forces behind feedgrain growth are the rising affluence of society, rapid urbanisation and rural consumers catching up to their urban counterparts.

Chinese farmers are generally less competitive in the production of land-intensive crops such as corn and beans, and China is likely to increase imports of feedgrains. This increase will of course be affected by uncertainties, including China's imports of meat and feed. As costs of production increase over time, more developed regions such as Shanghai, Beijing and South China may opt to buy feed or meat directly from the international markets.

As noted earlier, the findings in this chapter are subject to several technical assumptions in modelling, economic growth and policy development in China. However, the trend revealed in this chapter is the same under different scenarios and is consistent with findings in other studies. It can be anticipated that China's growing market for feedgrain creates opportunities for Chinese farmers as well as their foreign counterparts.

References

Fuller, F., Hayes, D. and Smith, D. (2000), 'Reconciling Chinese meat production and consumption data', *Economic Development and Cultural Change*, Vol. 49, pp. 23-43.

Huang, J.K. and Rozelle, S. (1998), *China's Grain Economy to the Twenty-first Century*, China Agricultural Press, Beijing.

Li, Y.Z. (1989), 'The structure of grain demand', in Liu, Z.C. (ed.), *China's Grain Studies*, Agricultural Science and Technology Press, Beijing.

SSBa (State Statistical Bureau), *China Statistical Yearbook*, various issues, China Statistics Press, Beijing.

SSBb, *Rural Household Survey Yearbook*, various issues, China Statistics Press, Beijing.

SSBc, *China Statistical Abstract*, various issues, China Statistics Press, Beijing.

Tian, W.M. and Chudleigh, J. (1999), 'China's feedgrain market: development and prospects', *Agribusiness: An International Journal*, Vol. 15, pp. 393-409.

Wang, J.M. and Fan, Y.L. (1999), 'A study on animal product consumption by rural and urban residents in China', Research Report for a project commissioned by the Ministry of Agriculture, Chinese Academy of Agricultural Sciences, Beijing.

Wang, J.M., Zhou, Z.Y. and Cox, R. (2004), 'Animal product consumption trends in China', AARC Working Paper series, No. 36, Asian Agribusiness Research Centre, University of Sydney.

Wang, L.M. and Davis, J. (1998), 'Can China feed its people into the next millennium? Projections for China's grain supply and demand to 2010', *International Review of Applied Economics*, Vol. 12, pp. 53-67.

Wu, Y.R. and Wu, H.X. (1997), 'Household grain consumption in China: effects of income, prices and urbanization', *Asian Economic Journal*, Vol. 11, pp. 325-42.

Yang, Z.H. (2003), 'China's feedgrain: production, trade, and its usage in the feed industry', in Zhou, Z.Y. and Tian, W.M. (eds), *China's Regional Feedgrain Markets: Developments and Prospects*, Grains Research and Development Corporation, Canberra.

CONCLUSION

Chapter 13

China's Grain:
an Issue that is Here to Stay

Zhang-Yue Zhou and Wei-Ming Tian

In this book, we examined how China's foodgrain and feedgrain demand and supply had evolved since 1990 and how such changes would impact on China's grain trade in the era of its WTO membership. In this final chapter, in Section 13.1 we summarise major findings and conclusions from our study and discuss their implications. In Section 13.2 we address remaining and emerging issues concerning China's grain economy. Finally, in Section 13.3, we draw attention to the fact that China's grain issue is here to stay and a concerted effort from all concerned is imperative to help China achieve a stable grain demand and supply.

13.1 Conclusions and Implications

13.1.1 Overall Balance of Grain Demand and Supply

In the past decade or so, China has enjoyed a comfortable grain demand-supply situation. The grain self-sufficiency rate was high. From 1990 till 2003, in only four out of the 14 years, China net imported grains. In balance, over the 14 years, China net exported 29 million tonnes of grains. China's high level of grain self-sufficiency was achieved without affecting the supply of other agricultural products. Indeed, in the same time period, the supply of non-grain agricultural products in China has been plentiful. This fact suggests that China has the capacity to achieve a high rate of grain self-sufficiency and may well be able to maintain a high rate of grain self-sufficiency for some years into the future should China choose to do so.

13.1.2 Foodgrain Consumption

Since 1990 per capita consumption of foodgrains has declined. Urban per capita consumption of foodgrains (processed) has declined from 131 kg in 1990 to about 80 kg in 2003. In rural areas, per capita consumption of foodgrains (unprocessed raw grains) has declined from 262 kg in 1990 to 224 kg in 2003. While the national total foodgrain consumption was still on the increase (only by a small margin from about 280 million tonnes in 1990 to about 285 million tonnes in 2003, representing the increased consumption resulting from population increase), the share of foodgrain consumption out of total grain consumption has declined continuously, from 62% in 1990 to about 53% in 2000.

In the near future, per capita direct consumption of foodgrains may decline further, especially as there is much scope for this decline in rural foodgrain consumption. Hence, the proportion of direct consumption of foodgrains out of total grain consumption is expected to decline further in the years to come. It is projected that this proportion will drop from about 53% in 2000 to about 43% by 2005 and to about 38% by 2010.

There have been notable changes in the composition of foodgrains demanded and also in the consumption patterns of foodgrains. With higher disposable income, consumers shifted away from coarse grains to demand for fine grains (rice and wheat) and also for grains of better quality. Direct human consumption of coarse grains has declined. However, in the meantime, recognising health benefits of consuming coarse grains, some consumers, especially urban residents, have created a strong demand for coarse grains of higher quality, indicating a future niche market for coarse grains (and their processed products) of better quality for human consumption. The consumption pattern with wheat as the staple food for people in northern China and rice in southern China is also evolving. Wheat consumption has increased in southern China and rice consumption has increased in northern China. Factors contributing to this change include: (1) changes in tastes and preferences induced by increased inter-regional movement of people and exchanges with foreign cultures; (2) market development that has improved the availability of different grains across regions; (3) migrating workers (northern Chinese who work in southern China demand more wheat; southern Chinese who work in northern China demand more rice).

While per capita direct consumption of foodgrains has declined, the consumption of other foods has increased steadily, including animal products. The demand for non-grain foods is expected to continue to increase and there is considerable latitude for non-grain food consumption growth in China, especially in rural areas.

13.1.3 Feedgrain Consumption

Per capita use of grains for feed purposes has increased steadily since 1990. In 1990, per capita feedgrain consumption was about 99 kg and this had increased to about 126 kg by 2003. China's total feedgrain consumption has also increased, from about 120 million tonnes in 1990 to about 163 million tonnes in 2003. The share of feedgrain use out of total grain consumption has also increased steadily from about 23% in 1990 to about 38% in 2003. The increased use of grains for feed purposes is caused by the increased demand for animal products.

Given that future demand for animal products is expected to continue to rise as a result of increased consumer income, feedgrain consumption in China is projected to increase. Total feedgrain consumption will increase to a little over 200 million tonnes by 2010. The proportion of feedgrain use out of total grain consumption will increase to about 49%, exceeding the proportion of foodgrain use.

Corn is the major item used for feedgrain purposes. Some other minor cereals are also used for feed but at a relatively very small proportion. In recent years, an increased amount of low quality rice and wheat has also been used for feedgrains. The use of rice as feed has been promoted, as feed rice is claimed to be nutritionally superior to corn and is more suitable to grow in southern China.

13.1.4 Grain Production

During 1990-2003, total grain output first increased but then decreased. Total grain output increased from about 450 million tonnes in 1990 to the peak of 510 million tonnes in 1998. Since 1998, total grain output has continuously fallen, to a low of 430 million tonnes in 2003, largely attributable to the significant decline in area sown to grain crops. The decline in area sown to grain crops was attributable primarily to changing relative returns from grain crops and other crops and government policy shifts, as well as to urbanisation and the use of arable land for non-agricultural purposes.

Although total cereal output has fluctuated over the years, the proportion of each of the major cereals (rice, wheat and corn) in the total output has remained relatively stable. Over the years, the share of rice in total cereal output tends to decline slightly from 46% in 1991 to 44% in 2002, while the share of wheat remained at about 25% till 2000 but has experienced a notable decline since 2001. The share of corn increases at the expense of rice and wheat crops and other minor cereal crops. At the aggregate level, the proportion of these three major cereals continues to dominate in total cereal output, accounting for 97% in recent years compared to 95% in the early 1990s. The other 3-5% of the cereal output is for minor cereal crops.

While there were abrupt changes in areas sown to grains between years, the proportions of area sown to major grain crops (i.e., rice, wheat and corn) have been relatively stable over the years. An emerging trend is that more land area has been devoted to corn production at the expense mainly of wheat. In 2002, the share of corn area in total area planted to cereals rose to 30%, compared with 23% in 1991. Meanwhile, the share of rice remained at about 35%, but the share of wheat declined from 33% to 29%. Apart from strong domestic demand for corn as feed, the increase in sown area to corn is induced by the relatively high price of corn in the domestic market, which is partially attributed to government policies in the late 1990s to support corn export.

Changes have occurred in the regional distribution of grain production. At the more aggregate level, grain production has shifted from the south to the north. In 1978, about 59% of China's grains were produced by 14 provinces south of the Yangtze River. The 15 provinces north of the Yangtze River produced the other 41%. However, by 2002, the proportion of grains produced by those provinces south of the Yangtze River had dropped by about seven percentage points, to being less than 52% while the proportion of grains produced by northern provinces had increased to 48.5%. At the less aggregate level, the decline in grain production in southern China took place mainly in the wealthier south-east coastal region while the increase in grain production in northern China mainly took place in the north-east provinces. If we divide China into east, middle and west, then the change in the proportion of grain production in each region out of the national total is nominal.

There has been increased attention to produce grains of higher quality, reflecting farmers' response to changing demand situations in the market. Increased production of higher quality grains (chiefly wheat and rice) will adversely affect the total grain output level due to lower yields of high quality grains. Although China's feedgrain consumption is projected to increase, whether more resources will be devoted to producing feedgrains is uncertain. Many factors affect China's choices between producing feed domestically or importing, or simply importing more animal products. In relation to feedgrain production, an emerging trend worth noting is that in some areas a growing share of land is used for production of hays or crops for silages, other than harvesting the crops for cereals. Hence, it is possible in the near future that outputs of cereals may not increase greatly, but that total nutrients produced with domestic resources for human and animals may actually continue to increase.

13.1.5 Domestic Grain Trade

The Chinese government started to introduce reforms to domestic grain marketing arrangements in the mid-1980s. Since the early 1990s, the reforms continued but there have been drastic policy shifts in response to the country's grain demand and supply situations. Such policy shifts have resulted in domestic grain trade being easier sometimes but difficult at other times. However, overall, China's inter-regional grain trade has become easier.

China's domestic grain markets have also become increasingly integrated. Market policy reforms, improved marketing infrastructure, and improved communication techniques have contributed to the increased market integration. Improved market integration has encouraged grain trade across regions. However, due to a lack of reliable regional grain trade data, we were unable to present accurate trade flows between regions. Nonetheless, in this book we attempted to construct a regional feedgrain demand and supply balance sheet for China in order to simulate and demonstrate inter-regional feedgrain trade flows. Our findings suggest that in the late 1990s, inter-regional feedgrain trade volume was in the vicinity of 30 million tonnes. This volume is projected to increase to about 35 to 40 million tonnes by 2010 assuming that a free grain trade regime is present.

Notable changes have taken place in the volume and varieties of grains traded between south and north China. Due to increased grain production in northern China, grains transported from the south to the north have been reduced and increased grains have been moved from the north to the south. Corn has been a major item transported to the south for feed purposes. As a result of increased consumption of wheat products in southern China and rice in northern China, varieties of grains traded between the south and the north are also changing. High quality indica rice produced in southern China is made available in northern China. In the meantime, high quality japonica rice produced in northern China is also transported to the south to meet increasing demand.

13.1.6 International Grain Trade

There has been no clear pattern in China's international grain trade in the recent years. Volumes of net import or net export and composition of grains imported and exported have tended to change rather dramatically between years. In 1995, China net imported about 20 million tonnes of grains but in 2003 it net exported about 20 million tonnes. In the early 1990s, China was a major wheat importer but in recent years its wheat import has dropped significantly and in 2003 China even net exported two million tonnes of wheat. In 2003, China also net exported 16 million tonnes of corn to the world market, although in 1995 it imported about five million tonnes of corn.

China's import source countries for rice and wheat have been relatively stable. Thailand is China's major source of rice import. However, the amount of rice import has been generally small. Import source countries for wheat are the United States, Canada and Australia. The amount of import from Australia has been quite unstable. Destinations for China's grain exports have tended to change frequently. This instability in export destinations is dictated by China's unstable export supply.

While China has been a net grain exporter in the past few years, China is likely to become a net importer in the near future. However, based on our simulations, China's grain import needs are unlikely to be very large in the near future. Uncertainty exists as to whether China will import foodgrains or feedgrains. China is unlikely to import foodgrains in large volume due to grain security concerns. China may increase feedgrain production based on regional comparative advantages while allowing feedgrain imports when necessary. Based on our study, China is soon to become feedgrain deficit from the present surplus due to faster growth of demand for feedgrains. How much feedgrain China may import will be significantly affected by China's choice of strategy to produce animal products domestically and by China's ability to increase its animal product exports to the world market. Assuming current economic and technological conditions prevail, China's feedgrain import needs by 2010 will be in the range of three to four million tonnes. Assuming that there will be a faster increase in consumer income and that China can increase its livestock product export, a further five million tonnes of feedgrain may be demanded and imported from the world market. This would lead China's feedgrain demand in 2010 to being in the vicinity of 210 million tonnes and its import requirement to being still less than 10 million tonnes. This suggests that, in the near future, China is unlikely to become a large net importer of feedgrains, or for that matter, grains.

As a member of the WTO, China is obliged to follow WTO rules in its grain trading. China has proven to be disciplined in following WTO rules. However, in terms of its current TRQ operations, it seems there is still a lack of transparency. Given that market access continues to be an important issue in the Doha Round and reforms on TRQ arrangements are under negotiation, it is expected that China's international grain trade operations will become increasingly transparent under the WTO framework.

13.1.7 Grain Policies

Grain production and procurement policies are the centrepieces in China's overall grain policies. Since the early 1990s, all other components of China's grain policies have revolved around them. Given the fact that some 60% of China's grain output is still consumed on farm, the amount of grains available for sale in the market to the non-agricultural population and also the amount of grains held by the government often trigger changes to procurement policies. When the government feels uncomfortable about the amount of grains available to the market (too much or too little), modifications are often made to the procurement policies, which then result in changes in production policies and other components of the grain policies.

Since the mid-1980s when the government began to reform the unified grain procurement system, China's grain policies have generally evolved from a strict control approach to a less controlled regime using increasing market forces. In the near future, China's grain economy and market are likely to become more liberalised. Consequently, there will be further changes to the government's approach to procuring grains. In particular, the government is likely to increasingly procure grains in the market other than through quota allocations. When the government becomes more proficient in using the market to secure grains for its own disposal and to influence the market, it may be that grain policy changes will be less abrupt than was the case in the past.

However, achieving grain security will continue to be the paramount objective of the government's future grain policy. When China's grain security is reasonably assured, the government's grain policy may increasingly accommodate the needs for (1) raising farmer income, (2) encouraging agricultural structural adjustments in line with industry comparative advantages, (3) fulfilling WTO commitments to further open up the grain market, and (4) protecting and rehabilitating the environment and natural resources.

13.2 China's Grain: Remaining and Emerging Issues

Our examination of the developments in China's grain economy shows clearly that China has managed its grain demand and supply reasonably well since the early 1990s. China was able to produce enough grains for domestic use, and even had a small amount to export to the world market. However, in spite of such a remarkable achievement, it is imperative to also note that some important issues remain unresolved, while others are still emerging, all of which deserve close attention.

13.2.1 Establishing a Self-adjusting Demand-supply Stabilising Mechanism for Grain

Maintaining a relatively stable grain market is an enormous challenge for governments of populous countries such as China. While China's grain market has been generally stable in most years of the past decade or so, occasional fluctuations have caused great concern to the Chinese government. A price increase in the grain market in late 1993 and 2003 caused the government to panic on both occasions. The 1993 price increase happened in a year when grain output was in fact higher than the previous year, while the 2003 price increase occurred in a year when China net exported grains to the world market. This suggests that there was a lack of a self-adjusting grain demand-supply stabilising mechanism and speculations in the market may have played a major role in bringing the price hikes. Added to this, quite often the government is unable to prevent misconduct of state-owned grain marketing enterprises and their misconduct may have aggravated the unstable grain market.

Admittedly, over the past two decades the government has made a great effort to establish a state grain reserve system with the intention of curbing any undue price fluctuations in the market. Yet the panic reactions to price hikes by the government indicate that the reserve mechanism is not working well to handle the market fluctuations. In our view, there is one important component missing from the mechanism, which results in the mechanism's malfunctioning. That is, there is a lack of information transparency in the government's management of its grain reserve system in that the information about the level of grain reserves held by the government is not available to the market. This encourages speculation which then leads to an unstable market; or the speculation forces dramatically magnify a small shortage or oversupply.

It used to be popularly believed that keeping grain reserve levels secret was of strategic importance. This may have been the case in the old days (1950s to 1970s). Given the fact that nowadays China has opened its doors to the rest of the world and its economy has increasingly integrated into the world economy, there is little strategic significance for keeping grain reserve levels secret, at least in peace time. Secrecy makes it difficult to stabilise the grain market due to speculation problems. When the Chinese market is not stable, it also affects the world market due to abrupt changes in China's imports and exports. The Chinese government should consider publicising the level of grain reserves to the market on a regular basis, as does the Indian government (Zhou 1997, pp. 73-75). This would discourage speculation in the market and in the meantime help producers and traders from both China and the rest of the world to adjust their production and business activities in response to China's reserve stock changes. As a result, this would help not only China to stabilise its grain market but also the whole international community to stabilise the world grain market.

It is fair to say that the Chinese government has brought more and more market forces into play in the grain market. However, the grain market reforms will not be complete unless the information regarding grain reserve levels is made available to the public on a regular basis. In addition, China needs to build a dynamic grain demand-supply forecasting system to regularly provide China's grain demand and supply projections to the market. Such information will be most invaluable not only for China's own grain economy management but also for business planning of producers and traders both in and outside China.

13.2.2 Improving and Protecting Grain Producers' Income

Since 1997, the increase in rural income has slowed notably. In the meantime, the rural-urban income disparity has been increasing. Given that grain production is still the major agricultural industry in China and is the major income source for many rural families, it is of great importance to increase and protect grain producers' income. This is simply because China cannot become prosperous if its rural areas are not prosperous. Recently, some measures have been undertaken to support farmers (direct payment linked to areas sown to grain; subsidy for the use of improved seeds, assistance to the purchase of farm machinery). In addition, the government is going to phase out agricultural tax in five years. One other important measure that can help grain producers significantly is the increased public investment in agricultural research, development and extension.

It is also important to protect grain producers' income when there are extraordinary circumstances. Farm production is a very risky business operation. Both bumper harvests and very poor harvests can harm grain producers. While there are measures that help farmers when their harvests are really poor, supporting measures also need to be devised when the harvests are extremely good, causing a supply glut in the market. Guaranteed government procurement of surplus grains at protecting floor prices is essential. Such floor prices need to be set by careful calculations, ensuring that they help small grain producers in their difficult times without inducing future oversupply.

Now that China is a member of the WTO, Chinese farmers are facing increasing competition from overseas suppliers. The Chinese government needs to be active in protecting Chinese grain producers from any unfair overseas competition by using measures as allowed under the WTO rules.

13.2.3 Using the World Market

To what extent can China rely on the world market to supply its grain needs? This has been a long debated issue. Given the increasingly integrating world economy and China's WTO membership, it has never been easier for China to make use of the world market. However, strategically, China may choose not to rely too much on the world market for its grain security for two major reasons. One is the sheer size of China's grain demand. According to FAO, total world cereal imports would be some 370 million tonnes by 2030 (Bruinsma 2003, p. 82). At present China's total grain demand has already been in the vicinity of 500 million tonnes. Various studies have pointed out that China's total demand for grain in the next couple of decades will continue to grow. As such, if a large portion of China's future grain requirements were imported, it would have a tremendous impact on the world market. Although China's import of a large quantity may be welcomed by a few major grain exporters, this scenario is unlikely to be welcomed by the rest of the world. The other reason for not relying on the world market concerns uncertainties in that market. Such uncertainties can be caused by adverse weather conditions in major grain-exporting countries, large-scale worldwide unrest, or even blackmail based on political considerations by some countries. Following the war on Iraq without a UN resolution, it is hard to guarantee what may happen and what may not happen in the present world; hence, "never say never".

13.2.4 Protecting and Increasing Grain Production Capacity

As the Chinese economy continues to grow, comparative returns from grain production are declining. There is increased competition for limited natural resources from grain production for use in other industries. Grain production is land and water intensive. Both land and water are precious resources in China. China's further industrialisation and urbanisation require more land, water and other resources. Declining comparative advantages in grain production will make it easier for such resources to be deviated away from grain production. Hence, for long-term grain security, China needs to preserve and even increase its grain production capacity.

To preserve its grain production capacity, the government should restrict the deviation of arable land for permanent non-agricultural uses. To best capitalise on the WTO membership and hence benefit from exporting labour-intensive agricultural products, in normal circumstances, land for grain production may be used to produce labour-intensive crops. In extraordinary times, such land can be reverted to grain production as necessary. China's grain production capacity can be increased by increased investment in agricultural and rural infrastructure, agricultural R&D, agricultural extension and farmer education.

Closely related to the protection of grain production capacity is the urgent need to protect the natural environment. China's rapid economic growth did not come without a cost to the environment. The achievement of a remarkable economic growth has been accompanied by severe and large scale damage to the natural environment and resources. Despite some recent efforts, environment pollution is still a major issue. Land degradation, water system pollution and depletion, and other environmental problems such as desertification and acid rains affect China's ability to produce grains. Increased efforts are needed to alleviate the environmental pollution problem and to rehabilitate damaged resources so as to improve the sustainability of China's grain production.

13.2.5 Exploring the Use of International Contracts and Joint Ventures

China's grain production capacity may be effectively "stored" for future use by presently producing grains overseas. In view of China's limited agricultural resources, it can be a useful option for China to form international alliances to produce grains in other countries for the Chinese market. Contracts may be used to have growers in other countries to produce grains that China promises to buy. Commercial joint ventures may also be used to produce grains in other countries (e.g., USA, Australia, Canada, Argentina) for export to China. Depending on the extent of such joint ventures, Chinese farmers' income and employment need to be protected because increased use of international alliances will reduce the demand for grains produced domestically.

13.2.6 Uncertain International Trade Environment

After the Uruguay Round of trade negotiations, a series of reforms were expected to be carried out to international agricultural trade. However, many reforms have not taken places as expected. Despite some proposals under the new Doha Round of negotiations, reforms to agricultural trade remain uncertain. Whether and how soon major grain importers and exporters will remove distorting domestic supports and export subsidies is yet to be seen. Such distorting measures affect China's grain imports and exports. As we have shown in this book, China will benefit from the removal of such measures in major grain importing and exporting countries. As such, China's fulfilment of its WTO commitments may be affected by trade policy reforms of some developed countries. For example, if heavy subsidy is provided by developed countries to their grain production and export, Chinese farmers will find it difficult to compete on a fair basis. This will affect farmers' income and also China's long-term grain production capacity. Another recent movement that will affect the broader world trade environment is the increasing tendency to negotiate bilateral or regional free trade agreements between two countries or a group of countries.

In addition to the issues mentioned above, other remaining or emerging issues that deserve attention include:

- increased consumer awareness for food quality and safety and thus the need for the industry to respond to consumer demand
- GMO issues and the ways the grains industry would respond
- increased demand for feedgrains and therefore whether and how the industry would adjust crop structures to produce more feedgrains
- the need to help small grain producers to cope with the increasingly competitive market
- the need to find alternative employment for workers becoming surplus to grain production requirements.

Resolving the above issues represents a significant challenge to the Chinese government and China's grains industry. Apart from various other constraints, whether China can achieve its grain security is the key factor that affects how the above issues may be resolved. If China's grain security is assured, it would be easier to solve most of the above issues. Hence, achieving China's grain security is the most important factor determining how many other issues will be resolved.

13.3 Looking Ahead

The recent success of China's grain economy by no means suggests that China has resolved its grain demand-supply problem. In the near future, further agricultural structural adjustments are expected. Resource allocation will be increasingly determined by comparative advantages and market forces. Unless the comparative advantages of grain production improve, potential to increase grain production in China is not optimistic. Accompanied by rising demand for grains, supply from domestic sources will not meet demand and imports will have to be sought. Indeed, China had already started to import more than it exports in the first six months in 2004. It is expected that in 2004, China will move from being a net grain exporter to become a net grain importer.

What matters in the future is the size of China's imports. If the size is small and China's grain security is not threatened, the government will be happy to accept this. If the size is large and China's grain self-sufficiency rate becomes too low, the government is likely to do anything to boost domestic grain production to ensure China's grain security. This should be understandable given that there are so many mouths to feed and there is a high risk associated with relying too much on imported grains to feed the large population.

Hence, in the future, the major objective of China's grain policy will still be to ensure China's grain security. The Chinese government is most likely to rely on its domestic resources first to achieve its grain security and to use international trade as a supplementary means. Given the likely strong impact of China's large grain imports on the world market, in our view, it is imperative for China to strive to produce as much grain as it can domestically so long as economic, social and environmental considerations permit. This is simply because China's grain is important not only for China itself but also for the rest of the world. Should China experience problems of serious shortages of grains, there may be serious ramifications for the rest of the world due to the sheer size of demand. In this regard, a high level of grain self-reliance in China is not only in the interests of China but also in the interests of the rest of the world, for the sake of global grain security and world development. As such, overseas governments and international organisations should encourage and help China to meet its grain requirements as much as possible with its domestic resources.

In the meantime, the Chinese government should further improve its grain economy management practice. Further reforms can be carried out to state grain-handling agencies to improve their efficiency and accountability. One other important area where improvements can be made and which will significantly help China to achieve its grain security is to increase the transparency in its grain policies such as grain reserve policies and international grain trade policies. Transparency in these policy areas will discourage speculation and rent-seeking behaviours, thus in turn greatly helping China to manage its grain economy.

To close the book, we reiterate that China's grain problem is far from over. It will continue to concern many people and will continue to be an issue for years to come. Researchers are encouraged to continue their efforts to study China's grain issues so as to contribute to achieving China's grain security and, in turn, global grain security.

References

Bruinsma, J. (ed.) (2003), *World Agriculture: Towards 2015/2030, An FAO Perspective*, Earthscan, London.
Zhou, Z.Y. (1997), *Effects of Grain Marketing Systems on Grain Production: A Comparative Study of China and India*, The Haworth Press, New York.

Index

Note: Italic page numbers refer to figures & tables. Numbers in brackets preceded by *n* are note numbers.